JOBS THAT DON'T SUCK

Jobs That Don't Suck

Charlie Drozdyk

BALLANTINE BOOKS • NEW YORK

A Ballantine Book
Published by The Ballantine Publishing Group

http://www.randomhouse.com/BB/

Library of Congress Cataloging-in-Publication Data
Drozdyk, Charlie
  Jobs that don't suck / Charlie Drozdyk.
    p.   cm.
  ISBN 0-345-42426-3 (alk. paper)
  1. College graduates—Employment—United States.   2. College students—
Vocational guidance—United States.   3. Job hunting—United States.   4. Career
development—United States.   I. Title.
HD6278.U5D76   1998
331.7'02—dc21   98-12736
                    CIP

Cover design by Barbara Leff
Cover photo © James Harrington/Tony Stone Images, NY
Text design by Debbie Glasserman
Illustrations by Shannon Wheeler

Manufactured in the United States of America

Contents

PART 8: MOVING UP THE LADDER: FROM BEING AN ASSISTANT TO HAVING ONE   263

Acknowledgments

First of all, many, many thanks to everybody I interviewed for this book. Without them this book would suck and wouldn't even exist. Thanks to: My agent, Marcy Posner, and also to Tracy Fisher at the William Morris Agency for being much more than agents. My editor, Peter Borland, and his associate, Emily Grayson, two unusually nice human beings. Rob Kleinman for his excellent satirical definitions scattered throughout the book. Shannon Wheeler for the great illustrations. Abigail Hirschhorn for giving *me* a job that doesn't suck. Sam Paul for encouraging me in everything I do. My brother John for all sorts of stuff. And to two nasty ex-bosses (both talent agents; I hope you're reading this) for showing me (by graphic demonstration) that being miserable, ugly, and mean is something *not* to aspire to. Cheers!

Assistant
Secretary
Job Description:
Answer phones
Open mail
Type
File things
Use 2% of brain
Salary:
$23,000
Job Description:
Answer phones
Open mail
Type
File things
Use 2% of brain
Salary:
$55,000
SHANNON WHEELER '98

Introduction

WHO I AM AND WHY YOU SHOULD LISTEN TO ME

I could tell you that I'm "qualified" to write this book because I've written another book about jobs called *Hot Jobs*. And because I've written for *Rolling Stone* on the subject and have appeared on TV and radio all across this country. Yeah, this stuff is true, but it's still no reason to listen to a word I say.

Here's why you should listen to me:

• **I can relate.** I completely and totally remember what it's like graduating from college and having absolutely no clue what to do with my life. I was not premed, I was not prelaw, I was not pre*anything*. I was clueless. I was a history major.

• **I was kind of a screwup. A definite late bloomer.** After I graduated, I went to an island and windsurfed for six months and then started waiting tables at night while writing crappy poetry and plays during the day. After about a year and a half of this, having done everything the wrong way, I somehow managed to join the "real" world.

• **I always got every job I went after.** From working on Broadway to Hollywood to advertising, I've always been able to land one cool job after another by doing things differently and by doing things that made sense.

· **I'm not a "career expert."** I don't make my living telling other people how to get jobs. Anybody who does this for a living can't possibly know what it takes to land one these days. I work in advertising. I've written two "career" books because work—what we do during most of our day—is a huge part of our lives. Our work, our jobs, define us. It's who we are. It can make us happy or make us want to blow our brains out. That and relationships. And since I suck at relationships but am really good at the work thing, I write about the work thing.

So that's enough about me for now. Let's concentrate on getting you a job that doesn't suck.

Part 1

In the Beginning

Chapter 1

GETTING STARTED

Looking for a job sucks. No doubt about it. I'm not going to give you worthless encouragement, as other career books might, like "Make it an adventure!" "Make it fun!" "Make it your job to find a job!" "Get dressed up every morning. Put on a tie!" "Form a support group!" Screw this.

You're going to get a job, so don't worry about it. You heard me, you *will* get a job. How do I know? Because you give a shit. The fact that you are reading this right now shows you give a shit. And if you give a shit, if you really want it, you will get it.

And giving a shit means working for it, which most young people don't do.

Most young people go about looking for a job either half-assed, totally inefficiently, or both. And this is great news. For you. If

---

"Shut Up and Listen"

Linda showed up for her interview with the president of a marketing company terrified of the questions she might be asked. So, not wanting to be caught off guard, she prepared answers to all the normal questions she could imagine she might be asked. But as it turns out, she didn't even get asked one question. Instead, "the woman talked about her vision for the company for over forty minutes and then offered me the job out of the blue. Maybe it was the expression on my face—intelligent listening or something. Maybe by not saying anything, [I let her project] all her answers onto me. By not saying anything, I had all the right answers because I agreed with everything she said."

you're hungry and aggressive and take advantage of your opportunities and don't make stupid mistakes and follow even a quarter of what I have to say, you are going to get a job.

But still, you have concerns. I'll address them.

FIVE REASONS NOT TO EVEN BOTHER LOOKING FOR A JOB; OR, WHY YOU MAY AS WELL END IT ALL RIGHT NOW

1. "There Are No Jobs Out There." Debunking the Fallacy

This has got to be the biggest excuse for hanging out on your parents' couch all day playing Microsoft Solitaire and watching Rosie O'Donnell. It's a great excuse and will probably buy you six months with your parents. However, it will eventually fail you. Why? Because it's bogus. People have been saying "Nobody's hiring right now" and "Oh, it's a really bad time to be looking for a job" for decades.

fact

Odd Jobs of Celebrities
<u>Warren Beatty:</u> dishwasher and cocktail lounge pianist.
<u>Marlon Brando:</u> department store elevator operator. He quit after four days because having to call out "lingerie" embarrassed him.
<u>Danny DeVito:</u> hairdresser in his sister's beauty salon.
—*The Book of Lists*

As Greg Drebin, senior vice president of programming at MTV, says, "When people say 'Well, now is a really hard time for the industry,' and all that—well, it's always a hard time. There's no such thing as: 'Oh, it's hiring season; we've got all these jobs that just became available. This year, for some reason, we have tons of jobs.' It's never like that. It's always hard. And you know what? There's always jobs and there's never jobs."

So don't be like others and use that as an excuse not to look for a job. People are always retiring, getting sick, quitting, dying, getting fired, getting promoted, moving to Tibet . . .

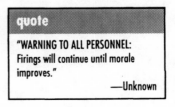

quote

"WARNING TO ALL PERSONNEL:
Firings will continue until morale improves."
—Unknown

2. "If I Pick the Wrong Career, Then I'm Doomed"

This is what I thought when I graduated from college *and* what made me so half-assed about my job search. I was so afraid of winding up in the wrong career. I was like "Shit, I don't know if this is *really* what I want to do, and if I do it, then I'm stuck in it for good." If this is what you think, get over it. There's no *one* right job or industry for you, so don't kill yourself worrying about it.

The important thing is to dive into a career and stop farting around waiting tables or working at Starbucks. It's better to go into some job you're not sure about and wind up hating it for six months than to continue serving up café lattes. (I talk about how to pick your first job in chapter 2, "Figuring Out What to Do with Your Life.")

3. "I'm Not Smart Enough"

You've got a problem: everybody in the field you want to get into is smarter and more talented than you.

This is what I thought when I got out of college. I probably would have pursued a career in arts management or film right away, but I was so intimidated by the idea of it. There was no way *I* could ever get a job in film. Impossible. That was for other, smarter people.

Well, if you're anything like I was, get over it. The people you'll be working with are no geniuses. The reason they have a job and you don't is not because they're any smarter than you. It's because they've basically said to themselves "If anybody is going to get that job, it may as well be me."

4. "I Can't Do Anything with My Degree"

Wondering what you're going to do with that sociology, history, or English degree? Think you're only qualified for teaching or social work or collecting recyclable cans from the trash? I hear this concern all the time. I'm always being asked "What kind of jobs can I get with an English degree?"

She's Got Balls

When Courtney graduated from the University of Michigan, she knew she wanted to go into journalism, but there was one problem: she didn't know what to write about. "I knew how to write, but I had no area of expertise," she says. "I wanted to learn about something that I love—food—so I went to culinary school. Writing about food is a little more specialized and less competitive than political journalism."

When Courtney got out of culinary school, she sent a letter to a contact at the Television Food Network and landed an interview. "How about an unpaid internship?" they said to her. How about not. "I *could* have gone in there as an unpaid intern, but I believed and portrayed that I had all these skills and that I should come in at a higher level than what people normally come in at. I had the attitude that I know too much and have too much education. And I don't have any more than anyone else. That's the thing; it's just a matter of believing it and positioning yourself and selling yourself in a certain way."

Actually, I can hardly believe people ask me this. It just seems so ludicrous. (Although I do remember asking the same thing myself when *I* graduated.) The truth is, you can do anything you want—banking, advertising, music, publishing, computer programming, sales . . . whatever.

> **quote**
>
> "I don't look for advertising degrees at all. In fact, I'm less likely to hire somebody with an advertising degree."
>
> —Director of personnel, Chiat/Day Advertising

A guy I used to work with at this Internet company was a music major in college. He had never taken a computer class in his life. In fact, he didn't know anything about computers until he graduated and started putzing around with them and eventually taught himself HTML (the language the Web uses). Now he's a Web producer at a top Web production company.

I was a history major in college, and now I'm in advertising. One of my good friends is an investment banker who was a photography major. So don't worry about your major. Nobody else does.

Check out this quote from a film executive at a major studio:

I couldn't care less what somebody's major was. I really don't think it matters. What impresses me is people who have a wide range of interests, a solid intellectual education, and who have ideas of what to make films about. No one in my department was a film major. Most of us were involved in theater at one point, in either writing or acting. Most of us were English majors.

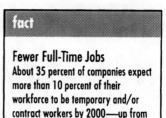

fact

Fewer Full-Time Jobs
About 35 percent of companies expect more than 10 percent of their workforce to be temporary and/or contract workers by 2000—up from 12 percent of companies in 1990.
—The Conference Board

5. "My GPA Is Too Low"

Another thing that a lot of college grads obsess on—something that keeps them from taking action—is the old GPA. "My GPA is just too low," they'll say. "Nobody will hire me with my grades."

definition

CARPAL TUNNEL SYNDROME:
Face-saving "ailment" for those individuals whom natural selection has deemed unfit for the modern workplace.

Well, I can't even tell you how little your GPA matters. In fact, if I had known how little it matters with respect to getting a job, I would have had a lot more fun in college. I also would have participated in a few more extracurricular activities, which would have helped beef up my résumé.

I graduated with a 3.5 average and thought that was too low to put on my résumé, so I simply didn't include it. I should have, but I didn't. Anyway, in all the interviews I've been on, not once have I been asked what my GPA was. People just don't give a shit. Sure, if you're planning on going to grad school, your GPA definitely matters. If not, don't sweat it.

The Real Skinny with . . . Farrah Greenberg, Fashion Editor

FROM INFORMATIONAL INTERVIEW TO JOB OFFER:
My aunt knows a lot of people in the industry. When I graduated, she introduced me to a senior fashion editor at *Glamour* magazine. She agreed to meet with me as a favor to my aunt, even though there wasn't a job available. So I went up there. We were chatting. I didn't even pull out my résumé, and before I knew it, she said, "I think you would be perfect for the job." And I said, "What job?" She said she needed an assistant.

DOING A LITTLE EXTRA:
I would volunteer to assist one of the stylists when they needed help, because it interested me more than what I was doing. This means assisting on the shoots: booking hair and makeup, finding locations, getting the clothes there, unpacking, ironing, sewing. Just dealing with everything that's involved in a shoot. So when an assistant stylist position became available, this stylist hired me because she knew I could do it.

IT'S WHO YOU KNOW:
When I hear about a position—say, Calvin Klein is looking for someone—I'll call a friend that I know from the industry and say "I know you're not happy where you are. Calvin Klein is looking; you should call over there." [With my assistant,] my friend said "My cousin has a friend who wants to get into the industry; will you meet with her?" So I hired her. Some people get it on their own, but a lot of people know people.

SCHMOOZING THE BOSS:
It was probably merit [why I got promoted] and because my boss and I had a good relationship. It really depends on your boss what's going to happen to you. You could do a hell of a job, and he or she might not like you for some reason. You can keep your job, but you're just going to stay where you are.

Chapter 2

FIGURING OUT WHAT TO DO WITH YOUR LIFE

The hardest thing about finding a job, by far, is figuring out what the hell to do with your life. Why? Because if you don't know where you're going, it's kinda hard to get there.

It's like that lyric from the musical *South Pacific*: "You've got to have a dream. If you don't have a dream, how you gonna make your dream come true?" Or something like that.

If you're one of those people who knows exactly what you want to do and where you want to work but don't know how to get it, skip ahead to the next chapter.

If, however, you're like me when I graduated—clueless—read on.

Keeping in Touch

"I was living in Boston waiting tables. I thought about being a cook and then decided that wasn't my thing. I always enjoyed making things and sewing and drawing, so I thought maybe I should get into that. So I decided to move to New York and told everybody I know to let me know if they heard of anything. One day my sister-in-law called and told me that a hat designer she knew might be looking for an assistant. So I called her. She needed somebody right away, but since I was still in Boston and couldn't start when she wanted me to, she hired someone else. When I moved to New York, I gave her a call. It turns out that she didn't like the woman she hired, and she asked me if I could come in to meet her. We met and she offered me the job."

—Bianca, twenty-four years old

"I'M A GRADUATE. I'LL GET A GOOD JOB"

I had absolutely no clue what to do with my life when I graduated with my history degree. Amazingly, I wasn't even that worried about it. I just kind of assumed (stupidly) that everything would work out. "Hey, I'm a college graduate! I'll get a good job for good pay, no sweat," I thought.

So why was I still teaching windsurfing and waiting tables and writing bad plays and bad poetry and partying every night until four in the morning a year and a half after I graduated?

I don't think it's because I was lazy, as my father probably thought. I think the reason I delayed the inevitable rat race was because I had absolutely no idea what to do with my life. And when you have no idea what to do with your life, it's hard to get motivated to go after something.

Sound familiar?

If you don't know what to do with your life, it's probably because you don't know what you *can* do with your life. You've been in school your whole life, isolated from the real world. Sure, you know what a few careers are, like doctors and lawyers and cabdrivers and strippers, teachers, cops, and garbagemen. But you probably have no idea what the hell the rest of the suit-wearing population who get in their cars and cruise up elevators in tall buildings all across the country do.

Yeah, I'd heard about "advertising and marketing executives," "financial planners and bankers," but I never had any contact with them, so I had absolutely no idea what they did. They were hidden away in these tall buildings that I wasn't allowed in.

Once you're in the working world, however, once you are no longer an interviewing fool but are actually drawing a paycheck at a company, the whole business world unfolds right before you.

Barfly to Manager

When Doug graduated from the University of Maryland, he continued waiting tables in town, where he had worked his last two years in college. He wasn't sure what he wanted to do with his life but wasn't too anxious to get a "serious" job anyway. He thought about learning the restaurant business and would have been interested in managing at the restaurant he worked at, but the manager had been there for a few years and wasn't going anywhere.

Every Thursday, after his lunch shift, he would go to this nice restaurant down the block for a drink. One Thursday he went in for a drink at around six P.M., late for him, and found the *owner* behind the bar serving drinks. Doug asked where the bartender was and was told he was out sick. "How about the manager?" he asked. He was out sick, too, he was told. Doug told the owner that he could help him out right then if he wanted. Desperate, the owner took him up on it. That night Doug alternated between bartending and solving problems on the floor and stayed until closing. The owner was so impressed with how he handled the pressure and the customers that he told him at the end of the night that if he was interested, he could have the manager's job. "You have a manager," Doug said. "Not if you say you'll take the job," the owner said. The owner was so pissed off at the manager for not coming in, especially since the bartender was sick, that he canned his ass and gave Doug the job.

YOU'LL MEET PEOPLE FROM DIFFERENT COMPANIES

After you dive into the nine-to-five thing, no matter what job it is, you'll start learning about jobs you've never heard of before. You'll be doing business with all sorts of people at different companies that your company does business with.

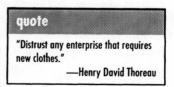

quote

"Distrust any enterprise that requires new clothes."

—Henry David Thoreau

For example, say you take a job at an accounting firm, and your firm does work for Evian. Now, even if you're just a phone picker-upper, you're probably going to be talking with Evian people every once in a while. And if you're smart, you'll be really nice and helpful and make friends with them. Boom, you now have an in at a company you might be interested in working for.

YOU'LL MEET PEOPLE IN YOUR OWN COMPANY WHO HAVE COME FROM OTHER COMPANIES

You'll also be working with a group of people who have come from a variety of companies, companies you might want to work for.

This is how I landed a job as director of development for a small film company in Los Angeles. I was working as an assistant at a talent agency, absolutely hating it, and one day at lunch I was talking with a cohort, telling him how I wanted to get into development. "My brother is the president of XYZ Pictures. They're actually looking for a development person right now," he said. Two weeks later I had the job.

---

definition

GOLDEN PARACHUTE:
Excessive bribe paid for the future silence of an incompetent senior executive, lest shareholders realize the board of directors is devoid of sound judgment.

JUST DIVE IN

So don't worry that you don't know what the hell you want to do with your life. Get off your butt and dive into something. Anything. It matters some, but not as much as you think. Remember, you're gonna change careers (not jobs, *careers*) at least three or four times anyway.

This is not to say, however, that it wouldn't be a great thing if you knew exactly what you wanted to do and got a job with a great company right out of college doing that. Sure, this is the ideal, but it rarely ever happens. And even if you think you know exactly what you want to do with your life, chances are you won't be doing it five years from now.

Creativity and Confidence

This was the dilemma: Lilly lived and designed children's clothes in Montreal but wanted to live and design children's clothes in New York City. But (a) she had no connections, and (b) she had no working papers. This is what she did.

First off, the résumé. "In the fashion industry you can't send your résumé on plain white paper, because it's a creative industry. You have to do more. My résumé was very colorful. It was for children's wear, so I had to make it fun-looking. It really said all over it that I do children's clothing. It showed my creativity right on the résumé. For instance, where it said my travel experience, I had a little airplane and a map. Where it mentioned my negotiating skills, it had a little mouth talking. It was just very fun and colorful."

Second, the interview. "I went in and was very confident. He asked me, 'What makes you think you'll come here from Montreal and get a job?' And I said, 'Because I'm extremely intelligent and very creative, and I know I can do well in New York.' Once he was hooked and ready to hire me, I slipped it in that I couldn't work here because I didn't have working papers. I wanted him to like me and want to hire me and *then* deal with the consequences. He wound up hiring me on the spot and sponsoring me."

PICK THE INDUSTRY, NOT THE JOB TITLE

I remember when I graduated I was fixated on what job title I'd have. I'd say to myself, "Do I want to be a 'marketing executive' or an 'account manager'?" all the while trying to suss out which sounded better. I didn't even know what either job was about. I just needed to know what I was going to be.

Well, when you're starting out, titles don't mean squat.

If I were starting over again, I'd pick the industry I most wanted to work in, like advertising, film, or radio. And then, instead of trying to come up with some job title that looked good on paper, I'd pick the companies in that industry I would most like to work for.

WHAT'S IN A NAME?

You see, you don't want to limit yourself with a job title by saying "I'm going to be a 'market analyst' or 'development executive.'" Sure, maybe you'll wind up doing that, but the truth is, you might wind up doing it with some crappy company that lured you in by offering you the title that you always wanted, and you'll end up hating it.

But the reason that you'll probably hate it is not because of the job title but because the product that your second-rate employer produces—whether it be TV shows, blouses, radio shows, whatever—is just that, second-rate. There's nothing like the excitement of working with a first-rate company, with first-rate clients, that does first-rate work—even if you're sweeping the floors.

I'll give you an example.

HOW I BLEW IT

With my first job out of college, I made the mistake of going with a title rather than a company. I accepted an offer with a very small, unknown public relations firm because they hired me straight off as a "copywriter." Skipped right over that "assistant copywriter" thing and landed the real deal. I was psyched. For about a minute. After three months, I quit. The job was a joke. I spent all day on the phone calling TV and radio stations all across the country trying to get our clients—a bunch of schlock doctors who cured hemorrhoids and came up with things called the "bikini diet"—on their news programs. I did zero writing. I was a telemarketer. It sucked.

Meanwhile, I had turned down an offer with a very big company with a great name because they told me I would be an assistant for at least a year before I would be doing much writing. What I know now is that I would have learned what real public relations was all about, and the reason I wouldn't be writing for the first year was because I'd be learning how it was done by people who know what the hell they're doing.

So I quit after three months, saying "Screw public relations. That blows," and went back to waiting tables.

Therefore, I think it's imperative that when you're starting out, you try to get a job with the most prestigious and most successful company possible—forgetting about the job title. Here's why.

This Is a Test

How's this for an interview? Marcy was working as an assistant to a talent agent at a big firm in Los Angeles. She wanted to transfer to the firm's London office as a full-fledged agent, so she arranged an interview with the president of that office. He had her fly out to New York, where he was going to be for the day. They planned to have breakfast on a Friday morning at 9:00 A.M., so she took the red-eye out Thursday night, getting her to New York by 6:30 A.M.—in plenty of time for the breakfast. She showed up on time. He, however, was nowhere to be found.

Not knowing what hotel he was staying at, she didn't know where to call. She called the New York office and talked to several people, trying to figure out where he might be staying. No one knew. So she called the top ten hotels and found out where he *had* been. She found the hotel and found that he had already checked out. Then she called the guy's office in London to ask his assistant what his schedule was for the rest of the day and what flight he was on, but the assistant was out sick. Marcy managed to get the assistant's home number after telling her story to someone in the London office. When Marcy reached the woman at home, she told her where her boss was going to be eating lunch. (Reservations had been made.)

Marcy showed up at the restaurant and found the man. "Oh, you made it," he said. "Actually, we had spoken about meeting for breakfast," Marcy said. "Yes, I know," said the agent. "I hope you don't get upset, but I wanted to see if you could figure out how to find me. My assistant called me and told me you got her." The whole thing had been a test. "As an agent, you need to open doors that are closed to you all day long," the man explained. If Marcy couldn't find her way to him, he didn't want her working for him. She got the job.

A MATTER OF PERCEPTION

One of the most important things about starting out your career with a great company is how it propels your career. The better the company you start out with, the better your second job is going to be. This is because people love hiring people from brand-name companies. It's all a matter of perception. People are shallow. People like names.

Say applicant 1 and applicant 2 are applying for the same job at Company X. And say applicant 1's first job was as an account executive at the number one advertising agency in New York and applicant 2's first job was at some unheard-of agency where he also was an account executive. Providing both make a good connection in the interview, who do *you* think is going to get the job?

You want to see how impressed people are by names? Check this story out.

When I was around twenty-two years old and in between jobs, I spent a total of maybe three days helping out a friend of mine who worked for this famous Broadway producer. In fact, I met this famous producer maybe twice. She never even knew my name. Well, when I was applying for a job at the Brooklyn Academy of Music, I lied and said that I was presently interning for this producer, and I mentioned her name. I remember that when I said this woman's name, they were both really impressed; you could see it on both of their faces. I hadn't even done anything for this woman besides photocopy a few things and do a few errands. It didn't matter. The name of this woman

fact

Sixteen Jobs with the Lowest Unemployment Rates

Dentists	0.0
Speech therapists	0.2
Radiologic technicians	0.3
Farmers	0.5
Supervisors of police and detectives	0.5
Pharmacists	0.6
Physicians	0.7
Police and detectives	0.7
Clergy	0.9
Water and sewer treatment plant operators	0.9
Dental hygienists	1.0
Mail carriers	1.1
Veterinarians	1.1
Lawyers	1.2
Registered nurses	1.3
Stenographers	1.3

—Unpublished tabulation, "current population survey 1993," U.S. Department of Labor, Bureau of Labor Statistics

alone was enough to impress them. They thought, wow, if he works for her, he must be good. They offered me the job that day.

DO IT FOR LOVE. THE MONEY WILL FOLLOW

Something to consider before you start your job search is this: If you don't like the career you pick, you're probably not going to be very good at it. So if your parents are putting pressure on you to go into banking or some career you have no interest in going into, then don't be an idiot and do it because they want you to. If you're not into it, you're going to suck at it.

A friend of mine proves this point beautifully. When he graduated from college, he decided to go to law school, partly due to pressure from his father, who had also been a lawyer. After he graduated *magna cum laude* from Columbia, he was heavily recruited by the top white shoe firms and got an offer from his first choice. Over the next year, eighty-hour workweeks were not uncommon. He worked his ass off. So a year later he was very surprised and pissed off when he received two unfavorable reviews from partners.

It wasn't until a year after he quit to pursue a career in music that he realized he deserved those bad reviews. "I was so miserable doing law. I thought I was doing a great job because I was working so many hours. I *did* deserve those bad reviews. I wasn't into it. I was working hard but I was miserable and it reflected in my work."

Money, Schmoney

"You've got to forget about the money. Don't think in terms of 'I'm working eight hours, and therefore, I should get paid for eight hours. If I work that extra hour, I want money.' The smart kid will say, 'I'm going to forget about the money and do what I can to make *The Toxic Avenger, Part IV* the best possible film.' If eighteen- to twenty-year-olds have got to make $500 a week, then they should become accountants or dentists or something useful."

—Lloyd Kaufman, president of Troma Films

FEATURE INTERVIEW

Jane Ridge
Nike
29 years old
Product line manager of walking
Saint Norbert College, Wisconsin
Communications major

When Jane was a junior in college, one of her marketing professors told her that she needed to get an internship with a good company in college if she planned on getting a good job when she got out. All she had to do was figure out what companies, out of the millions out there, she wanted to work for.

Not a problem for Jane. Since she was fifteen years old, she knew exactly what industry she wanted to work in: athletic shoes. Sounds a bit specific and focused for a fifteen-year-old, I'd say. Jane doesn't think so. "I loved sports and I loved athletic shoes. You put these two together and it makes sense." Well, when you put it that way.

So, heeding her professor's advice, Jane wrote and called every athletic shoe manufacturer on the East Coast from her dorm room in Wisconsin. The response? Zilch. Zero. Nada. So, when summer came around, it looked like it was back to working retail, selling sneakers for the fifth summer in a row. Or not.

Instead, Jane hopped on a plane to Boston "to see if I could persuade someone to let me work for them." She arrived on a Friday, shacked up with relatives, and called Reebok on Monday morning. Being that her chances of getting an internship were slim, since it was already summer, Jane knew she had to be aggressive. "Look," she said to the personnel person at Reebok, "I'll wash your windows and scrub your floors if you hire me as an intern." Luckily, the woman was cool and laughed at Jane's bravado. "Come on in and let's talk," she said.

They met, they talked, and Jane walked out of the interview with a paid internship. For the next three months Jane worked in the special projects division, helping with fashion shows, sales meetings, and the U.S. Open, which Reebok was sponsoring that year.

Jane was right all along. Sneakers *were* her thing. She loved the internship and loved Reebok, but unfortunately, she had to go back to college for one more year. She was determined, however, not to be forgotten as just another intern, for she wasn't done with Reebok yet. So in January of her senior year, knowing there was a big sporting goods show in Atlanta coming up that Reebok would be participating in, Jane took action. She called up her old boss and said, " 'You're probably going to need some help with the event in Atlanta, right?' And she said, 'Yeah, why don't we fly you down?' "

Two months after the Atlanta show, Jane called her old boss again, this time regarding the next show taking place in Chicago. "I called them up again and said, 'Do you need help with the next show?' And they said, 'Yeah.' So they flew me to Chicago." Something Jane was learning was, if you don't ask, you don't get.

But Jane wasn't done asking. During her Chicago trip, she let Reebok know that she'd like to work for them full-time after graduation. Though she'd known since her first day of her internship that this is what she wanted, she waited until then because, as she says, "I wanted to prove myself and build a name for myself first." Her strategy worked. After a summer and two trade shows, Reebok saw what Jane could do and told her they *would* be interested in talking to her after graduation.

Right before graduation, Reebok flew Jane out to Boston and wound up offering her a job in L.A. as a field service rep, a position she held for two years until they eliminated all field service rep jobs. Not wanting to lose her, however, Reebok tapped Jane to help launch new Reebok concept stores across the U.S., which Jane did for another year and a half.

Then came the phone call: "Would you ever consider leaving Reebok?" It's something Jane hadn't really thought about. But after Sun Country Sales—a sales agency that reps Avia footwear, Vuarnet sunglasses, and other lines—made her a sweet offer, Jane thought to herself, "Maybe it is time for a change."

Change came again six months later, when Avia decided to bring their sales in-house and tried to lure Jane away from Sun Country. After they agreed to relocate Jane to the East Coast, where she'd been wanting to live, Jane accepted the offer, packed up, and moved to Connecticut.

Then, two years later, someone *else* came knocking on her door. This time the knock came from *within* the company, however. A knock that most sales reps pray for but never hear. The marketing group at Avia asked Jane if she'd be interested in moving out to Portland to be marketing manager in cross-training. To put it plainly, most sales reps dream of crossing over from sales to marketing. It's more responsibility, more fun, and your ass isn't on the line at the end of every month. The reason *she* got the job is pretty simple, Jane says. "I always gave them marketing information. I always gave them feedback about what worked and what didn't. I was there to help."

Apparently, nothing could help the ailing Avia, however. Eight months into her job, they got rid of cross-training in an effort to redefine and save the company. Though they offered Jane several different positions, none of them interested her.

When an old associate from Reebok who had gone to Adidas got wind of Jane's situation, he hooked her up on an interview there. As it turns out, another person whom Jane had worked with at Reebok had also gone to Adidas. So when *she* heard that Jane was interviewing there, she put in a good plug for Jane as well. In the "big, but small" athletic shoe industry, had her past associates not liked her, Jane would have been screwed.

People don't dislike Jane, however. Take the Adidas interview. Had the interviewer not liked her, she never would have gotten away with saying this to him: "A number of years from now somebody's going to come to you and say, 'Who hired that person?' [meaning her]. And you're going to be able to say you're the one who did it." Though she laughed when she said it, it's something she believes. "There's good apples in a company and there's bad ones," she says. "If you can pick the good ones, that reflects well on you."

After six months at Adidas, Jane was tapped to head up the international kids' unit, where she was responsible for deciding what sneaker designs to go with, how to build the best shoe for the best price, and how to market them. And how do you pick the shoe that's going to break through and be the hot seller? "It's tough. That's what we're here for. We do tons of research and testing, but in the end it's a very well thought out educated guess."

Along with the guessing came tons of hours and market research and traveling. Trips to Asia and Europe were part of the routine. Tough life, right? Actually, it takes its toll. Especially on relationships. "You go out with someone and they ask you, 'Do you want to go out again?' And you're like, 'Yeah, can you call me in two or three weeks?' Like this person is going to be around then."

Five months after I interviewed Jane and one week before this book was due, I found out that Jane was recruited by Nike to help build their growing walking line. Again, the opportunity came from someone Jane worked with. This time it was a friend from Avia who had gone to Nike to work on the walking line. When this friend gave Nike her notice, they asked her if she could recommend anyone, and she gave them Jane's number. "So they called me and asked if I would be interested in interviewing," Jane says.

From Reebok to Avia to Adidas to Nike. Who's next? According to Jane, no one, at least for a while. "I took this job because of the long-term attractiveness," she says. Not only is the walking market growing, but right now, Nike is number three in the category. "I have an opportunity to make a difference," Jane says. "There's a lot of potential for the category and for Nike, and I want to be a part of it."

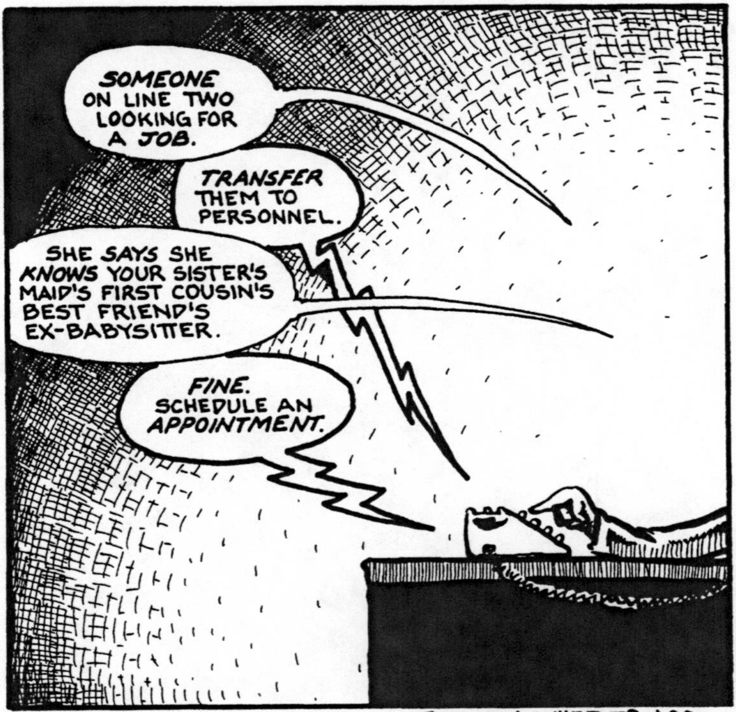

SHANNON WHEELER '98

Part 2

Finding the Job: The Passive Approach

Chapter 3

INTRODUCTION

Man, anybody can find a job. You want to find *the* job. You want to find the job you're going to be psyched to go to every day. A job that isn't going to rot your brain and turn you into a bitter, middle-aged alcoholic. Basically you want a job that doesn't suck.

> **definition**
>
> COPY MACHINE:
> 1. Electronic trickster with a black sense of humor and impeccable comic timing. 2. Japanese-manufactured paper-cut factory.

YOU AND THE BUSINESS WORLD

The first thing to know about the business world is this: It's a strange place unto itself where honesty is laughed at, cruelty is tolerated, and no one can be trusted. There are no rules. There's no such thing as fair. There is no accepted standard of behavior. It's dog eat dog, kill or be killed.

NOBODY CARES IF YOU "MAKE IT" OR NOT

It's sad but unfortunately it's true: the only people who care whether or not you succeed are your family, and you can't be too sure about them sometimes. Nobody else cares. You wish somebody would just give you a break. Sorry. You have to make your own breaks.

"Have a Drink. How About a Job?"

"Sit down and have a beer. It won't kill you," said Beth's friend. Beth had walked into the bar to use the phone to call her boyfriend because her car had broken down. But before she could, her friend, who happened to be there with coworker friends, grabbed her. "Hang out. My boss will be here any minute, and he'll pick up the tab. Drinks, dinner, whatever." So Beth forgot her car problems and stayed. As she says, "The guy shows up and starts talking about his company, and at the end says to me, 'Why don't you come talk to me about a job.' I wasn't even *looking* for a job. But I went to meet him and he offered me a better salary and a better opportunity, so I took it. You never know where opportunities are going to come from."

Now that I've said that, I'm going to contradict myself. Finding a job is about *making* people—certain people, a few people—care about you. It's about making people want to help *you*. *You,* as opposed to someone else. This is why some people get hired easily and right away and why some don't—even though they both might be going about their job hunt with the same amount of gusto.

> quote
>
> "Every time a friend succeeds, I die a little."
>
> -—Gore Vidal

BE THE PERSON PEOPLE WANT TO HELP

Each of the ways of finding a job—whether it be through recruiting, interning, temping, letter writing, cold calling, connections (all of which will be discussed, and more)—all share one thing in common: they all deal with people. Using your college career center might be a good way to find a job, but a college career *counselor* is the one with the power to tell you or not to tell you (i.e., they can tell someone else) about an opening at a cool company.

Using a recruiter can be a good way to get a job, but a *person* is either going to go out of their way and tell you about an excellent recruiter who got them a job—or not. You get what I'm saying?

Finding a job is about having someone—a person—giving you a job or giving you information about a job. It's about people wanting to give to *you*.

WHO IS THE PERSON PEOPLE WANT TO GIVE THINGS TO?

In no particular order, this is the kind of person I go out of my way to help. And I don't think I'm that atypical.

Someone who's

> **fact**
>
> ## Odd Jobs of Celebrities
>
> <u>Cyndi Lauper:</u> cleaned dog kennels
> <u>Steve Martin:</u> eight years at Disneyland selling Mouseketeer ears and Davy Crockett coonskin hats
> <u>Groucho Marx:</u> cleaned wigs for a theatrical wig maker
> <u>Gregory Peck:</u> carnival barker at the world's fair and tour guide at New York's Rockefeller Center
> *—The Book of Lists*

- Ambitious
- Modest
- Confident
- Smart
- Kind
- Joyous
- Optimistic
- Grateful

The reason I mention this is because I think a lot of college graduates *aren't* these things. Opinionated, moody, ungrateful, and insecure would be a decent way of describing a lot of college graduates. You see these people all the time. They think somebody owes them something—a great job, in particular. Do I sound like an old fogy? Tough. It's true. Having the right attitude is at the core of finding a job. Your attitude affects the way you'll *look* for a job and determines how successful you'll be at finding one.

Again, your attitude affects the way you'll *look* for a job and determines how successful you'll be at finding one. It's all about appreciating what a job is and why jobs are "handed out."

Passive-Aggressive Job Hunting

Talk about passive-aggressive job hunting. Jen's got it down to a T. After a few weeks in New York, having moved from Canada, she was at this swank SoHo party where she met this television director. Instead of asking him if he had any jobs available, Jen decided instead to work herself into this guy's life. She called him the next day and asked him if she could come in to his office to borrow his *New York Production Guide,* which she was going to use to cold-call people in the film business.

After a few days of going in to his office and using his resources, she started to get to know him, and he let her sit in on a couple of meetings. Then, out of the blue, he told her he was doing a film about women in their twenties in America and asked if she wanted to produce it. After all, she was a woman, and she was in her twenties. As Jen says, "I didn't walk up to him and say, 'Can you give me a job?' I said, 'I'm looking for a job. Can I use your resources, and can you give me advice and counseling about what to do?' I let it come from him."

JOB APPRECIATION

Before you call me a pedantic preacher for trying to tell you to be grateful—or whatever you think I'm going to say—and skip ahead to a more sexy chapter, don't. Read this.

People, including myself when I was in my early twenties, take jobs for granted. That would be okay, except for the fact that it keeps them from finding one. For when you have the proper appreciation for what a job is, you're going to be more prepared to get one. So, what is a job?

A "Job." My Definition

A job is a product of somebody's hard work and inability to do everything on their own. For example, say Jill and Jane start a design company out of their living room. They max out their credit cards and eat peanut butter sandwiches for two years before they start making money. Their hard work pays off, and now they have more clients and more work than they can handle on their own. They take a look at their books and decide they can *just* afford to hire somebody to take up the extra load of work. They don't want to give up their profits to pay somebody—they'd rather buy decent, new cars—but they have no choice.

This is what a job is, no matter if it's a two-person mom-and-pop shop or if it's a two-thousand-person company. They're dipping into *their* profits to give *you* a job. The job that has your name on it out there exists because of someone's incredibly hard work and possible near poverty. Somebody worked their ass off so they could give *you* money so you can live and pay your rent.

"You Owe Me"

I think most people, young and old, lose sight of this. Everybody thinks they're owed a job. Nobody owes you a job. Figure out how to make your *own* money. Make something, invent something, sell something—whatever. If you can't, then go work for somebody who's done it for you.

Politicians aren't helping matters. You're always hearing them say that people should have the right to a job. It's just not true. Jobs are created and companies exist because people, owners of companies, needed to find a way to pay for food and rent, so they created something out of nothing. Who do you think you are to think that you shouldn't have to do the same?

If you're with me on this whole job appreciation thing, it's going to affect your success in finding a job. It will affect the way you interview, for

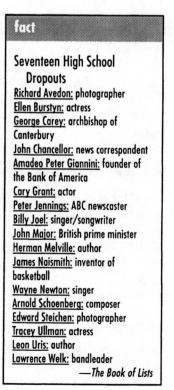

fact

Seventeen High School Dropouts

Richard Avedon: photographer
Ellen Burstyn: actress
George Carey: archbishop of Canterbury
John Chancellor: news correspondent
Amadeo Peter Giannini: founder of the Bank of America
Cary Grant: actor
Peter Jennings: ABC newscaster
Billy Joel: singer/songwriter
John Major: British prime minister
Herman Melville: author
James Naismith: inventor of basketball
Wayne Newton: singer
Arnold Schoenberg: composer
Edward Steichen: photographer
Tracey Ullman: actress
Leon Uris: author
Lawrence Welk: bandleader
—The Book of Lists

sure, but it will also affect the way you deal with people who can help you land jobs, such as college career counselors, recruiters, friends' parents, professors, etc. And this is important, because anybody in a position to help you get a job will only do so if they know these two things:

1. You're hungry for one.
2. You don't think you're owed one.

"But I'm a College Graduate"

I've actually heard this used as a reason why this kid thought he "deserved" a better job than the one he had selling ladies' shoes. He's not alone. But not only this, many graduates are under the false impression that college has in fact *prepared* them for a good job—a job where they don't have to answer the phones and make copies and file things. "I mean, I went to college so I could avoid that crap, right?" Wrong.

A college degree is simply a way of allowing you to get an entry-level job that requires no college education. An employer will say "college degree required" as a way of weeding people out. But it's not a requirement as though college has given you anything that could be of value to them. Because it hasn't.

The Real Skinny with . . . Ray Rogers, Editor, *Interview* Magazine

"CAN YOU TYPE?"
I moved to New York right after college without a job. I interviewed with Condé Nast, and it seemed really promising. They said that they had a job that I'd be perfect for, but I couldn't pass their typing test—a big faux pas.

WHAT'S SURPRISING ABOUT THE MAGAZINE WORLD:
I guess what surprised me is how gay it is, which is great. Just how open it is about everything. I guess just coming from a small town where it's sort of conservative, and then coming here and half the staff is gay. It's so cool. And nobody thinks twice about that.

IT'S THE END OF YOUR LIFE AS YOU KNOW IT:

The hours can be a real problem if you can't handle it. Sometimes you don't have time to even do your job—going out to see music and to be on top of things—if you're here until all hours. You're exhausted, but you have to come in the next day and do it all over again. And the next day, and the next day, and the next day. People get burned out.

FRUSTRATING POLITICS:

What's frustrating at some magazines is when you see that so-and-so's friend got assigned a story because it's their friend or their boyfriend or something. It's frustrating and kind of gross. If you have a real sense of integrity, it can be frustrating to see that go on.

SHOW ME THE MONEY:

You don't go into publishing if you want to be rich. Don't go into publishing if you want to even live a comfortable life for the first few years. But my entertainment's free. Whenever I want to see a band, I just call up and they put me on the list.

Chapter 4

INTERNING

Whether you're in college or you've already graduated but don't have the job you want, you should be interning. In the seventies and eighties companies would interview scores of graduates, spend thousands of dollars on training them, and pray they worked out. Not so in the nineties. More aware and more concerned with the bottom line, companies have trimmed costs wherever they can, and employee training has not gone unscathed.

The old "hire, hope, and pray" hiring methods don't cut it anymore. Companies want guarantees. They want people they *know* will succeed in the job. They want someone who can, and will, come in and hit the ground running. This is why interning has become a very, very important source of recruiting for many companies. In fact, in a survey by the College Placement Council, employers say that three out of ten new hires will be former interns. You got that? For every ten people hired at any given company, three of them will have interned at the place.

> quote
>
> "Only dead fish swim with the stream."
>
> —Unknown

GETTING THE INTERNSHIP YOU WANT

Internships these days can be harder to get than a job. The competition is stiff. Use your college career center if you're still in college (and even if you've graduated) to find out what companies they have relationships with. If none of the companies interest you, don't waste your time going for an internship with them. Get off the mind-set of doing an internship to get "experience"—in other words, something to put on your résumé. Since companies love to hire former interns, you should aggressively be going after internships with companies you actually want to *work* for.

HOW TO FIND OUT ABOUT INTERNSHIPS YOUR COLLEGE DOESN'T LIST

Call the Company's Human Resources Department

Ask to speak with a human resources manager. Tell them (or their assistant) that you're interested in interning at their company and you were wondering how you can do that. Don't let them blow you off by saying "Well, we only take interns from certain schools," or something ridiculous like that. If they sense your enthusiasm—and they will only know you're enthusiastic about interning there if you tell them—they will probably go out of their way to help you get an internship with them.

Call the Department Head at the Company You Want to Work For

If you don't get anywhere with human resources, call the department—e.g., marketing, advertising, sales, public relations—you want to work for directly. Ask for the "head of marketing," for example, and start a dialogue with them or their assistant. Just be honest with them and tell them who you are and what you want. You'll be surprised who will talk to you and offer you help. Why shouldn't they, after all? You're offering to come help them, to make their lives easier for no pay.

Check the World Wide Web

Here are some good Web sites to find out about internships that don't suck:

- **Cool Works**

www.coolworks.com

A source for seasonal employment opportunities in national parks and ski resorts: Yellowstone, Grand Teton, Acadia, Vail, Grand Canyon, Rocky Mountain, Mesa Verde, Denali, Big Sky, Sun Valley, Mount Rainier, Mount Rushmore, and Winter Park.

- **Internship and Fieldwork Listings Nationwide**

http://minerva.acc.virginia.edu/~career/intern.html

A great list of internship opportunities and internship sites put out by the University of Virginia.

- **GoodWorks at Tripod**

www.tripod.com/work/goodworks/search.html

A very easy-to-use database where you can look for job opportunities and specify full-time, part-time, internships, volunteer, what kind of compensation, benefits, and where you want to work.

- **Entertainment Recruiting Network**

www.showbizjobs.com

A good area for entertainment jobs that also posts internships. Companies that list include Sony, DreamWorks Animation, E!, Turner, MTV, and Warner Bros.

INTERNING RULES: THINGS YOU SHOULD BE DOING AS AN INTERN

Let me just start off by saying that if I had ever interned at a company when I was nineteen years old, I would most likely have been thrown out after a day or two. Offices aren't made for your average teenager.

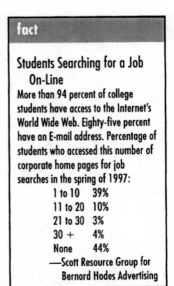

fact

Students Searching for a Job On-Line

More than 94 percent of college students have access to the Internet's World Wide Web. Eighty-five percent have an E-mail address. Percentage of students who accessed this number of corporate home pages for job searches in the spring of 1997:

1 to 10	39%
11 to 20	10%
21 to 30	3%
30 +	4%
None	44%

—Scott Resource Group for Bernard Hodes Advertising

How do I know this? Because I have heard so many, I mean tons of stories about how interns have either made complete idiots of themselves or have simply guaranteed that they will never be hired by that company after graduation.

Rule 1: Don't Be an Idiot

Listen to this interning story about idiots from Spike Feresten (writer of the "Soup Nazi" *Seinfeld* episode) from when he was an intern on *Late Night with David Letterman*.

Me: *Any advice on how to get a full-time job from an internship?*

Spike: Just don't be an idiot. We had a couple of interns stealing shirts. Just do a good job and get along with people and show you're not just doing this to get free T-shirts and dates with models. When you're there in the internship, you've got to know where to make the right moves—it's your call. You can't just come in the first day and go, "Here, I've got jokes [for Letterman to use on the show]," because they're gonna look down on you for that. There's nothing wrong with being ambitious, but it's got to be the right place at the right time, and make the right move at the right time.

      You'd be really surprised what some interns would do. You have to understand what your position is. When I was an intern, I was like, "Whatever you want me to do, go ahead and ask me. I'm going to do it. I'm not going to be an idiot. You want me to get coffee, I'll get coffee. You need me to get this photo, I'm not gonna come back 'til I have this photo." You'd be surprised. I've heard interns say, "I'm not gonna do that." And then years later this person is suddenly up for a job on the show, and someone says, "Oh, yeah, she was your intern, she used you as a recommendation." And you're like, "No, tell her to go fuck herself." [Laughs.] I don't know. I wouldn't really do that.

Don't make a nuisance of yourself, but at the same time, if you have an idea, don't be afraid to push it through. It can't hurt to show it to someone. Just find a way of not being a pain in the ass and still getting your ideas in.

Rule 2: Make Yourself Indispensable and Make a Good Impression

Be the intern that everybody in the department you're working in goes to. You need to think of each internship as if it were an audition, because that's what it is. You have to make a strong impression on them, such that when you go back to school (if you're still in school) they remember *you* over all the other interns they'll have. Or if it's postcollege, that they offer *you* a job over the other interns.

Getting Aggressive

When Jeremy was in college, he sent his résumé "all over the place" for internships—ABC, NBC, CBS, etc.—but never heard from anybody. So he followed up with phone calls. "Generally, what I got from each place was 'We'll call you if we're interested.'" Realizing he had to get a little more aggressive, he called Fox, got the personnel director on the phone, and told her he wanted an interview. "I felt that I interviewed very strongly and I needed to get in and meet with these people in person," Jeremy says. Well, he got the interview and was offered an internship on *A Current Affair.*

From May through August he worked fifteen-hour days, five days a week. "I was there constantly. I lived there. I worked around the clock." And all for no pay. "I made five dollars a day for transportation, and it cost me ten dollars. I lost money by working there."

Although he says he had no problem "running personal errands and getting coffee," he wanted to "milk" the internship for all it was worth. So he started setting up stories—something an intern normally doesn't do. Why did they let him? He asked. "I said, 'Hey, can I start working on some stories?' At first they were hesitant. They're not going to let an intern do this. But they trusted me, and they let me do a couple."

More than happy with his work, they offered Jeremy a full-time job as a segment producer at the end of the summer.

---

definition

SENIORITY:
Windows, doors, plants, speakerphones, laptops, and cell phones—or any combination thereof.

Here are some basic interning tips:

• Never complain about how little money you're making. Nobody cares.
• Don't think you're above doing anything—even picking up someone's dry cleaning.
• Make sure you stay later than all the other interns.
• Make sure you get there before all the other interns.
• Always seek out work and initiate projects. Often, people don't have the energy to keep thinking up projects for you to do. They want to see you're a self-starter, a project initiator.
• Always dress as well as everyone in the office, if not better.

Rule 3: Let Them Know You're Interested

Make sure you let the people you're working for know that you're interested in working there full-time when you get out of school, assuming you're not out of school yet. Just because you're interning there doesn't mean they'll assume you want to work there full-time. For all they know, you're just doing the internship for credit or for a résumé filler. You need to pick an opportune time and tell them flat out that you'd love to work there, that you'd love to be considered for a job when something becomes available.

Rule 4: There Are No Rules

Just because your internship ends without your being offered a full-time job does not mean you have to disappear from these people's lives. It doesn't mean you're done trying to prove yourself. In fact, it shouldn't. You should expand your internship until you're offered a job. If you've done your job and have made yourself indispensable, but they just don't have money in their budget to hire you at the moment, they will find a way to extend your internship. If they can't extend your normal internship, suggest to them the following:

• If they say you can't intern because you're out of school, look into taking a night class at a nearby college and have the company pay for it.

• If they say they can't pay you a full salary, suggest that they give you an apprenticeship and pay you a partial salary.

• If you have to work at a McJob to pay your bills, offer to go into the office two days a week. Remember, out of sight, out of mind.

Rule 5: If All Else Fails, Have Them Get You a Job Somewhere Else

If there's just no way for them to hire you, ask your closest ally there if they could make a couple of calls to their friends in the industry to see if *they* have something available. You might not even need to ask them. At two different companies I've worked at,

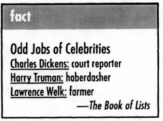

fact

Odd Jobs of Celebrities
Charles Dickens: court reporter
Harry Truman: haberdasher
Lawrence Welk: farmer
                    —The Book of Lists

there were a couple of really great interns who were just a pleasure to have around. Since we didn't have any jobs to offer them, we practically made it our mission to find these people jobs with friends of ours at different companies. You should make it your mission to be the type of person others will do this for.

This is how Michael Meisel (see interview on pages 277–280) got his job at a high-powered Los Angeles talent agency. He was interning at a reputable but small talent management company that just didn't need one more paid body. So they said to Michael, "Well, we have friends at Triad [a talent agency now part of William Morris]. Why don't we try to get you a job there?" That was Michael's next job.

Chapter 5

COLLEGE RECRUITING

College recruiting has, in my opinion, destroyed lives once full of promise and has, maybe more than anything else, assured the vitality of Alcoholics Anonymous in this country. Each year, thousands of college students walk through their campus to the college center like lambs to the slaughter, their heads and spirits bowed to the reality of broken dreams and uninteresting careers.

Why is this? Because very often companies that recruit on campuses aren't the ones you've always dreamed of working at. They're sensible careers with paper and railroad companies, insurance and pharmaceutical companies. They're the companies that generally have a hard time attracting students were it not for recruiting.

If you really don't give a shit what you do with your life and who you work for as long as you get a steady paycheck, go ahead and make college recruiting your main focus, 'cause you can probably land a job from it. If, however, you're a little more selective about what you're going to do most of your waking

quote

"Ya gotta do what ya gotta do."
—Sylvester Stallone in *Rocky IV*

hours, and aren't ready to sell your soul to the recruiting devil, college recruiting may not be for you.

I said *may* not be for you. Occasionally a company you find interesting in an industry you want to work for will show up at your college. Maybe even more than occasionally, depending on what industry you're interested in working in.

Squeaky Wheel Gets Grease at MTV

"I think the squeaky wheel gets the grease in terms of getting your foot in the door. Specifically, bug people in terms of calling and sending your résumés and checking up with them. Remind people. People ask me about positions here and send me their résumés, and they may be very qualified but I don't have anything available. Unless they are constantly reminding me that they're out there, they're going to fall in a pile of résumés like everybody else."

—Greg Drebin, MTV

A HIRING FREEZE SAVED HER LIFE

Here's a case in point. Lauren Marino (whose interview you can read on pages 61–64) got offered a job with a printing company based in Tennessee that had recruited at her college. The company had to rescind the offer, however, due to a hiring freeze, and Lauren was forced to start a proactive job search. After some thought, she realized she wanted to be a book editor. Now she is a successful book editor in New York City. If that offer at the printing company hadn't been rescinded, according to Lauren, she'd be living in Kingsport, Tennessee, a member of the Junior League, and would have ten kids.

"Influential" People

Gail's father owns a successful design company in New York with a staff of around twenty-five. She and her father are pretty close and talk on the phone with each other at work at least twice a week. I wouldn't say that Gail is overly demanding or picky. It's just that, as a person who also works in an office, she knows how things should be done.

So when the new receptionist at her father's office (a) hung up on her twice (by accident), (b) transferred her to the wrong extension, and (c) didn't even know who her father *was* ("You're looking for Mr. *who*?"), Gail felt she had to say something to her father. The very next day somebody new answered the phone when Gail called.

TAKING ADVANTAGE OF RECRUITING

Okay, now that I've totally trashed recruiting, here are a couple of *good* things about it:

> • **Good interview practice:** Sign up for some interviews with companies that show up on your campus and brush up on your interviewing. Get used to the type of questions interviewers ask. Get over your interviewing fears and nervousness. Interviewing is like making a cap-

fact

Balancing Work and Play

Over the past twenty years, Americans say they've increased the number of hours spent at work while cutting back on time devoted to leisure pursuits.

Year	Work	Leisure
1995	50.6	19.2
1993	50.0	19.0
1989	48.7	16.6
1984	47.3	16.6
1980	46.9	19.2
1975	43.1	24.3

—USA Today

puccino: the more you do it, the better you get at it. The first couple usually suck, so you might as well practice on a job you don't really care about getting. Depending on how big your college is, you *may* be able to get feedback from your career center person on how you interviewed.

definition

E-MAIL
A written message intended to insulate sender from project responsibility while falsely creating the appearance of informality and utter lack of concern.

• **Paid ticket out of nowheresville:** If your family's home *and* your college are not near where you want to settle down for the next few years, recruiting can be beneficial to you. Snag a job with the company that will send you to the city you want to go to and have *them* pay for your relocation expenses. Moving to a new city without a job can be a daunting and expensive prospect. Showing up with a job and a steady income will make the whole thing bearable. Even if it's a crappy job, at least you'll be where you want to be. Once you're there, you'll meet people and make friends in different industries who can help you get the job you really want. It's better than showing up with no income and having to wait tables.

F E A T U R E   I N T E R V I E W

Chris and Paul Weitz
Hollywood screenwriters
Ages 26 and 30, respectively
Cambridge and Wesleyan, respectively

Introduction: This hot Hollywood writing team's credits include *Ants,* the animated feature starring Woody Allen, which DreamWorks is producing. They also wrote (ghostwrote, actually) *A Very Brady Sequel* and several other screenplays bought by major studios (for which they paid them a lot of money) that have yet to be produced. Paul's play *Captive* was made into a movie with Stanley Tucci and Ron Eldard.

Chris and Paul piss off a lot of people without even knowing it. They're great guys, don't get me wrong. It's just, they're succeeding at what most of us dream of doing—writing screenplays for like, $250,000 a pop.

Why them and not you, you ask?

As Chris says, "It probably all boils down to us doing little disco dancing performances for our grandparents to the sound track of *Saturday Night Fever* at home—just being *on* for five minutes at a time." Huh?

What he's talking about is the classic Hollywood pitch meeting, where, in front of a bunch of studio execs, you act really excited about a movie idea you have. A movie idea that you want them to pay you a shitload of money to write. "I don't think we're good at it," Chris says regarding the pitch. "We're actually pretty good at it," Paul corrects. "We're pretty dour people when you meet us at first, but we have this reputation out here as being the funny guys—the hilarious Weitz brothers."

"It's a lot to live up to, actually," says Chris. "Every time we go into a room, they're [the movie executives who are considering buying their script idea] like 'So, make me laugh.' "

When I ask Chris if that can be a difficult thing—getting a studio executive to laugh—he says, quite diplomatically, "A sense of humor is not universally applicable to everyone. You answer that, Paul."

In fact, a diplomat was exactly what Chris came close to becoming upon graduating from Cambridge University. But after passing the physical, written, and clearance exams, he ultimately opted out of it because "I didn't want to be stamping passports somewhere on the border of the North Pole," he says.

Paul, on the other hand, had been writing since he was in high school and had his first play produced in Los Angeles while he was still in college. After he graduated, however, he found himself working in bookstores in New York City and bumming off his parents—much to their chagrin. "My parents definitely thought there was a chance I was going to be a loser," Paul says.

"I think the jury is still out on that one," says Chris, in perfect, rim-shot timing.

"I was totally out on a limb," Paul continues, quite used to Chris's one-liners. "Playwriting is totally impossible to make a living at, unless you're maybe one of two people in America. At the same time, though, I was determined that I wasn't ever going to do anything but write for a living."

That's when Paul decided to give screenwriting a shot and convinced his younger brother to write a comedy with him. As Chris says, "Comedies are good for us to write as brothers because we've shared the same sense of humor since we were born. The lucky thing is that other people seem to find it funny. At least they're paying us to expound upon it in 120 pages, which to us is kind of bizarre."

Bizarre indeed for a Cambridge English literature major and his brother, a writer of dramatic theater. You'd think, with their backgrounds and education, that they'd kind of look down on Hollywood genre films. Not the case at all. As Chris says, "I think a lot of people in New York who want to be screenwriters secretly harbor this grudge against Hollywood and don't like the Hollywood genre pictures—and I've always loved them. I never feel that I fit into the stereotype of the writer who's prostituting himself. I'm just totally into what I'm doing."

"You're pimping yourself," says Paul.

"Right," says Chris. "I think of myself as a pimp rather than a whore."

Pimp, whore, writer, whatever. Whatever they choose to call themselves, they know exactly what they're doing and exactly what their role is. They've got it down to how they're supposed to *dress.*

"We have to dress down for a lot of meetings, intentionally," says Paul. "It's best to have like three days' stubble and be slightly out of it. I think people would be really annoyed if we came in wearing suits," adds Chris. "They'd think we were rude," says Paul. "They'd be like, 'What the hell are these guys doing coming in dressed like executives when they're supposed to be writers?' "

But even though they have the luxury of writing in their underwear if they want to, they still keep business hours, taking turns writing at each other's houses. The difference between working in an office and at home? "We have to pay for the coffee. And there's no office gossip, 'cause it's just us," says Chris.

When I ask if it bothers them not having a normal job, writing freelance, project to project, Chris makes a good point: "There's really no job security anywhere in the entertainment industry."

This alone explains why many of the scripts that Chris and Paul have written for studios have failed to make it to the screen. "In the process of writing an idea into a script, what always seems to happen is, everyone at the studio gets fired," says Chris. "Then, your script gets put into turnaround (a polite way of saying "We're not making your script into a movie") because there's this turnover every six months of studio executives. So it's just impossible to get anything made."

"I don't know why people want to be writers," adds Paul. "Most screenwriters say that it's hell. Most screenwriters are tortured."

"Chris, are you tortured?" I ask.

"The only thing that bothers me is when I tell people I'm a screenwriter, the immediate assumption is, I'm actually doing something else to make a living. And I always want to say, 'But I'm paid for it.'"

Chapter 6

WANT ADS

You know how everybody says that finding a job through the want ads is like winning the lottery? Well, it is, kind of. But I, for one, have landed three jobs by answering ads in newspapers. And I know several people who have landed decent jobs from want ads also. But there are millions of people who have sent billions of résumés to addresses listed at the bottom of tiny boxes in classified sections all across the country who have never even gotten as much as a rejection letter.

The basic problem with answering want ads is that it's a passive approach to job hunting, which this book is definitely not about. Since 80 percent of the jobs out there are never listed in want ads, it's also a very limited approach.

So, should you or shouldn't you play the want ad game? Yes, but only if you spend the least amount of energy playing it and if you expect the least from it. You cannot make it the center and focus of your job hunt, because you will most likely not find a job from one.

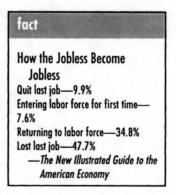

fact

How the Jobless Become Jobless

Quit last job—9.9%
Entering labor force for first time—7.6%
Returning to labor force—34.8%
Lost last job—47.7%
—*The New Illustrated Guide to the American Economy*

Great Memories

"The most successful businesspeople I've ever met have incredible memories. They can quote figures from deals from twelve years ago. Rupert Murdoch, Ted Turner, any of these guys, they have the greatest memories alive. Power is knowledge. And the more knowledge you retain and the more details you remember about things is everything."
—Lisa Katselas, entertainment lawyer and film producer

YOU CAN'T GIVE A SHIT. THERE'S NOTHING TO LOSE

Now the question is, why are some people like me and some of my friends successful with the want ad game? I'll tell you why—because we don't give a shit. And neither should you. Since it's not your focus, since all your employment opportunity eggs aren't in the want ad answering thing, you can afford *not* to give a shit. In fact, this is how you *have* to approach it. If you send a standard (boring) cover letter to some pissed-off personnel person who is getting hundreds and maybe thousands of them, you're going straight into the circular file. Imagine how glazed over this person's eyes must be. They're probably half asleep while they're going through them.

This is why your cover letter has to literally jump up and bite their nose. It's got to be different. It's got to have personality. It's got to be creative. You can't worry about them thinking you're an idiot. Some people might hate a creative, ballsy cover letter. But the 20 or 30 percent who get off on it are going to notice you over the hundreds of others. It's all in the odds. And I think the odds are in your favor if you piss off the majority but catch the eye and create a fan in the minority.

For examples of creative cover letters, turn to page 167.

"No Calls, Please"

You either see this admonition "No calls, please" at the end of an ad, or you get some P.O. box number. You rarely see the name of the company you're sending your résumé to. Often, though, you get an actual address, but without the name of the company listed. They assume this is going to keep everyone from knowing who they are so they don't get any phone calls or unwanted visitors. They assume wrong.

If you live in the area, take a drive down to the address and figure out what company put the ad in the paper. Look at the list of companies in the lobby of the building. If it's for a job in advertising and there are two advertising companies in the building, you've got a fifty-fifty shot at being right.

Now, You Can Do Two Things with This Information

1. Show Up

This is a very ballsy move, but I've heard it work for several people. You get all dressed up as if you had an interview, and you simply show up at the address listed in the want ad. You walk up to the receptionist and, in your nicest voice possible, you tell him you're there for the "marketing position," or whatever the job is. When he asks whether or not you have an appointment, you say, "No, I don't, but I was wondering if there was any chance of having one now or scheduling one." The receptionist will probably say, "No, leave your résumé." To this, you say, "I don't mean to be pushy, but could you possibly call the person interviewing to see if they *might* meet with me?" On this, you've got a fifty-fifty shot. If he says no, say, "Could you at least tell me the name of the person hiring?"

If he tells you the name, go home and call this person and ask for an interview. If he says, "No, send in your résumé," at least you're sending it to the person who's actually hiring.

If the receptionist won't tell you who's hiring, go ahead and leave your résumé with him. But make sure you send another one in the mail, just in case you've pissed him off and he threw it out.

If this hiring person is desperate to find someone—which they might be since they advertised in the paper, after all—they might see you if they're not busy. Why not? Remember, people who work and hire are just people. Maybe they're bored and feel like killing time. Maybe they're intrigued that someone would just show up. You never know how they're going to react. Don't assume that showing up is some evil act, because it's not. You want the job and you're there. End of story.

2. Call

You've gotten the name of the company by going to the address listed. Now call information and get their number. Call the receptionist and say, "Hi, I'm calling regarding the 'marketing position' listed in the paper. Could you transfer me, please?" If you get transferred, tell them why you're calling and request an interview. Just be charming and nice. You never know what you'll get. If they ask how you got their number, tell them the honest truth. If they're smart, they'll think it's creative and resourceful of you, and maybe they'll give you an interview because of it.

"Wait, Whoa, Hang On"

After Bruce graduated from Arizona State, he got an interview at Xerox through and with his brother's fraternity brother. The frat brother pulled an associate in the room to interview Bruce with him, and the both of them wound up cracking jokes and goofing off. Bruce felt intimidated and didn't get to say much. When he got up to leave, he knew he hadn't sold himself very well. "I knew the guy wasn't convinced," he said. So when he walked out of the room, he pulled his brother's frat brother aside and asked if they could go back into the room alone to talk. "We went back into the room and I sold myself. I got real passionate about who I was and what I could do for him. I was bummed that I hadn't been able to convey to him the winning qualities I felt I possessed. So I sat him down and finally came out of my shell. Because of this, he said to me, 'I'm putting your résumé at the front of my drawer. You're the first person I'm going to call.' And I was. I got the job."

True Story

I landed a job by simply showing up at the address listed in the ad. It was as a production assistant for the Big Apple Circus. I was busing tables at the time and saw the ad in the *Village Voice*. The ad said "Big Apple Circus" and gave the address, but it also said, "No calls, please." Whatever.

I got dressed up the way I thought a circus production assistant would dress (sweater and jeans) and showed up at their offices. The receptionist asked me if I had an appointment, and I said no. I remember she asked me, "Do you realize how many ré-

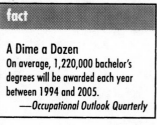

fact

A Dime a Dozen
On average, 1,220,000 bachelor's degrees will be awarded each year between 1994 and 2005.
—Occupational Outlook Quarterly

sumés we've received for this position?" She didn't say it mad-like. I said, "Tell me." "Over 300," she said. "Not very good odds," I said. "But how many people cared enough to show up like me?" I asked her. "You're it," she said. Then, to break the ice further, I said, "Listen, if you just call the person doing the interviews and let them know I'm here, I'll run out and get you a coffee or soda or anything really cheap." She laughed.

Anyway, I interviewed with the guy and was offered the job that day.

The Real Skinny with . . . Laurence Schwartz, Film Producer

CREATING A POSITION FOR YOURSELF:

When my internship was over [at New Line Cinema], I didn't want to leave and they didn't want me to leave, so we sort of figured out a way for me to stay. We came up with this idea for an apprenticeship, which had never been done. This was an idea I had so that they could keep me but wouldn't have to pay me a full salary while I did more of trying to prove myself.

ON WHY HE'S BEEN PROMOTED:

I hope it's because of the work that I've done. It's a political business. Why people get hired, fired, and promoted, I'd be a fool to say it's because of the work that they do. There's a lot of other reasons why this happens. It's a great mystery.

THE TYPE OF PERSON HE WOULD HIRE:

I look for someone who has really good ideas, good writing skills, good communication skills, is a really good spotter of talent, is really plugged into pop culture etc. . . . I think a good liberal arts education is crucial. A background that has a little bit more wit than just studying and watching movies; certainly literature and history. No one in my department was a film major. Most of us were English majors.

THE SHARK MENTALITY:

I think you have to have a certain amount of self-confidence. I don't think you have to be a killer. That's not appealing to me—people who have that shark mentality. Although I can't say that that's not a good thing to have, because a lot of people that make it are all about that.

BACKSTABBING:

You have to be careful. It's a tough industry. It can be very cutthroat. You have to be slow to trust people. You've got to have your guard up at all times. You have to look before you walk, because you can step in shit. And there's a lot of it out there.

Chapter 7

THE INTERNET

The Internet, baby. That fast-paced, fast-changing highway of information and downloadable pictures. Like it, hate it—it doesn't matter. It's now an essential part of the job search.

Why is it now an essential part of the job search? Because it has become an essential part of many companies' recruiting. So if many companies have found that they like recruiting via the Internet, you'd better be there.

HOW COMPANIES USE THE NET TO RECRUIT

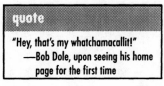

quote

"Hey, that's my whatchamacallit!"
—Bob Dole, upon seeing his home
page for the first time

On Their Own Corporate Web Site

As you probably know by now, everybody and their hamster has a Web site. From IBM and British Airways to Mom and Pop's Dry Cleaning in Podunk, Kansas. Many, if not most, of these sites have an "Employment Opportunities" area, where they list positions that are available at their company. IBM, for example, knows that someone interested in working for them will most likely (or should) visit their Web site to learn more about them and to see if they have an employment area.

fact

Odd Jobs of Celebrities
<u>Telly Savalas:</u> Peabody Award—winning executive with ABC News and State Department employee
<u>Sylvester Stallone:</u> gym instructor and dorm bouncer at a girls' boarding school in Switzerland
<u>Brad Pitt:</u> worked as a giant chicken in front of El Pollo Loco
—*The Book of Lists*

Good News for Jocks

When Chris graduated Radford College, he was kind of worried about the fact that he didn't include his not-so-stellar GPA on his résumé. Playing varsity lacrosse six days a week, five hours a day, in addition to bartending thirty hours a week didn't leave much time for the books. So as a way of explaining a lowish GPA, Chris included the lacrosse *and* the fact that he bartended throughout college on his résumé.

Good thing. On his second interview for the job he's at now, he was allotted five minutes with the president of the company. "I walked in there and the first thing he said was 'Tell me about playing lacrosse.' He was a seventy-year-old man who had no clue what the sport is but had heard of it. I told him what I got out of it and answered the question great. I told him it was a great sense of pride accomplishing a goal, working with a great group of guys, doing something you absolutely love. Getting thirty-five guys together and going after a goal."

The second question didn't go quite as well, however. In fact, he bombed it. The question? Oh, just that not-so-important one (yeah, right), "What do you want to do with your life?" A question you should have an immediate answer for. Incredibly, says Chris, it didn't matter that he couldn't answer it. He had connected on the sports thing.

Chris's direct boss (the first guy he interviewed with) also liked the lacrosse thing. "He liked my sports experience because he knew I could work on a team," Chris says. Unfortunately for Chris's boss, not everybody at the company benefited from playing on a team. "My boss argues with the MIS manager all the time. He's very selfish, and he doesn't accept criticism very well. And my boss always says it's because he was never part of a fraternal organization such as a sports team where you took criticism on a regular basis. That's one of the reasons my boss likes me. I take criticism really well."

And when you're new, accepting criticism is a must. "Accepting criticism when you're brand-new is essential because you're going to get barraged with criticism. You have to be able to go with the flow," Chris says.

On a Job Site Database

There are all these Web sites out there (I've picked the best of them and listed them below) that list job openings. The site puts all the jobs into a database and creates a type of search engine that allows you to find the jobs in there based on different criteria, such as location, salary, job title, and industry. These sites generally charge the companies to put their job openings in their database, thus making it free for you and me.

If you're looking for a job in computers, new media, engineering, accounting, or any applied science, for example, going through the job site databases should be a main component of your job search. Any company that is technical-, math-, science-, or computer-oriented has probably been using the Internet for a few years now to recruit people. Since knowledge of computers and the Internet is a basic requirement to work in one of these industries, what better way to find your new hires than that medium?

For you nontechies, job sites can be a very important job search tool, too. Since you're basically expected to be computer and Net literate no matter what industry you work in, even the most nontechnical companies are turning to the Web to recruit as well.

WHY COMPANIES ARE USING THE NET TO RECRUIT

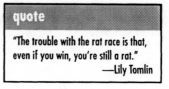

quote

"The trouble with the rat race is that, even if you win, you're still a rat."
—Lily Tomlin

It's Cheap

Paying a company a few thousand dollars a year to list many jobs, or a few hundred dollars per job listing, is nothing compared to paying a recruiter a percentage of a new hire's pay. And listing job opportunities on your own corporate Web site is free.

They Reach Educated, Computer–Savvy People—the Kind of People They Want

Whether it's Microsoft looking for an entry-level programmer or Nike looking for a marketing assistant, the people who wind up finding their "ads" are generally the kind of people they're looking for. (A) They're computer-savvy. (B) They're resourceful. The fact that they're *using* the Net as a search tool is impressive to a lot of companies.

There's No Paperwork

If the company is smart, they'll have you respond to their job listing by pasting your résumé into a "box" or into an E-mail instead of having you fax or mail it (which some still have you do). This makes storing résumés and responding to résumés a lot easier than if they were to place an ad in the paper and get tons of paper résumés.

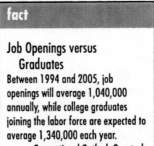

fact

Job Openings versus Graduates
Between 1994 and 2005, job openings will average 1,040,000 annually, while college graduates joining the labor force are expected to average 1,340,000 each year.
—*Occupational Outlook Quarterly*

definition

PERFORMANCE BONUS:
Timepiece made by Swiss Germans, or other token sum, given employee to reward entrepreneurial initiative, which earns employer hundreds of thousands of times the value of aforementioned bauble.

JOB LISTING SITES

Here are the best job listing sites on the Web (in my opinion), in alphabetical order:

- **America's Employers**
http://www.americasemployers.com
    - A fairly comprehensive company database divided by state and industry.
    - Advertises positions by computer and tech-related companies for computer and tech-related jobs.
    - Résumé bank. Post your résumé for HR people to browse. Divided up by industry.
    - A list of recruiters for different industries all across the country.
    - "Electronic Networking." A bulletin board where you can ask your peers about working in different parts of the country or whatever. A lot of good dialogue going on here.

- **America's Job Bank**

http://www.ajb.dni.us/

Brought to you by the U.S. Department of Labor. Boasts that it contains information on approximately 250,000 jobs, of which 5 percent are in government, the rest in the private sector. "Listings come from 1,800 state employment service offices around the country, representing every line of work from professional and technical to blue collar and entry level."

- **Boldface Jobs**

http://www.boldfacejobs.com

A good place to look if you're a software developer or engineer, accountant, or any other type of computer geek or engineer. You can also enter your name and résumé in their database.

- **Broadcast Employment Services, a.k.a. TVJobs**

http://www.tvjobs.com/index_a.htm

A great place to look if you're interested in getting into television, radio, cable, education, postproduction, corporate/industrial video, or multimedia. If you want to work at a TV station, this is a great place to go.

- **CareerCity, a.k.a. Adams JobBank Online**

http://www.adamsonline.com

Mainly job listings with computer and tech-related companies. A nice feature of the site is their search engine to over a hundred job newsgroups on the Internet.

- **CareerMosaic**

http://www.careermosaic.com

A very well designed site created by Bernard Hodes Advertising, one of the leading employment advertising agencies in the United States. Their J.O.B.S. database is not as large as Online Career Center's or E-Span's but is definitely worth looking through. Search by job title, description, company, city, state, zip code, and country. In addition, CareerMosaic's Usenet Search lets you search national, regional, and local Usenet newsgroups for job opportunity postings. Their International Gateway provides access to jobs in Canada, United Kingdom, Japan, Hong Kong, and France. You can also add your résumé to their database.

- **CareerPath**

http://www.careerpath.com

Check the want ads in twenty-four major-market papers, including: *Atlanta Journal-Constitution, Denver Rocky Mountain News, New York Times, Baltimore Sun, Detroit News and Free Press, Orlando Sentinel, Boston Globe, Fort Wayne Newspapers, Philadelphia Inquirer, Charlotte Observer, Hartford Courant, San Jose Mercury News, Chicago Tribune, Sacramento Bee, Houston Chronicle, Cincinnati Enquirer/Post, Los Angeles Times, Seattle Times/P-I, Columbus Dispatch, Miami Herald, South Florida Sun-Sentinel, Denver Post, Minneapolis–St. Paul Pioneer Press,* and *Washington Post.*

CareerPath offers search capability by newspaper, job category, and keywords.

- **Chronicle of Higher Education**

http://chronicle.merit.edu/.ads/links.html

Lists teaching positions in universities and colleges. You can search by the field you're interested in or by the location where you want to work.

- **Cool Works**

http://www.coolworks.com

Cool Works℠ includes seasonal employment opportunities in national parks and ski resorts, including Yellowstone, Grand Teton, Acadia, Vail, Grand Canyon, Rocky Mountain, Mesa Verde, Denali, Big Sky, Sun Valley, Mount Rainier, Mount Rushmore, and Winter Park.

- **Crew Net**

http://crew-net.com/

Lists job openings in feature films, television shows, commercials, and music videos all over the world. All major job titles are represented in the database, from production assistant to producer. Fee of $19.95 per month.

- **Entertainment Recruiting Network**

http://www.showbizjobs.com

A great site for entertainment job listings. Companies that list include Sony, DreamWorks Animation, E!, Turner, MTV, and Warner Bros. Also has internship listings.

- **E-Span**

http://www.espan.com

E-Span provides a fully searchable jobs database. You can also enter your personal profile (including your educational level, years of experience, current job level, salary requirements, geographic areas desired, and job keywords). E-Span will then keep you posted via E-mail on all new job opportunities added to the database that match your profile. Participating employers can conduct a search against the résumé database, then post a job that will "troll" for new résumés as they are submitted.

- **Federal Jobs**
  http://www.fedworld.gov/jobs/jobsearch.html
  Maintained by the U.S. Department of Commerce. Lists positions with government agencies across the country.
- **GoodWorks at Tripod**
  www.tripod.com/work/goodworks/search.html
  A very easy-to-use database listing job opportunities with special-interest groups, environmental groups, and every do-gooder society or association you can think of. You can specify full-time, part-time, internships, volunteer, what kind of compensation, benefits, and where you want to work.
- **Heart (Career.com)**
  http://www.career.com
  A good place to look for computer-related jobs.
- **Jobtrak**
  http://www.jobtrak.com
  A great source of job listings for college students and new alumni. Access is limited to participating schools. However, most major universities participate.
- **JobWeb**
  http://www.jobweb.org
  Sponsored by the National Association of Colleges and Employers (NACE), JobWeb offers a variety of job and employer listings for entry-level seekers. You can search by keyword and geography, or you can view the entire database of jobs and employers.
- **The Monster Board**
  http://www.monster.com
  With over fifty thousand job listings, this is the first place I would probably go if I were looking for a job. They even have a separate entry-level job opportunities section. You can also submit your

résumé to their employer-searched database on-line and surf through over three hundred different employer profiles.

• **Online Career Center**

http://www.occ.com

Between individual companies that pay a few thousand dollars a year to list jobs and recruitment companies, 4,500 different companies placed ads last year. Also has an okay recruiter list. Post your résumé and learn of career fairs and events. Skewed more to tech-related companies but lists nontech jobs within these companies along with the tech jobs.

• **Online Technology Employment Center**

http://www.hotjobs.com

Very easy to use. Mainly computer-related jobs. If you're a computerhead, this is a great place to find work.

OTHER USEFUL SITES TO CHECK OUT

• **Job Hunt**

www.job-hunt.org

The assistant director of residential computing at Stanford University has put together a comprehensive list of over six hundred Web links. It includes job lists in all fields, classified ads from newspapers, commercial services, meta-lists, résumé banks, university career centers, and reference material. The site is updated weekly.

• **EnviroLink Network**

http://envirolink.org/orgs/

A comprehensive listing of Web links to more than 250 not-for-profit environmental organizations. Does not contain job listings but is a great resource.

• **Environmental Organization WebDirectory**

http://www.webdirectory.com/Employment/

Lists top environmental job-postings sites as well as links to environmental magazines. A must if you're a greenhead.

• **Professional Association List on the Web**

http://www.yahoo.com/Economy/Organizations/Professional/

Yahoo has done a good job of compiling a list of professional organization sites in all major industries. For example, if you're interested in advertising, then you should check out the advertising associations on the Web and become a member. Professional associations can be a great way to network with people in the industry via conferences and other events. Associations can often give you a list of all the best companies and names of executives in their industry.

• **Internship and Fieldwork Listings Nationwide**
http://minerva.acc.virginia.edu/~career/intern.html
A great list of internship opportunities and internship sites put out by the University of Virginia.

• **International Homeworkers Association**
http://www.homeworkers.com/
Group health insurance, speakers, job opportunities, etc. A good site to check out if you're committed to going it on your own at home.

• **Relocation Salary Calculator**
http://www.homefair.com/homefair/cmr/salcalc.html
This calculator uses cost-of-living differentials to let you easily compare salaries between geographic locations.

• **City Net**
http://www.city.net/
Provides access to information on travel, entertainment, local business, government, and community services for hundreds of cities around the world.

• **RentNet**
http://www.rent.net/ctg/cgi-bin/RentNet/Home
RentNet is an on-line national database that includes furnished and unfurnished apartments in all fifty states, in Canada, and overseas. Database is searchable by city/area, apartment size, and price. Some listings provide pictures.

• **Chambers of Commerce**
http://www.careers.org/catg/06bus-02.htm
Learn about that city you're thinking about moving to, or being forced to move to. Find out about businesses in the area, the school system, what percentage of townies go on to college, and stuff like that.

- **Securities and Exchange Commission Information**
http://www.jobweb.org/sec.htm
A searchable database of financial filings (including annual reports) for public companies.
- **Graduate and Professional Schools (by Peterson's Education Center)**
http://www.petersons.com/graduate/gsector.html
Thinking of going to graduate school? Check out this site, where you can search by programs, location, or alphabetically.
- **List of Franchisers**
http://www.careers.org/gen/all_fran.htm
Interested in starting your own business or buying one? Search through this mammoth list of franchise opportunities. Supplies addresses and phone numbers only.
- **Business Job Finder**
http://www.cob.ohio-state.edu/dept/fin/osujobs.htm
For those of you interested in careers in finance, accounting, and management, this is the place for you.

Topics covered include: skills and requirements, key job areas, print resources, Internet resources, salaries, facts and trends, and top corporations.

Areas covered within these fields include:

Finance: corporate finance, commercial banking, insurance, investment banking, money management, and real estate

Accounting: public and managerial accounting

Management: management consulting, strategic planning, and logistics

BUSINESS FORUMS ON THE INTERNET

- The *Washington Post* Business Talk (http://www.washingtonpost.com/) hosts discussions with prominent people in the business community.
- *Entrepreneur Magazine* hosts a Small Business Forum (http://www.entrepreneurmag.com/forum.hts), where entrepreneurs can

discuss a variety of topics from starting a business to managing current operations.

• *Pathfinder* (http://www.pathfinder.com) is an excellent gateway to discussion forums and live chat sessions hosted by popular magazines such as *Life*, *Money*, *People*, and *Time*.

• *Advertising Age* (http://adage.com/interactions/) provides a discussion forum on issues important to marketing, media, and advertising.

FEATURE INTERVIEW

Lauren Marino
Senior editor
29 years old
Broadway Books
Providence College, English literature

Some of the books Lauren has edited include *Cindy Crawford's Basic Face*, *Webonomics*, *The Complete Geek: An Operator's Manual*, and *The Heart's Code*. Look for them today!

When Lauren hit her senior year of college, she still had no idea what to do with her life. She loved being an English major; she just couldn't figure out what to do with it. Then, in February of her senior year, it just came to her: she would become a book editor. It fulfilled two of her favorite things to do—reading and writing.

Knowing that the title "editorial assistant" was the entry-level job in publishing, having no connections, and not yet ready to move to New York City, she scoured the papers desperate to find it. "Anything with 'editorial assistant' in it," she says. Then, one Sunday she saw it in the local Providence paper and "went crazy." She ran down to the address written in the ad the next day, filled out an application, took their required grammar and spelling test, and got the job. The job? Writing greeting cards for $14,000 a year.

To supplement this paltry salary, Lauren bartended at night and often found herself falling asleep at her desk during the day. She didn't blame this on the bartending gig, however. "Writing greeting cards is not the most exciting job in the world," she says. "There's only about a hundred words you can use in the English language—and they're all nice ones."

Basically, she hated it.

"You would sit there and hope stuff comes to you in an inspirational moment. It was horrible, and I wasn't very good at it either." Her "claim to fame" was a card that involved Woody

Woodpecker flying through the air on some sort of rocket that said, "Woody's flying through the sky with a happy birthday hi." The job wasn't a total bust, however. Lauren received a bit of advice that she has carried with her to this day. "My boss told me, 'The squeaky wheel gets the grease.' It may sound corny to me now, but back then I was shy and naive, and that was very good advice for me."

Lauren's boss also encouraged her to go for the editing job she really wanted—being a *book* editor. "I wanted to hang out with brilliant writers and exchange ideas and talk about philosophy—all the glamorous stuff I thought book editing was about." In other words, she wanted to get as far away from Woody Woodpecker as possible. To do this required moving to New York, where most of the big publishing houses were—something Lauren was afraid to do without a job. So she sent a hundred cover letters and résumés to every publishing house in New York, hoping to at least snag an interview. She got nothing. Not even a rejection letter.

Undeterred, she hopped on a bus to New York, got a crappy apartment, and found a publishing placement agency that sent her out on some interviews. Problem was, all the jobs she went out for were for marketing assistant jobs within publishing houses—something Lauren had no interest in. She wanted an editorial position.

Eventually, she got a job with Kathy Robbins, a top-notch literary agent. It wasn't an editorial job at a publishing company, but it was an introduction and an "in" into publishing. Though she didn't really know what a literary agent did, she did know she would somehow be working with writers.

It was also a crash course on how business was done in the New York publishing world. "It was totally foreign to me," Lauren says. "It was really schmoozy, and that was something I didn't know how to do. I didn't even know how to answer the phone correctly! It was really hard."

"Your boss ever make you cry?" I ask Lauren.

"Oh, yeah. I would go into the bathroom and cry probably twice a week," she says. "I can't blame her for being tough on me, though. Who has time for some dumb assistant who doesn't know what the hell they're doing?" Though she might have been green and ignorant of the way things were done, one thing her boss said she had was "stick-to-itiveness." "I think I survived there and made it on pure, blind determination in the beginning," Lauren says.

After two years, Lauren knew it was time to go out and try to get an editing job. So, after trying to interview on the sly a few times, she sat her boss down and told her that she wanted to be an editor and not an agent. Much to her surprise and relief, her boss said, "Fine, we'll help you find a job if you'll stay and train whoever replaces you."

As it turned out, it didn't take much looking. One day, an editor at HarperCollins Publishers called Lauren's office and told the receptionist the following: "I'm looking for an editorial assistant. Pass the word around, would you, please?" The receptionist—someone Lauren was very friendly with—ran over and told Lauren about the job. Lauren met with this editor and, right away, sent him a nice thank-you letter. Turns out, it was the thank-you letter that got her the job, she says. "I asked him months later why he hired me, and he said it was because of the thank-you letter I sent him. It was between me and another person. The other person didn't write a thank-you letter, and I did."

Lauren had arrived. She finally had her foot in the door and could now see that corporate ladder, just waiting to be climbed. Sure, she was only making just over $20,000 a year, lived in a "crappy" walk-up apartment with four other women, ate baked potatoes for dinner, and couldn't even afford going to the movies. It didn't matter, though. She loved the work.

After a year of busting her butt, things were looking real good for Lauren at HarperCollins. As she says, "I was starting to make an impression there." She had acquired five books for the company and had just gotten her own office. So, when her boss told her that he was leaving HarperCollins to go to work for Hyperion, a different publishing house, and that he wanted her to come with him, she was torn. Leaving would mean having to turn down a promotion and some great opportunities. She would also have to give up her office and go back to cubicle life. But leaving *would* mean continuing to work with her mentor, somebody who "really cared about my career. Someone who gave me a lot of responsibility and trusted me." Lauren went with her gut and followed her boss.

At Hyperion, Lauren had to prove herself to more people now. She also had tons more work to do and found herself working until eleven o'clock many nights and on weekends as well. It all paid off in spades a year later, however, when she was promoted to associate editor. But it wasn't the long hours and weekends in the office that got her promoted, as if she were being rewarded for being a great assistant. In fact, Lauren was promoted because she *refused* to be a great assistant. "I took on as much of my boss's job as I possibly could. I started editing his books and reading all the submissions that came in for him," Lauren says. Sure, she did her job well, but if she hadn't started doing her boss's job, too, she'd probably still be an assistant.

The other reason she cites for being promoted was because of her mouth. "You have to be very vocal," Lauren says. "You have to have strong opinions about the kind of books you want to publish, and you have to make these opinions known. You have to be very hungry. It's very clear who is going to make it—who is really hungry—and who isn't."

Incredibly, two weeks after she was promoted to associate editor, Lauren was promoted again. This time they took "associate" out of the title and made her a certified editor. Here's how it happened. An editor whom Lauren had become friends with told her that she was going to be quitting the next day. So, at her friend's suggestion, Lauren walked into the boss's office immediately after she quit and said, "I know you're upset right now, and I'm here to offer a solution. And that solution is that I'll take over her responsibilities and you can promote me to editor."

Sure, Lauren snagged the job because she played the situation perfectly. But if she hadn't made a name for herself in the office, she never would have gotten the job. In fact, before the guy took her up on her idea of promoting her, he checked with other people first, to see what *they* thought of her. As Lauren says, "Having relationships with the other editors was very important to me. They helped tip the scales in my favor."

In one swift change of a title, Lauren got her own office, her own assistant, and a whole lot more pressure. "All of a sudden my job completely changed," she says. "It was a total change. Now I was expected to acquire books that were going to sell. My entire career was now based on what I acquired and how well my books sold in the marketplace." And in addition to acquiring her *own* books, she was also responsible for maintaining the Miramax Books imprint, which published film tie-in books such as the *Pulp Fiction* and *The Piano* screenplays.

Though Lauren was now an "editor," with "associate" nowhere in the title, she was not interested in coasting. So, when Bantam Doubleday Dell announced they were starting a new division, Broadway Books, Lauren put the "squeaky wheel gets the grease" principle into practice and sent the head honcho a note. Three interviews later, Lauren had the job.

Now at Broadway Books, the most difficult thing, she says, is time management. It's a never-ending process of reading submissions (books and proposals) from agents, reading and editing her authors' books, dealing with the contracts, the jacket, the packaging, the marketing, and the publicity. "It can be overwhelming at times," she says. "I don't think many people really understand what a book editor does. During the day I try to make deals and take care of business. I'm an acquisitions person. I bring in the product." The reading and the editing part of the job—the things Lauren originally *thought* editors did all day—is actually done at night and on the weekends.

"Does that leave much time for a social life?" I ask her.

"My bed and the stack of books and manuscripts next to it are my social life," she replies drolly.

Not that she's complaining, however. "I couldn't think of a more interesting job," Lauren says. "I get to work with intelligent and creative people, and I'm constantly reading and learning about new subjects. I feel like I'm in school forever. Which, for me, is great!"

Chapter 8

TEMPING

If you're a liberal arts grad who doesn't really have a clue to what you want to do, then you can thank God for temping. It is an amazing way to learn about different companies and careers—while getting paid for it. It is also an amazing way to land a full-time position.

fact

Temps
By the year 2000, half the U.S. workforce will be temporary employees.
—National Association of Temporary Workers

Temping is a super–fast-growing industry. I recently heard that it's now an $80-billion-a-year industry. I don't know about that (numbers like this mean nothing to me), but the fact is, it's grown by huge numbers in the past few years.

definition

401(K):
Inconsequential, time-released monetary fund designed to trap employees within their existing organization.

TEMPING IS A REFLECTION OF THE (EMPLOYMENT) TIMES

The fact that temping has become so big is an indication, or a reflection, of the changing employment scene. In the late eighties, early nineties, companies started canning people left and right. Companies like to call it "downsizing" or "rightsizing." Whatever you call it, one person today is often doing the work of three people ten years ago. Sure, Microsoft Office and voice mail have helped to make this possible, but the point is, there's just nobody around to pick up the slack anymore. No one to do that stuff nobody else wants to do. So what do you do? You call in a temp.

But the thing is, companies are using temps like full-time employees, with the benefit of not having to pay insurance or into a pension plan. Therefore, some temp assignments

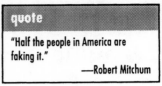

quote

"Half the people in America are faking it."

—Robert Mitchum

can last up to a year or two. I know someone who temped at Sony Records for a year and a half in the same position. It's kind of screwed up and not fair to do this, but this is the way employment is going.

For you, right now, it's good. For the millions of people who have lost their full-time jobs to temps, it's bad. But we won't get into that.

TESTING DIFFERENT COMPANIES AND CAREERS

Almost all companies have at least one temporary, personnel, or recruitment agency they use. Inevitably someone's assistant gets sick, pregnant, run over by a truck, or suddenly quits, and they need to be able to get a replacement in right away. Or else some department needs to redo all their files or has some equally boring task that no one has the time to do. In either case, they call their temp agency and tell them to send their best person right away.

Even though most temp work is usually boring and monotonous, it's still a great way to see firsthand what a company is like, what a company in a given industry does, and what the people who work there are like.

FINDING A FULL–TIME JOB THROUGH TEMPING: "TEMP–TO–PERM"

As mentioned above, companies also use temps as a way to fill full-time positions. Instead of interviewing like thirty people for a position, hiring one person, and hoping they work out, many companies

"Don't Mind the Blood"

"About a month ago I went into a temp job that was supposed to be indefinite," Amy says. "I go in, the guy sits me down and says, 'OK, I'll explain to you why you're here. You're replacing my assistant, who was murdered in her office by her ex-husband who'd been stalking her.' I turned my head and there are carpenters and painters painting and spackling the room. My boss told me that they'd be delivering my new desk and chair. It was a bloodbath. They had to throw away everything. I was definitely freaked out, but I had already agreed to the job so I had to take it."

Fortunately for Amy, that temp job only lasted a week. Now, she loves temping. She's currently temping at a financial company where she answers the phone maybe six times a day and makes $16 an hour. "I get to spend my day reading and looking for a job. It's great. It's amazing these people don't have voice mail. But I'm glad they don't, because then I wouldn't have a job. Temping is never hard. Every single job that I've taken, they've demanded that I know a bunch of software, but I've never used it."

are going the way of "temp-to-perm." They'll try out a temp in the position they're trying to fill and basically use them until they screw up or until the company simply realizes they can find somebody better. It's like test-driving a car. Once they find the perfect temp, they offer them the full-time job.

fact

Wanted: Priests
The number of men becoming Roman Catholic priests is not enough to fill the need. In other words, we've got a priest shortage.
—*Occupational Outlook Quarterly*

YOU AND YOUR TEMP AGENCY

Be Proactive: Two Scenarios for Choosing Your Temp Agency

1. You sign up with a temp agency that has associations with sucky companies you have no interest in working for.

2. You sign up with a temp agency that has associations with

really cool companies you'd love to work for for the rest of your human life.

Yeah, you want your life to be like "2." Trouble is, there are so many damn employment agencies out there. How do you find the ones that work with the companies you want to work for? Here's how.

Think of the company you'd most like to work for and call them up. Get someone from personnel on the phone and ask them what temp agency they use. Tell them you're interested in working there as a temp and therefore would like to know the agency to call. Then, call that agency and make an appointment to come in and take their typing test and all that. (You'll be expected to type at least forty words per minute.)

Manage (Schmooze) Your Temp Agent

A temp agent gets into the office by around 7:30 A.M. They check their voice mail to see what company called the night before requesting a temp. And by around 9:00 A.M. they start getting calls requesting temps to fill in for people who are out sick. Now, let's say your temp agent has ten spots he's got to fill right away. Out of the ten, one, maybe two, of the temp jobs are going to be with companies you'd potentially like to work for full-time. Meanwhile, this temp agent has around forty temps he can call for these ten jobs. Sitting back and hoping you're going to be the one this temp agent calls for one of these ten assignments, let alone the best one, is not going to cut it. Unless you badger/schmooze/charm/beg your temp agent, you are going to get the crappy assignments with the crappy companies, but chances are you won't even get one of those. You'll probably get "Sorry, it's kind of slow right now. I don't have any assignments." So what do you do?

1. You have to make their experience of working with you enjoyable, if not fun.

You have to make them feel good about themselves by constantly thanking them and being genuinely appreciative. Most temp agents (not all) hate their jobs. They'd love to do something else, but they're too afraid to quit. Asking someone how their day is going and thanking them in advance for helping you out will make anyone happy, especially someone who feels unappreciated. (Remember, a bunch of their temps know that they must schmooze them to get the good temp jobs, so if you're not one of these, you're dust.)

2. Call them every morning.

One fear a temp agent has is not being able to fill a temp position in a nanosecond. If they get your answering machine, you're dead. If they get your roommate who says "I don't know where he is," you're also dead. They want to know they can always get you at the drop of a hat (this is why you must have a beeper as a temp). Calling them every morning and asking them if they have anything for you will make them think you are (a) dependable, (b) hungry for work, (c) available. Not only will it make you shine in their eyes, but if you call them in the morning, if they have a job that just came in, you are likely to get it: it beats having to pick up the phone and track someone down.

Be Honest with Your Temp Agent about Your Career Goals

Think of your temp agent as a manipulative, capitalist pig who's only out for the quick buck. Because this is what they are. This is not an insult. If they weren't like this, they wouldn't have a job. The bad part of this equation is that they don't really give a shit about your happiness in a job as much as they do about eking out a percentage of your hourly income. This is not to say, however, that you can't *make* them interested.

Here's a quick story that made a big impression on me. I was at this temp agency in Los Angeles, the Friedman Agency, a really good agency that places a lot of temps at studios and really good entertainment companies. I had just taken my typing test (I scored 75 words per minute by cheating: when the buzzer went off and the scorer person didn't come in the room, I kept on typing) and was waiting to meet with an agent. I was outside his office listening to him speak with another young guy like myself who also wanted to go temp-to-perm with a good company. Here's how their conversation went:

Agent:	Okay, I've got a position open in the marketing department at Sony Studios. They'll want to try you out for two weeks, and if you perform well, they'll make an offer.
Guy:	No, I'm not interested. I'm really not interested in marketing. I want to get a job in creative development or with a really good producer as their assistant.
Agent:	But this is Sony. You don't do better than Sony. Plus, the benefits are great.
Guy:	I'm sure it's a great job, but I don't want to be locked into a job I have no interest in working in. I'd be wasting my time and theirs.
Agent:	But once you're in, you can always transfer departments.
Guy:	Maybe after a year. What else do you have?
Agent:	Okay, I've got a position with . . .

---

definition

HEADHUNTER:
Shameless liar who earns commissions by successfully placing incompetent individuals in bloated corporations and then subsequently placing their replacements.

I couldn't believe the balls on this guy. I thought he was crazy not to jump at the Sony job. I also thought he was crazy to challenge this agent. But after a few months of temping, I found myself doing the same thing with this guy, the agent. He'd try and sell me on some job I had no interest in, and I'd have to be very firm and remind him what I was looking for—a film development job. He didn't get these positions in very often, but when he did, he knew whom to call first. Me. And why not? Since I was very specific with him about what kind of job I wanted, he knew I would work my butt off once

---

"You're Cool. You're Hired"

After Rob graduated from law school, he started temping at different law firms until he got a decent offer. At one temp job at a decent firm, Rob was, unbeknownst to him, working at a desk that was within earshot of one of the firm's senior partners. That's why it kind of shocked him when she came up to him after two weeks on his temp assignment and said, "You're funny, you're charming, you're smart—I want you to work for me." "I am?" he said. "How do you know?" She told him that she'd been eavesdropping on his phone conversations and she loved the way he dealt with people. "It could have gone either way," Rob says. "If she didn't like my sense of humor, I'd have been kicked out on my ass. Instead, I was offered a full-time job."

I was given the shot. So don't be afraid to tell your agent what you're looking for, and don't be afraid to shoot him down when he tries to sell you on a job you're not interested in, just so he can get the commission.

YOU ON THE TEMP JOB

All right, as I believe I've said, there are two types of temp assignments. The first one is a real temp assignment where a company has you come in to fill in for someone who's either sick or on vacation, or because they need you to do some mammoth filing assignment. It lasts a week or two, maybe a month, and that's it. The second kind is where they have a full-time position to fill and they're going to try out temps until they find someone they like. Now here's the thing: sometimes you know going in that it's a temp-to-perm situation, and sometimes you don't. Sometimes they don't tell the temp agency (for what reason I'm not sure) that it's a temp-to-perm situation.

Therefore, assume that each temp job is a temp-to-perm

> **fact**
>
> **Workers Who Ask for a Raise**
> Men: 20%
> Women: 24%
> *Those who are successful:*
> Men: 59%
> Women: 45%
> —*USA Today*

situation—that there's a full-time job available. If you're a good worker, they'll offer you the job or else keep you in mind for a job somewhere else in the company. If you're not a good worker, not only will you not be offered the job, but they will tell your temp agent that you suck and you'll never be sent out by that agency again.

> **quote**
>
> "There is no happiness; there are only moments of happiness."
> —Spanish proverb

A Few Temping Dos and Don'ts

Never arrive late. This is one of the first things your supervisor is going to judge you on. As ridiculous as this sounds, it's true. Always arrive at your temp job at least five minutes early.

Never get caught on a personal call, even if you're just sitting there on your butt doing nothing.

Seek out work. As soon as you've completed an assignment, go to your supervisor and ask for something else to do. Most temps don't do this. They wait for the supervisor to check on them. As a temp, it is so easy to impress people and make them think you're hot shit by being merely mediocre.

Get to know as many people as you possibly can in the company if it's someplace you want to work. If you're temping in accounting but want to work in design, after a few days, go over to the design people and introduce yourself if the environment looks friendly. If you find a nice person there and have a good rapport, express your interest in working in that department and let them offer to help you out.

Never chew gum. For some people, it's a pet peeve.

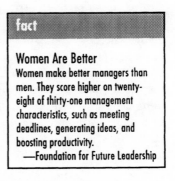

fact

Women Are Better
Women make better managers than men. They score higher on twenty-eight of thirty-one management characteristics, such as meeting deadlines, generating ideas, and boosting productivity.
—Foundation for Future Leadership

If your temp assignment ends but you're interested in working there full-time, then tell your supervisor. Ask her to keep you in mind if anything becomes available, and ask if it would be all right to check in with her every few weeks.

Just don't be an idiot. (This includes, but is not limited to, talking too much, picking your nose, and telling stupid jokes.)

TEMP POOLS

Instead of paying a temp agency up to $30 an hour for a temp (of which the temp gets around $18), many companies are hiring people in-house to act as temps, filling in where they're needed. They're often called "floaters." This can be a great way to get in the back door of a company. These floater positions are rarely advertised, so call the companies you'd like to work for and ask them if they have an in-house temp pool—that is, after you've asked them what temp agency they use.

The Real Skinny with . . . Woody Nuss, Rock-and-Roll Tour Manager

STARTING AT THE REAL BOTTOM:
I had a friend who was in a band, and I figured out a way of putting together a sound system for him. And that was it. I started doing sound for a bunch of fifteen-year-olds with shitty equipment, playing backyard parties. It was a way to have fun, hit on women, and party with the guys in the band.

HIS FIRST TOUR—PAYING HIS DUES:
It was complete poverty. It was six guys in a van with all the gear. Sleeping on top of the gear. You know, you'd build a little shelf where you could lie down over your gear. You throw the mattresses on the floor, and two guys sleep on the box springs and two guys sleep on the mattresses. You get stranded in Arizona sleeping at a girl's place that the guitarist used to go out with but doesn't anymore, sleeping on her floor.

JOB REQUIREMENT:
You've got to be a control freak, and you've got to be organized. You wake up the band in the morning and make sure they eat and have clean clothes and all that stuff. Try to give them enough time to party, which there's never enough time, because you've always got to be somewhere else. You've got to find time for them to go sit in a laundromat. Get

them across the borders, you know, arrange all the immigration paperwork. Check and make sure there's no roaches [pot] in their pockets. Keep them from buying drugs, if that's their situation.

BEING HATED:

There are plenty of tours I've done where the musicians hate me by the end of the tour. Because you're the one that's saying "Get your ass out of bed" and "No, you don't have time to have a long breakfast; you're just going to have to grab something quick." And you know, "I'm sick of your bullshit. Just wash your clothes in the sink and get moving."

Part 3

Finding the Job: The People–Using, Proactive Approach

Chapter 9

INTRODUCTION

Hi, and welcome to the next part of this book. The last part of this book (you presumably just read) was called "Finding *the* Job: The Passive Approach." It included finding a job through interning, college recruiting, want ads, the Internet, and temping. What I mean by its being passive is that you are *responding* to jobs that companies are listing. Jobs that they are having a hard time filling for whatever reason. Why do I say that they're jobs they are having a hard time filling? The mere fact that they're advertising them suggests so. You see, most jobs are filled via word of mouth—i.e., connections—especially the most sought-after ones.

---

definition

SOCIAL SECURITY:
That portion of your paycheck forcibly shot down a black hole by unindicted politicians, ostensibly for your benefit.

While the aforementioned, passive (except interning and temping, which are semipassive) ways of landing a full-time gig are acceptable and will probably find you a job, they lack in proactive specificity. "Proactive specificity"? Yes. The act of your aggressively going after your ideal job at your dream company in the industry you most want to work in.

Schmoozing on the Water

John took a job teaching sailing with me after he graduated from the University of Connecticut. Even though he wasn't the best sailor of all the instructors, he got way more requests for private, one-on-one lessons. He was good-looking—fit and tan—but he also had a habit of not wearing underwear underneath his cutoff jeans. Now, I'm not saying this was why he got more private lessons than the rest of us, but I don't think it hurt him. Anyway, John met a lot of young, professional women that summer and a few men, too. He learned about all kinds of jobs and industries. At the end of the summer, he started to think about getting a real job and remembered that someone he had taught told him that they thought he would be a good advertising account executive. He looked through the registration cards, found the person's name and address, and sent them a card with the *Titanic* on it. Inside he wrote something like "Summer's ending and this career is starting to sink fast" and asked if he could come into the city to talk with them about advertising. One month later John was hired at that person's agency.

FOOT IN THE DOOR

As a recent college graduate, or even as a forty-year-old who's thinking about changing careers, you need to forget about job titles and what you think you may be "worth," and concern yourself with doing whatever it takes to get your foot in the door. Instead of thinking about getting a specific *job title*, concern yourself with getting into the *department* you want to work in. And if you can't get into the specific department, then simply concern yourself with getting into the *company* you want to work for. As mentioned earlier, what good is a great job title in a shitty company that does something you couldn't care less about? The proactive job search is about doing whatever it takes to get into the company you want to work for, proving yourself, and maneuvering into a better job once you're there.

WHAT FINDING A JOB IS ALL ABOUT

The proactive job search is about:

- Making someone want to help *you* get a foot in the door of their company (as opposed to someone else).
- Getting someone to notice *you* above all the other people out there who want a job at their company.

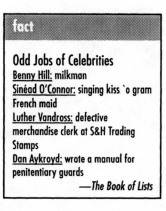

fact

Odd Jobs of Celebrities

<u>Benny Hill</u>: milkman

<u>Sinéad O'Connor</u>: singing kiss `o gram French maid

<u>Luther Vandross</u>: defective merchandise clerk at S&H Trading Stamps

<u>Dan Aykroyd</u>: wrote a manual for penitentiary guards

—*The Book of Lists*

- Getting someone to tell *you* about an opening at a company instead of them telling their other friends who are looking for a job.
- Making friends with the right people.

As you can see, getting a job—not just any job, but the job you want—is all about dealing with people. Connecting with people, getting information from people, and getting people to help *you*. In other words, it's all about connections, which is the title of the next chapter.

Chapter 10

CONNECTIONS

For some reason, *connections,* or *contacts,* for a lot of young people is a dirty word. Friends will snivel, "He only got that job because he knows somebody." Damn right. Get used to hearing this, 'cause it's how the world works, baby.

Before I go on, when I use the word *connection* or *contact,* I don't just mean someone who works at a company you want to work for. What it also includes are people who *know* people at companies you want to work for. A direct contact at a company is obviously a great thing to have, but it's also very rare. A contact who *knows* somebody at a company you want to work for is a much more common thing. These people become referrals because they *refer* you to somebody. I know this is an insult to your intelligence, but I needed to say it. Read on.

PEOPLE LIKE TO PLAY GOD

This is why people don't mind being used as a contact, referring somebody to a friend or an associate. People like to play God. People like to help the little guy. Generally speaking, people get a vicarious thrill out of helping someone get a job. Sure, you hear stories about idiots who won't even help their own son or daughter get a job, but most people get off on it. I'm always helping friends of friends find a job.

> **fact**
>
> **Fastest-Growing Industries**
> Multimedia: 3.6%
> Environmental technology: 4.8%
> Computers: 3.3%
> Electronics: 3.3%
> Telecommunications: 2.7%
> Bioscience: 1.1%
> Tourism: 0.6%
> Banking and finance: 0.3%
> —*USA Today*

Why? Partially because I'm a good guy. Partially because I remember what it's like being in their shoes. Partially because it makes

Word of Mouth

After Rob graduated from architecture school, all his jobs came to him via word of mouth. He never even sent out a résumé and hasn't still to this day.

Job 1: Rob heard about his first job from an old karate class friend whom he ran into at a mutual friend's wedding. The friend happened to be the head of personnel at Estée Lauder and called around to the heads of the design offices for him. Rob got an interview with this guy who "loved to talk about himself." So Rob listened to the guy for an hour straight. "I didn't even say anything. He didn't even look at any of my drawings until after he hired me," says Rob. Even though the job was only a six-week project designing countertops and things for their showrooms—"nothing terribly exciting"—it led to job 2.

Job 2: Two of Rob's associates he had gotten to know at Estée Lauder went over to Swatch to design prototypes of their watches. Luckily, Rob stayed in touch with them, because after a little while, one of them realized she didn't like it and told Rob she'd be leaving. So Rob called his other friend there to let him know of his interest. The guy liked Rob but didn't know what their plans were—whether or not they were going to replace her. So Rob called faithfully every four days to find out what was going on, so *he* would be the first person on their minds should they decide to hire someone. After a few weeks they made up their minds and offered Rob the job. This was another free-lance project that was *supposed* to last for only two months but went on for five months.

Job 3: I love the way Rob landed his next job. It's just so ballsy. A friend of his had received two offers at the same time, so Rob asked her if he could call the company she rejected and try to land the job for himself. She said sure. So Rob called and said, "Hi, I'm a friend of so-and-so's, and I would love to interview for the position she wasn't able to accept." He got the interview—which lasted for two hours—and got the job. What did they talk about for two hours? "He had hired someone six months earlier who had fought with everyone, and it made him very cautious about hiring someone that could fit in with the group. So I tried to be very polite. I definitely tried to make him feel comfortable. If I went in there and really tried to toot my horn, he would have been like 'Thanks, have a nice day.' "

me feel like God. Partially because they're going to owe me one. And partially because it adds to the network of people I know in the business world. So if I ever need something from a company where I helped someone get a job, I can call them up and cash in a favor.

PEOPLE HATE HIRING

In general, executives hate hiring people. It's not what they're paid to do. It's one of those burdens that come with success and power. When they could be doing their job actually making money for themselves and their company, they have to take constant time-outs to interview people.

> **definition**
>
> FICA:
> Act under which involuntary "protection money" is extorted by U.S. government and subsequently used to subsidize millionaire farmers and purchase Department of Defense double-cheese pizzas costing tens of thousands of dollars.

This is why connections are so important for someone like you who is looking for a job. When someone at a company needs to fill a position, they usually start by calling all their friends and associates and asking "You know anyone who needs a job?" It saves them the hassle of dealing with their personnel department and meeting a bunch of strangers, most of whom they will hate.

WHY YOU NEVER HEAR ABOUT MOST JOB OPENINGS

This is why you usually never *hear* of most of the jobs that are getting filled every day. As soon as a person realizes they need to fill a position, they don't say, "Okay, let's go out and do a search for the most qualified person." Nope. They get on the phone to their buddies, and everybody else who works at that company gets on the phone to *their* buddies as well, and tell them about the job that is available. Employees are actually encouraged with cash money to keep out outsiders like you and me by referring their friends.

PEOPLE TRUST REFERRALS

This is why companies encourage their employees to tell their friends and relatives about jobs. It's not because the human resources department is completely lazy. It's the club mentality, basically. Well, maybe not entirely a club mentality as much as it is this: "If Bob's a smart, eager fellow, then his friends and associates probably are as well. A person referred by Bob is a much safer bet than someone with a glowing, fantastic résumé."

> **quote**
>
> "If you have a job without aggravations, you don't have a job."
> —Malcolm Forbes

BUT YOU HAVE NO CONNECTIONS

When I started looking for a job a year and a half after college, I didn't think I had any contacts. My older brothers and sisters lived far away in places I didn't want to move to. My parents weren't particularly social people, so I didn't know many friends of theirs. The only friends my father had worked for IBM anyway, the last place on earth I wanted to work.

Neighbors, Friends' Parents, Etc.

But what about my neighbors? Did any of them work for, or own, a company that I would be interested in working for? How about my high school friends' parents? Or my brothers' and sisters' ex-boyfriends and -girlfriends? Thinking back on it, some of them *did* work in advertising and public relations, two fields I had an interest in getting into (although film, at the time, would have been my first choice). All I had to do was call them up or drop by some weekend and ask them if I could come to their office and meet with them.

Schmoozing at the Dentist's Office

After Karl graduated from Tulane, he went back home to live with his brother and sister-in-law in Detroit. He wanted to get into radio sportscasting and figured there would be more opportunity back home than in Tulane. After he was home not even a week, a cap fell off one of his teeth, so he went to his dentist. His dentist asked what he was up to, and Karl told him he wanted to get into sports radio. "Yeah? My wife's brother works at a station in town," the doctor told him. Not in sports, though. Karl asked if he would call the guy on his behalf, and the doctor said sure.

After Karl left the office, he went straight out to a store and bought a thank-you card and wrote: "Thanks for the cap, and thank you in advance for calling your brother-in-law on my behalf. I appreciate it very much." Karl dropped off the note the next day and two days after that got a call from the doctor's assistant with the name and number of his wife's brother. Karl met with the guy and was brought on as an intern. He was hired full-time seven months later. "Some of my friends thought I was crazy to work for free for seven months," Karl says. "My best friend said he didn't spend $90,000 [for a college degree] to work for free. But he's still sitting on his parents' couch looking for a job a year later, and I have the job I want."

You're probably thinking "Yeah, right. Like I'm going to call the guy down the street who remembers me as the kid who threw snowballs at his car. He'll never help me."

You're wrong. The fact that you are a neighbor or his daughter's friend from high school is enough of a connection for you to call. They're not going to think you're being a pain in the ass; they're going to think that was very resourceful of you to call, and they'll respect you for it. Businesspeople like resourcefulness.

College Buddies

I hate sounding like an opportunistic, predatory jerk, but if you recently graduated or are about to graduate from college, then you've got to take advantage of your college friends' parents. That's all there is to it. The mere fact that you went to college with their little

Bobby or Jane warrants a meeting with them. Remember, most parents love their kids, so they'll do it as a favor to them. If you've picked your friends correctly (just kidding), you'll have either informational or formal interviews set up at the hottest companies months before you even graduate.

Let Your College Buddies Do the Groundwork for You

Thinking about taking a year off after graduating and doing that Europe thing but feel anxious because you're going to fall behind in the rat race? If your friends aren't slackers, but are moderately savvy and ambitious, you might want to reconsider. Go to Europe and enjoy yourself and let your friends bust down the doors at all the hot companies for you. Give them at least a year to get their act together and comfortably settled in a job. Then stroll into town, tan and fit, and check on their progress. If they're doing well at their jobs, their human resources departments and/or bosses will welcome the opportunity to meet with you. As mentioned earlier, companies actually encourage employees to recommend their friends for jobs at their companies. They figure if you're a hard worker, then your friends will probably be also. And since a lot of companies give cash money to employees who recommend someone who gets hired, you can feel less guilty that they did all the hard work while you were busy having the time of your life.

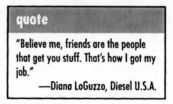

quote

"Believe me, friends are the people that get you stuff. That's how I got my job."

—Diana LoGuzzo, Diesel U.S.A.

Friends and Acquaintances

Everything I said about college buddies and how to use them applies to your friends also. Even if you've been out of school for ten years, you're much more likely to get a job through a friend or a friend's friend than you are by going it alone sending out résumés or answering want ads. Somebody had it right when they said someone's success can be measured by the number of their friends. I don't think they meant it the way I'm using it, but it fits.

Paaaarty!

So if you're unemployed or in a job that you hate and are trying to get out of, get your butt off the couch, stop feeling sorry for yourself, and start socializing. I don't think there are statistics on it, but the percentage of people who find out about job openings and make connections that result in interviews and jobs from attending parties or social gatherings is huge. Ironically, parties at someone's apartment or house or office are attended by most people because of their hope of meeting that special person—or at least getting laid. But the truth is, you're more likely to get a cool job lead than you are a date.

> **fact**
>
> **Middle Manager Blues**
> At least 1.4 million white-collar professional and management positions have been eliminated by corporate restructuring during the past five years. Middle managers have been three times more likely to be put out of work by "reengineering."
> —U.S. Department of Labor statistics

> **definition**
>
> PERSONAL DAY:
> Bad hangover.
> SICK DAY:
> Severe alcohol poisoning.
> VACATION:
> Severe alcohol poisoning in another state.

Too Bummed to Party

The problem is, however, that when you're out of a job or in a job you hate, if you're like me, you don't really feel like going to a party where you're going to meet a bunch of people who have better jobs and lives than you. You're not up for the humiliation of trying to answer "So what do you do?" You'd much rather watch MTV *Real World* reruns and feel strangely superior. (The fact that they're on TV and you're not, in this instance, does not bother you.) But when you need something, like a job and a life, this is the most important time to be on the social circuit. Just make sure you know how to schmooze correctly. And this is what the next chapter is about.

F E A T U R E   I N T E R V I E W

Jennifer Bretan
Publicist
Jason Weinberg and Associates
27 years old
Cornell, English major, 1991

Jennifer's Work Life: A Docu-Interview

Note to the reader: The following interview is different from the others in form. All of Jennifer's quotes are real. What's not real is the Host, who was created by me as a means to string together Jennifer's story (interview) in an interesting and different way.

>   **Scene 1**
>   Reenactments (Jennifer plays herself in all reenactments):
>   Jennifer graduates from Cornell. Jennifer opens the *New York Times* classifieds. Jennifer sees an ad for a job at CBS. Jennifer answers ad. Jennifer interviews for job. Jennifer gets job.

HOST: Why do you think you got the job?
JENNIFER: It was the interview. I told the guy that I really wanted the job and that I would be better than anybody he could find. I said, "Look, I'm smart, I pick up things without you having to tell me twice, and I want to be part of this company. That's what I want, and I'll do everything in my power to make it happen." I think he liked my moxie.
[Jennifer steps away to make a phone call.]
HOST: First interview and four days later a job at CBS? Kinda makes you want to beat the crap out of her, doesn't it? Yeah, you would, *if* she hadn't been so absolutely miserable after one week. That's right, the job sucked.
[Jennifer returns from phone call.]
HOST: So how was the job?
JENNIFER: I was miserable. I hated it.
HOST: Really. That's too bad.
JENNIFER: My second week of work I had a crying fit in the bathroom, going "Why did I do this? I need out!"
HOST: Why?
JENNIFER: I had assumed that a job at CBS would be a cool job. But what I didn't realize was there's a business side that isn't very interesting. It was a very hard comedown for me to go

from thinking I would immediately have some creative position to realizing I was someone's secretary.

Scene 2 (ten months later)
Jennifer starts hanging out with rock band. Jennifer gets a meeting with her friend's boss—a very famous music manager—so she can play the guy her friends' demo tape. Jennifer meets the guy and plays the tape. The guy says no to the band but offers Jennifer a job as his assistant. She'll help with the music stuff, plus, he's starting a new magazine, so she'll help out on that, too. Jennifer quits job at CBS and accepts job with music manager thinking her life is going to rock. Shot of Jennifer walking down the street smiling. Smiles turn to tears.

HOST: What went wrong?

JENNIFER: I thought it sounded like the coolest fucking job in the world. Go work with this guy who had discovered everybody and who was friends with John Lennon. . . . So I took it, and it was crazy.

HOST: Explain.

JENNIFER: He had his office up in the penthouse of this open apartment and he'd sit up there and say do this and do that.

HOST: What else?

JENNIFER: Nobody knew what they were doing. The guy had made a lot of money in the music business, but now he wanted to be a magazine mogul. But he didn't know what he was doing. It was utter chaos.

HOST: Tell them about the pot.

JENNIFER: People would get stoned at work. At first, it was great because it was exciting and loose. But then it became completely irrational. People can't be smoking pot and then making important decisions and looking at numbers. He'd think that he told me something, which I know he never told me, and then he'd say, "Is it done?" And I'd say, "What are you talking about?"

HOST: So the job sucked.

JENNIFER: It made me crazy.

HOST: How crazy?

JENNIFER: I would quit constantly. I would walk out the door saying "I quit," and by the time I had reached home, his girlfriend would call me trying to talk me into coming back, and I'd go back. One day I said, "I'm leaving," and he said, "Okay," and I'm like "Bye," and I walked out and never spoke to him again.

Scene 3 (eight months later)
Jennifer leaves the country. Goes to Europe for two months "to ruminate." Jennifer comes back to the States in debt and takes a temp job at Chase Manhattan Bank. They

like her so much, they offer her a full-time position writing their company newsletter. Jennifer is happy.

HOST: What was so good about this job?
JENNIFER: The guy I worked with was brilliant. And since they really wanted me to work there, I negotiated a really high salary and got myself out of debt.
(*Note to myself:* Possible theme: money = happiness for Jennifer.)

Scene 4 (six months later)
Jennifer still dreams of getting into the entertainment world. The only person she knows in entertainment is a film publicist. Jennifer thinks this sounds glamorous. She calls friend and asks how she got into it. Friend says, "Oh, wait a second. My friend who is also a film publicist is looking for an assistant." Jennifer calls friend. Jennifer gets interview. Jennifer gets job.

HOST: Is it time to hate Jennifer again? No! Stop the hate.
[Jennifer returns from offscreen.]
HOST: Okay, moving on. Why did you get the job, do you think?
JENNIFER: I went into the interview and tried to charm her. It's all about charm, whether or not you can work somebody. I was also very eager. I said, "Okay, look. This is the job I've been waiting for. This is the job I've been thinking about for two years. This is the job I'm willing to give up a $60,000-a-year salary to take. This is how committed I am. If that desire is any indication of how I'll do on the job, then I think I'm the right person for it."
(*Note to myself:* Scratch possible theme of money = happiness. As Jennifer says, "I went from a lot of money to barely subsisting money. It's not the money, it's the job. Because if you're good at the job, the money will come.")
HOST: So how was this job?
JENNIFER: At first, I loved it. The second day I was there, I worked a film premiere, and I was very excited. I met movie stars, and I saw the director. When I was at CBS, there was one time I walked down the street past the Ziegfeld Theater and *The Prince of Tides* was opening, and I was standing near the window watching the movie stars and the guests walk in. I was also watching the people who were working, and I was saying to myself, "Who are these people? How do you get that job? Who do you apply to?" I was working in this corporate environment a block away, and I wanted to know who that girl walking next to Barbra Streisand was. Then, all of a sudden, that's me.
HOST: Was it as glamorous as you thought?
JENNIFER: Well, it's still work. On nights of premieres I'd get to work at nine A.M. and not get home until two in the morning. And then, when I'd have a film junket, I'd also work all weekend.

HOST: For you people out there who don't know what a film junket is, that's when the stars of the film all fly into one place and the press from all over the world takes turns interviewing each of them for their magazine, newspaper, and television show. Very well, let's move on. What really sucked about the job? Anything?

JENNIFER: One of the bad things when you're an assistant is that there's no credit involved. The credit reverts to the person you're working for. You're also dealing with major attitude in this business. And it's not a real business environment, so there's not a business format for the work.

HOST: So it was frustrating.

JENNIFER: With this particular boss, yes. She was very successful, but I didn't agree with the way she did things. I sound like a really difficult person, don't I?

HOST: Kind of.

JENNIFER: I was just really ambitious. After three months I felt I could do my boss's job, which made it really difficult to keep working for her. Eventually we came to blows. I couldn't stay there any longer.

[Jennifer walks off camera to say hi to somebody.]

HOST: So what happened was, Jennifer quit—without anything else lined up, mind you. Two weeks later the president of that same company calls Jennifer at home and says, "Would you please come back and work for me as *my* assistant," or something close to that.

[Jennifer returns.]

HOST: Jennifer, continue with the story. You're working for the president—take it away.

JENNIFER: I was thrilled to come back. I moved twenty feet across the room, and my job was completely different—so much better. But this never would have happened if I hadn't . . . quit. She never would have been able to take me away from my old boss. Too many politics.

HOST: Jennifer, tell them about how there was a film your company was supposed to be doing publicity for, but nobody was doing anything, and how you took it upon *yourself* to do the publicity on it—as an assistant! Tell them how you got *Vanity Fair* and *Interview* and *Premiere* to do pieces on the film. Forget it, don't tell them. Tell them why you quit six months later.

JENNIFER: After six months (which was actually a year and a half, considering I had worked there before), they still hadn't even made me a *junior* publicist. Then, I found out they were rehiring someone who had been an assistant there for a shorter time than I had been, and now they were bringing her back as a publicist. They completely passed over me.

HOST: Jennifer? How did that make you feel?

JENNIFER: I was furious. Sometimes people see those who have left as more worthwhile than the people who are there.

Scene 5
That very week Jennifer runs into Jason Weinberg—a young guy who has his own very successful PR firm—at a party. (She had met him months earlier at a premiere and several other times as well.) They have a drink, and then another drink, and end

up having dinner at three in the morning. A few secret dinners and lunches later, Jennifer is offered a job as a publicist with Jason's company.

HOST: Okay, girl. How come he hired you, an assistant, instead of someone with more experience? Not that you're not smart, darling.

JENNIFER: I didn't tell him that I was still an assistant. I told him the things I did. Even though I wasn't officially a publicist, I said, why should I sell myself short?

HOST: Darling, we've only got a minute left. Tell us about what it's like being a publicist. Any pressure?

JENNIFER: The pressure is huge. When you work with an actor, you're dealing with their agent and manager, and you have to make sure everyone is happy with the way things are developing. Because press can make someone's career.

HOST: So that's your job, to get them press.

JENNIFER: You get them press, but it's also about knowing what press to get and how you want that client portrayed and what would be important for that client's career. And also give them advice and guidance. It really runs the gamut. From helping them find the right designer to dress them for the Oscars to talking to them at four in the morning from a film set because they don't like the director. It's a twenty-four-hour-a-day, seven-day-a-week job.

HOST: Is that what you hate?

JENNIFER: I hate having to be friendly when I'm not feeling friendly, introducing myself to someone when I'm feeling shy, and more than anything, having to be fake sometimes. Publicity is like running an obstacle course of other people's arbitrary design.

HOST: Is there anything good about it?

JENNIFER: Yes. Seeing my client on the cover of a magazine is one of the greatest feelings in the world. That's the kind of thing that makes it worth it.

HOST: Out of time. Good-bye, world!

Chapter 11

BASIC SCHMOOZING: MAKING "CONTACTS"

All right, I'm not going to insult your intelligence here, but since I've encountered idiots at parties and other places who are looking for a job (and I'm not saying everybody looking for a job is an idiot), I figure there's got to be a couple of thousand of you out there who need to hear the basics about schmoozing and networking.

BE ON YOUR SCHMOOZING GUARD

One of the hardest things about schmoozing is that you don't know when you're going to be doing it. There are obvious times when you know you're going to be, like parties and weddings, but there will be plenty of times when you'll be caught off your schmoozing guard. You're going to run into somebody's sister whom you haven't seen in years, wind up talking to her, and

fact

Famous People Who Never Graduated from Grade School
Andrew Carnegie: U.S. industrialist
Charlie Chaplin: British actor
Charles Dickens: British writer
Isadora Duncan: American dancer
Thomas Edison: American inventor
Claude Monet: French painter
Sean O'Casey: Irish playwright
Alfred E. Smith: American politician
John Philip Sousa: American composer
Mark Twain: American writer
—*The Book of Lists for Kids*

find out that she works for a company you'd kill to work for. Oh, yeah, meanwhile, you're doing your grunge thing, and you smell like beer. Sure, you could call her at the office a few days later or send her a note saying how great it was to run into her and how much you'd appreciate five minutes of her time. But chances are, she'll blow you off hard. (If you just asked "Why?" and really mean it, then you should make a great effort to try to get your money back for this book, because nothing I can say is going to help you. Tell them this book is defective or something.)

The Answer

Okay, here's why she'll blow you off. She'll look at you and say to herself, "Oh, he's just a kid who isn't ready to grow up and join the real world. He's too immature." Sure, she might be wrong. She shouldn't judge you based on the way you look. But she will.

Think of it this way. Imagine your father isn't working for whatever reason and is looking for a job. He's walking down the street one day and runs into a guy he used to work with years ago who is now at a company where your dad would love to work. Oh, yeah, your dad is wearing ripped jeans, his hair is all over the place, and he hasn't shaved in days. This person is going to think that your dad has fallen on hard times. He'll think, "Since he looks like a mess, his life must be a mess, too. God, I hope he doesn't call me." Sure, your dad might be judged a little harder because he's "expected" to look a certain way. But now that you're in the real work world, you're going to be held to the same standards. Sucks, doesn't it?

It's insane to say be ready to schmooze and impress at all times.

fact

Percentage of People Satisfied with Their Jobs
Yes: 85%
No: 14%
Not sure: 1%
—*Time*/CNN poll conducted by Yankelovich Partners, Inc.

This would mean never going out in public unkempt, ugly, smelly, and unstyled—which, of course, is impossible and frankly not a fun way to live. I will say, though—and I can't believe I'm about to say it—that when you go to the mall or to a movie or to a party, you should dress in such a way that you can answer the following question with a yes. "If I run into someone I kind of know who can help me in any way at all to get a job, will I look okay?" In other words, it may be time to grow up.

Schmoozing Soccer Mom

After Krista graduated from Vassar, she took a job teaching junior high at a private school in New Jersey. After two years of teaching, Krista had had enough. No more kids. She wanted to get into magazines but didn't know anybody in the magazine world. She tried sending letters and résumés to *Vogue, Cosmopolitan, Esquire,* and a bunch of others but couldn't even land an interview. Then one evening she was reading the masthead (the page that lists who works at the magazine) of a fashion magazine and noticed that an editor at the magazine had the same last name as a student of hers. So, one day after school, Krista stayed to attend this young student's soccer game, hoping his mother would show up so she could ask her. She had met the woman before, so she knew what she looked like, but didn't know her well enough to call her at home. It also didn't seem appropriate to bother her at home.

Sure enough, the kid's mother arrived at the end of the game, Krista positioned herself next to her, and struck up a conversation. Krista told the woman that she had seen someone with the same name in a fashion magazine just the other night. "That's me," the woman said. Krista went on to tell her that she had wanted to go into magazines after college but didn't know anybody in the industry. "Now you do," the woman said, or something like that. Krista went in to interview with her a few times that spring and was offered a job when the school year was over.

BE UPBEAT, OPTIMISTIC, ENTHUSIASTIC

What I'm about to say is one of the most important factors in getting a job and moving from job to job. People like to hire and recommend people with good attitudes, not negative, cynical intellectuals. This is kind of weird advice to give because, if you're cynical and/or negative, it's hard to say, "Don't be." All I can say is fake it.

I've had a lot of different jobs with good companies. I've been in a position many times to get people jobs at my company or at companies where I know people. Now, just because I kind of know somebody does not mean that I'm going to recommend them for a job or get them an interview with a company. If I don't think this person will be a great addition to somebody's staff, I'm not going to ruin my reputation by recommending them. It's just not going to happen. And if this person says, "Hey, Charlie, do you know anybody I can meet with at X Company?" and I think they have a chip on their shoulder, then I'll say, "I'll see what I can do," and then call them a few days later and say, "Sorry, they're not interviewing," or something like that.

Now, why is this such a big deal, you ask? Because if I'm not going even slightly out of my way to tell you about a job lead—and remember, most people land jobs through connections and word of mouth—then there's most likely a bunch of other people out there who are not going to tell you about job leads either.

Hopefully, you're wondering if you're this person whom people won't go out of their way to help out jobwise. Hopefully, you're slightly concerned. How do you know if you are or not? Let's do this, let's have an attitude check.

An Attitude Check. Are You Someone People Will Help to Get a Job? Or, Schmoozing 101

Pretend you're at a party where there are like thirty people, and you know five of them. Most of these people have jobs that you want, and you kind of hate them for it. We'll also assume that:

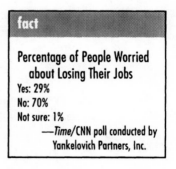

fact

Percentage of People Worried about Losing Their Jobs
Yes: 29%
No: 70%
Not sure: 1%
—*Time*/CNN poll conducted by Yankelovich Partners, Inc.

- You are twenty-two years old.
- You graduated with a major in English.
- You are living with your parents.
- You want to get into something "creative" like advertising or public relations, but you're not sure.
- You've been interviewing for the last eight months. You've come close to a few jobs but haven't received an offer yet. You're extremely frustrated.
- You're waiting tables at night for dough.

• The party is completely boring, the beer is warm, and the food sucks.

Now pretend someone comes up to you and asks you some questions. What follows are the right and wrong ways to schmooze with this person. Let the schmoozing begin!

---

definition

"A LITTLE CHAT":
The conversation where "probation status" officially attaches to employee.

Question 1

Jerk who has a job you want (we'll call her Jill): Hi, how you doing?

Good answer: Great. How about you?
Bad answer: Eh. Not bad.
Analysis: You've got to be positive! Sure you want to put a gun to your head, but you can't let *her* know that. The first thing to do is engage somebody, to get them to like you, to take an interest in you so they'll want to help you. Nobody is going to help you out of pity. They're going to walk away.

Question 2

Jill: So, what do you do?

Good answer: There isn't one.
Bad answer: Any answer you give.
Analysis: Since you're not 100 percent sure what you want to do, you might be interested in potentially working for this person's company. So, if you make them tell you what they do first, then you can answer, "Really? That's funny. That's just what I'm looking to get into."

Question 3

Jill:	Why do you want to go into cosmetics? [This is assuming she said she worked in cosmetics and you said that's what you wanted to get into.]
Good answer:	I've just always been interested in it. How do *you* like it?
Bad answer:	I don't know. You gotta do something, right?
Analysis:	If you don't have a good answer for this question, get out of it quickly and get her talking about herself. Do not come across as apathetic or unfocused.

Question 4

Jill:	So, how's the interviewing going?
Good answer:	It's going okay. Just not getting *enough* of them.
Bad answer:	Sucks. I'm losing my mind. These people are a bunch of idiots. They don't know what the hell they're doing.
Analysis:	Never, ever appear desperate, frustrated, or angry. If you give the bad answer as written above, they'll say to themselves, "Well, no wonder she doesn't have a job yet. She's a loser." The good answer lets the listener know that you're frustrated without your having to say it. It also lets them know that you could use a little help in the connection department.

Question 5

Jill:	So, quite a party, huh?
Good answer:	Yeah. How did you wind up here? Do you know Bob? [the host]
Bad answer:	I'm not certain, but I don't think I've ever been to a worse social event in my life.

Analysis: For all you know, this person helped organize the
                     party and was looking for some encouragement.
                     Avoid all foot-in-the-mouth answers.

Question 6

Jill: I can't believe Clinton isn't behind bars. He's a . . .
                     [She gives a list why.]

(*Note:* You're a Clinton supporter.)

Good answer: Oh, my God, can you hang on a second? I've got
                     to tell somebody something right away.
Bad answer: Any answer that disagrees with her political
                     opinions.
Analysis: Some people take politics very seriously and will
                     judge you based on your party affiliation. It's true.
                     For example, if somebody told me in an interview
                     that they voted for George Bush, I really don't
                     think I'd hire them on that alone. Swear to God.

Question 7

Jill: Listen, it was nice meeting you. I'll see you later.

Good answer: Yeah, you, too. Listen, do you think it would be all
                     right to call you sometime? I'd love to take you to
                     lunch and find out more about what you do.
Bad answer: Yeah, you, too. Listen, do you know if you guys
                     are hiring right now? I'd love to work over there.
Analysis: People are always hiring, and people are never
                     hiring, remember? You're setting yourself up for
                     rejection here. You need to get to know this per-
                     son more and show them you are very interested
                     in their company.

Liar, Liar

Manny was going for a job at a big music management company—a much more corporate company than the one he'd been working at. But the fact that he never went to college worried him. So on his friend's advice, he lied on his résumé and said he went to college. "My friend told me, 'Don't worry, they're never, never going to check.' "

Well, after they narrowed it down to two people, Manny wound up getting the job, partially because they liked the fact that he had an English degree, he says. An English degree he didn't have. As Manny says, "If you were applying for a job as a biomedical researcher at Harvard, then you can't lie because you have to know things. I could spell and write very well. I *could* have had a degree. I just didn't."

BE LIKE ANTHONY ROBBINS (THAT INFOMERCIAL GUY)

Now, I'm not an Anthony Robbins kind of guy—my teeth aren't as big, and I'm not as preppy and tall—but the kind of person I will recommend for a job is someone like him, not somebody who thinks he's real cool and above it all. I've never read his books or anything, but I will say that I love his energy and optimism. This is a guy I'd want on my team. And if you want people—friends and acquaintances alike—to recommend you for jobs, or tip you off to a job opening, then you should act a little like Anthony. And I'm not kidding.

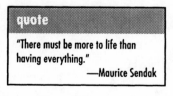

quote

"There must be more to life than having everything."

—Maurice Sendak

I don't want to toot my own horn, but the reason I've never had a problem getting jobs is because I'm a very upbeat, optimistic guy. (Sure I get depressed like everybody, but I try not to let people other than my closest friends see me that way.) I have a bunch of friendly acquaintances out there—around twenty or so—people I know from past jobs. I see them maybe once every other month at the most. Some maybe once a year. We talk on the phone a little more often, however, checking to see what's going on in each other's lives. Every time I see and talk to these "friends," I put on a kind of game face. I try to make sure I'm very energetic and upbeat, even if I'm having a bad day and everything sucks. It's not that I'm lying or being fake, I don't think. What it's basically about is appearing like a winner. Like you're on top. People like to be around winners.

definition

CHRISTMAS PARTY:
Opportunity to drink with coworkers you've seldom spoken to and then have sex with them.

Take This Scenario

Let's say I just had lunch with my brother-in-law who is head of programming for MTV. At lunch he mentioned to me that he's looking for an assistant—the job he started out in ten years ago. Now, imagine I go home and call two people I went to college with whom I haven't spoken to in months, people who I know are looking for jobs. Or say I just happen to run into both of them on my way home from lunch. Keep in mind that these people are friends of friends, and not good friends of mine. The first conversation goes like this:

Conversation 1, with Bobby

Me:	Hey, Bobby, what's up?
Bobby:	Nothing, man. Just hanging out.
Me:	Yeah? What's going on? [With this question, I'm feeling him out to see where his head is at before I mention the job at MTV.]
Bobby:	Nothing much. Partying. Going on the road with Phish for a month or two. See what happens.
Me:	How's the job search going?
Bobby:	Screw it. I don't even know where to start. Nobody's hiring anyway.

Conversation 2, with Cindy

Me:	Hey, Cindy, what's up?
Cindy:	Nothing much. How are you?

Me: Great. What's going on?

Cindy: Jan broke her nose again, so that's a drag. Other than that, I'm just pounding the pavement, looking for a job.

Me: Yeah, how's that going?

Cindy: You know. It's tough. I'll land something soon, though. How about you? How's your job going?

Analysis

Bobby:

I would never, ever recommend Bobby for any job. Period. He may be the greatest guy in the world, but he's apathetic and pathetic at the same time.

Cindy:

Now, Cindy, on the other hand, had enthusiasm and optimism. She sounded like she really cared about finding a job and wouldn't embarrass me if I told her to call my brother-in-law. I want to help Cindy because she is trying.

BE LIKE RICHARD SIMMONS—I.E., DON'T BE A JERK. BE NICE

Richard Simmons. This guy is my hero, and not because I'm overweight. What can I say? This world would be a better place if people were just a smidgen like Richard. This is one guy who will never be out of a job. He does so many good things for so many people that people would give their right eye for him.

You know, this whole schmoozing chapter is turning out to be like part of a self-help book, what with all the optimism and good energy advice. And you know, that ain't bad. Because I think if you go through your life giving off good energy—with optimism and enthusiasm—people are going flock to you and give you things. My friend Bruce is a great example of this. He is the most optimistic, energetic guy I know. Even when things look real bad for him, he keeps plowing along. He is motivating to me and many others, and because of this, everybody I know who knows him wants him to be successful and does things for him so that he will be.

YOU NEVER KNOW WHO SOMEBODY IS, SO BE NICE TO EVERYBODY

Life is a series of coincidences and happenstances and chance encounters all thrown together. Or not. Let's take this past weekend as an example. I was hanging out in a bar in the East Village in NYC, and I happened to meet Rupert Murdoch's nephew and his friends. This was a chance encounter. What wasn't chance about it was how we became friends. He spilled his beer on my pants by accident. And instead of being a prick about it, I said, "No problem," when he apologized. My saying "No problem" was not by chance. That was an intentional action of being a decent guy. We wound up hanging out the rest of the night. It wasn't until six in the morning that I found out from his girlfriend that he was Rupert Murdoch's nephew. This was a great guy and a great contact. He said, "If you ever move to Australia, I'll set you up." The point is, nice guys finish first.

Consequently, if you're a prick who brings unhappiness to the world by being rude or indifferent, not only will you miss out on untold job opportunities, you're going to have a crappy life, and I hope you do it somewhere far from me.

Tell Everyone

An important thing to remember about connections is this: you don't know who is connected where. This counts for strangers, as mentioned in the story above, but it also counts for friends and everybody we come in contact with. You never know whom somebody knows. Therefore, if you're jobless, you want to tell everyone what kind of job you're looking for.

For example, the first time I moved out to Los Angeles, I didn't know anybody. I was moving out there without a job, and I had no connections. Connections of my own, at least. As soon as I knew I was moving out there, I told everybody I knew and everybody I didn't know what I was up to. This included people whom I talked to on the phone and did business with at my job but had never met. I figured somebody had to know somebody in the entertainment business in L.A. Sure enough, two people I knew, from the phone only, gave me the names and numbers of two people who would have huge influences on my life.

Granted, the people who gave me the names of people to call were people I knew from a job. Maybe you're saying "Sure, it's easy to make connections when you already have a job." But since I was going for entry-level jobs, these people could have been anybody—a guy I sold a cappuccino to, a guy whose car I cleaned, or my dry cleaner.

"I Think I'll Get a Job"

Dana graduated from Carnegie-Mellon with a painting degree and had no idea what she was going to do. She wasn't too worried about it either. One day while she was kicking back with her roommate, her roommate dared her to get a job on Wall Street. Why Wall Street? "She thought I was too artsy and that I could never get a 'real job.'

"So the next day I answered an ad in the *New York Times* for an entry-level bonds broker. I called the guy and went in that day for an interview. I didn't even have a résumé. We met and for an hour and a half we talked about sailboats. My family has a big sailboat in Greece, and he thought that was so cool because he had a boat as well. So we just sat around and talked about boats. We didn't even discuss the job. At the end of the interview, he said, 'You're hired. Come in tomorrow and see so-and-so, and he'll tell you what to do.' I think he wanted interesting people to work for his firm instead of the usual account types. I was different, I guess."

definition

OFFICE BONDING:
Heavy intake of drugs or alcohol shared with coworkers.
SUBSTANCE ABUSE PROBLEM:
Heavy intake of drugs or alcohol not shared with coworkers.

From Bartender to *Pulp Fiction*

The second time I decided to move to Los Angeles, I was bartending twice a week. I had gotten to know some of the regulars and told them I was planning on moving to L.A. Francine, who is now a close friend, said, "You should call my old boyfriend when you get there. He produced *Reservoir Dogs*, and now he's producing a new movie with Bruce Willis and John Travolta"—i.e., *Pulp Fiction*.

I wrote down her number and said I'd call her when I got out there to get his number. I called her, I called him, and I got a job on *Pulp Fiction*. How? This is the subject of the next chapter, "Contacting Your Contacts."

The Real Skinny with . . . Emily Gerson, Talent Agent, William Morris Agency

COLD CALLING FOR A JOB:
I went through the *Ross Reports* [a little book that lists producers and agents] and called everybody that I possibly could. I got one very famous producer on the phone directly. His assistant just put me through for some reason, and he had me come in to meet him. He said, "Come on in. Let's talk." He didn't know me from a hole in the wall. He wound up sending my résumé around New York to various important people.

THE BENEFIT OF WORKING LONG HOURS:
[While at the talent agency ICM,] I was one of the few people who was working long hours. Therefore, when Sam Cohn, who was running the office, needed something late at night, he would come over and I would get him whatever he needed on the computer or with anything. He and I developed a relationship which was very instrumental for me, and I'm very grateful for it.

DEALING WITH THE COMPETITION:
All you have to do is your job, and do it better than anybody else possibly can. You never want to bad-mouth anybody. Let everybody have a chance to succeed. Just do your job, and do it well.

ON DECIDING WHICH OFFER TO TAKE:
I go with my heart. I've taken jobs that weren't financially the best offers. I've wound up making more money by taking a job that initially offered less money and a year down doubling my salary.

GETTING YOUR FOOT IN THE DOOR AT A COMPANY YOU WANT TO WORK AT:
I went from paying $20,000 a year for an education to becoming a secretary. And if I'd had to start as the receptionist, I would have. Go in, answer the phones, type, get into the environment. And then you can talk to people about what they do. Slowly but surely, you'll learn what they do. And when you're ready to do what they're doing, they'll let you if you're smart. But you have to be in the right place.

ON BECOMING AN AGENT:
No one just goes down the hall and says, "Oh, you're next in line, you're an agent." You have to figure out how to be indispensable to the company and show signs of promise. You've got to be aggressive about it, but with finesse.

Chapter 12

CONTACTING YOUR CONTACTS

WHOM TO CONTACT

Before I get into how to contact your contacts—which may seem like an obvious, basic thing, but believe me, it isn't—let's first look at *whom* you should contact.

Let's say you want to get into public relations. (If you *don't* want to go into public relations, stay with me, I'm just making a point.) A lot of people, including myself when I graduated, limit themselves by a type of linear thinking that goes something like this: "I want to go into public relations, so I'm going to try to get interviews with public relations companies."

> **definition**
>
> NEW HIRE:
> Fresh meat.

So we make our list of contacts—friends' parents, neighbors, college buddies' parents—and figure out who, if anyone, works in public relations. And we find that nobody does. So we continue working at some lame-ass job.

What a lot of people forget, or don't know, is that companies, large and small, do many things. Let's take Nike, for example. Sure, Nike makes sneakers. But Nike also *markets* their sneakers, *advertises* their sneakers, *sells* their sneakers, etc. There are all sorts of different departments and jobs available at a company like Nike.

So go over your list of people to call and expand your thinking a little bit about what opportunities might exist at that company you thought you had no interest in working at.

Okay, Here We Go. Contacting Your Contacts

Making a contact is a great thing. Meeting somebody at a party or running into an old buddy's mother who works somewhere you want to work, or knows someone at a company you want to work at, is by far the most common way to find a job. It may not be with your first job, but it will definitely be with your second or third, which might be two months after your first.

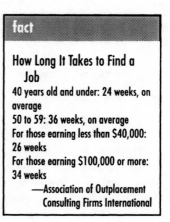

fact

How Long It Takes to Find a Job

40 years old and under: 24 weeks, on average
50 to 59: 36 weeks, on average
For those earning less than $40,000: 26 weeks
For those earning $100,000 or more: 34 weeks
    —Association of Outplacement Consulting Firms International

The problem is, believe it or not, most people blow it with their contacts. They get a phone number from somebody who says, "Call me," and it basically ends there. It happens all the time. If you have a contact at a company you want to work for, it should always end up in a job offer for you if you handle the situation right. There's no reason it shouldn't. Really.

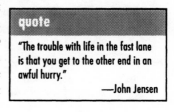

quote

"The trouble with life in the fast lane is that you get to the other end in an awful hurry."
    —John Jensen

Some Things People Say That Sabotage Their Success with Contacts

"They Were Just Being Nice. I Don't Want to Bother Them"

All right, here's the deal. If somebody says, "Call me," then you call them. Yeah, maybe they were just being polite. Yeah, maybe the last thing they want to do is take five minutes from their day to help you. So what. It's not going to kill them. And your calling them is no different from what they do at their job often—calling people who don't want to talk to them. Remember, they once relied on someone to help *them*. Give them the opportunity to help someone else now—namely, you.

"I Called, and They Didn't Call Me Back"

This is so common. Somebody's being nice, and they say, "Call me." So you call them, leave a message on their voice mail or with their assistant, and they never call you back. This is the way it's going to go with most people you call. You're at the bottom of their list as importance in calls goes. You are going to be the last person they call back—and then it will be under duress. Usually it takes around three calls over the course of a month for them to feel guilty enough to call you back.

They Might Not Have Gotten the Message

Sometimes they never get the message that you called. Think about it. Who are you usually leaving a message with? Somebody's assistant, right? Some bored, competitive, pissed-off phone-answerer who's probably frustrated in their career and would eliminate all of their competition with a sawed-off shotgun if they knew they wouldn't get caught. In other words, when you call this person's boss for a job, what they're hearing is this:

> Would you mind having your boss call me—a stranger who happens to know somebody they know, which therefore makes me more important than you—so I can take your job as soon as you get fired for screwing something up, or else take the job that you've been dying to get? Thanks a lot.

Maybe you think I'm exaggerating. I'm not. Check out this obnoxious little story.

A Guy I Should Have Killed

When I moved to Los Angeles, I called this woman named Lisa who worked on a TV reality show for CBS. She was friends with this guy I had spoken on the phone with back in New York a few times—this guy named Bryan who was friends with, and did business with, my boss. He said, "When you get out there, call her. She's really nice; she'll help you out." Great, I thought.

I got to L.A. and dialed her up. Here's what happened:

"Lisa Reilly's office. This is Barry," some young guy said.

"Hi, is Lisa available?" I said.

"Who's calling, please?" said the guy, very nicely.

"My name is Charlie Drozdyk. Lisa's friend Bryan so-and-so suggested that I give Lisa a call when I arrived in Los Angeles and gave me her number. Is she around?"

"I see. She's in a meeting right now," he said very nicely. (I liked this guy.) "Can I have her call you back?" he asked.

"Sure. My number is . . ."

"Great. I'll give her the message."

"Great. Thanks a lot, Barry," I said.

One Week Later . . . A full week goes by, and I don't hear from Lisa, so I call her again. I talk with her assistant again. He remembers who I am and apologizes that Lisa hasn't gotten back to me yet, as she is really busy. He says she is currently in another meeting. He takes my number again and says he'll give her the message, again. "Great, thanks a lot," I say. "I really appreciate it." "Sure, no problem," says Barry.

A Week after That . . . Another week goes by, and no word from Lisa. Not doubting that she received the messages (I trusted Barry), I decided to call her after hours when perhaps Barry had left for the day. Maybe she'd pick up her own phone. I called at around 7:00 P.M. and got Barry, so I hung up. Same thing at 7:30. I tried again at 8:30 P.M. and got this:

"Lisa Reilly."

"Is this Lisa?" I asked, incredulously.

"Yup. Who's this?" she asked very nicely.

"This is Charlie Drozdyk," I said. "Listen, I hope I'm not calling too much. I just figured you were really busy and thought I'd give you a shot after hours."

"Charlie who?" she asked.

"Charlie Drozdyk. Bryan so-and-so's friend from New York?"

"I'm sorry. I don't know who you are," she said.

"I know, we've never met. He told me to call you when I got out here about meeting with you. I left you a couple of messages."

"Really? When?"

"One last week, one the week before."

"Never got 'em."

"Oh. Well, I left them with Barry. Anyway, Bryan said I should give you a call since I don't know anybody out here."

We went on to talk for a few minutes about Bryan. I never mentioned that I had never actually met him in person. I let her assume we were better friends than we were. I told her that I was looking for any entry-level job and asked if I could come to the office and meet with her. The next day I met with her, and the day after that I was offered a job as a production assistant.

Why Lisa Never Got My Messages— and Why the People You *Call May Never Get* Your *Messages:* About five months into the job, Barry and I were having lunch. By then we had become pretty good friends. He was a really sweet, great guy. A kind of guy you could trust with your teenage sister. I asked Barry, point-blank, if he had given Lisa the messages I left when I first moved out. He admitted that he hadn't. "Why not?" I asked. "I don't know. I didn't like your voice. You sounded, I don't know. I just didn't like your voice," he said.

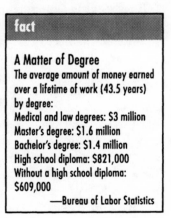

fact

A Matter of Degree
The average amount of money earned over a lifetime of work (43.5 years) by degree:
Medical and law degrees: $3 million
Master's degree: $1.6 million
Bachelor's degree: $1.4 million
High school diploma: $821,000
Without a high school diploma: $609,000
                —Bureau of Labor Statistics

Can you believe it? I couldn't. And this from a really, really nice guy. So don't give up until you get the person on the phone directly. There are a lot of Barrys out there.

---

definition

IN-BOX:
Your problem.
OUT-BOX:
Someone else's problem.

"They Said There Are No Jobs Available"

Say you don't have trouble with an evil assistant and are able to get
your contact on the phone. You tell them you're interested in working at their company and you would love to meet with them. They
tell you there's nothing available right now but ask you to send them
your résumé. You say, "Great, I'll do that. Thanks a lot." Congratulations, you're dead. Flip to the next chapter, "From Contact to a
Face-to-Face Meeting," to save yourself from this kiss of death.

FEATURE INTERVIEW

Ronnie Kimm
Producer, Agency.Com
24 years old
Cornell University
Government major, 1994

At ten years old, Ronnie wanted to be a spy, a dancer, a corporate lawyer, and a social worker.
When she took the Myers-Briggs career aptitude test in college, it recommended she become a
journalist, teacher, researcher, or minister. By the time she graduated, all Ronnie knew was that
she wanted something creative and fast-paced. So, after a few months in Europe and six months
at home in Oklahoma after graduating from college, Ronnie hit the Big Apple—a city not
known for being dull and slow.
     She enrolled in an eight-week publishing course at NYU in order to get into the city, learn
her way around, and get an apartment. Oh, yeah, she also thought that magazine publishing
might be the way to go, considering they're graphical and the work (content) is always changing. Creative and fast-paced, you know?
     But then Ronnie started to hear the roar from the fast lane on the information superhighway
called the World Wide Web, a place in cyberspace that was redefining the terms *creative*

and *fast-paced* every few months. Ronnie didn't have to look very far for the on-ramp. Her roommate was interning at an Internet service provider start-up company in lower Manhattan. So, with her roommate's okay, Ronnie called them up and said, "I hear you're a start-up company, and I know you don't have any ads out, but are you looking for an administrative assistant?" In fact, they were. "I showed the initiative, I was clean, and I presented myself well, so they offered me the job."

It seemed almost too good to be true. Assistant to the president, starting in the high twenties—far more than she would have made at a magazine—at a hip, young, friendly, and laid-back company in a huge loft in TriBeCa. "I thought, 'Wow, I could not have done better for myself,' " says Ronnie. But then the nail of life punctured a hole in the tire of the start-up company—i.e., the Japanese investors pulled out—and the company started to crash. Slowly. But instead of bailing out right away, Ronnie (and others) stayed for six weeks without getting a single paycheck, hoping other financing would come through. None did.

Instead of freaking and running home to Oklahoma, Ronnie took to the quick-cash temping road. A seventy-word-per-minute typist, she had no problem getting work. And temping, which originally started as a way to pay the rent while she looked for a *real* job, became the *way* she looked for a real job. "It's a great way to learn about different companies and industries and also a great *in* into a company," she says. In fact, in the first three months of temping, Ronnie was offered three full-time jobs.

This time, however, Ronnie wasn't about to jump at the first offer. Now that she was making steady cash, she could take her time, try out a bunch of companies, and wait for the right gig. Actually, instead of waiting for what they might *offer* her, Ronnie would scope out the company and talk to people in different departments to see if there was something that *interested* her. "I would just be nosy and curious and look around and talk to people and tell them who I was," she says. "They would offer me a job, and I'd say, 'No, this isn't what I'm looking for.' And they'd say, 'Well, what *do* you want?' "

Good question. She was still interested in the Internet, but she was also interested in design. However, not having any experience in design, at all, she wasn't in any position to land a design job. Or so you'd think. When the direct-marketing company she was temping for offered her a full-time job in the account department, Ronnie said no thank you but added, "If you're interested in having me work here, I'd like to work in design." Ronnie got an interview with the creative department, which included a test on the design program Quark, which she taught herself over the weekend. "I had no portfolio and no experience, but they knew I was going to work hard. Plus, I showed an aptitude for it," she says.

In that same week, Ronnie landed an interview (through the *New York Times*) with a trade magazine publishing house that was looking for a production editor in their Internet division. Like the design job, this job *also* required her to know computer skills she didn't know—specifically, HTML, the language the World Wide Web uses. "I said I knew it," Ronnie says. "I didn't. But I taught myself real quick. You can always learn something new; it's just a matter of whether or not you want to."

Life's tough when you get everything you want, or both things that you want, anyway. Really. "It was a really tough position to be in, because here's someone offering me a great job where they're going to teach me everything on the job. But the Internet seemed to be the thing of the future. I wanted to move forward in an industry that was taking off."

She didn't get left behind. In fact, after six months Ronnie felt she had outgrown her job. "I started getting really bored," she says. "I wanted to learn the industry, and I did. They taught me everything I wanted to know. Everybody was great, but I was ready to move on."

She didn't want to get off the highway; she just wanted to change into a faster lane. When Ronnie read a story about a hot, young, innovative Internet company called Agency.Com, Ronnie knew that this was the place for her. "They were small and aggressive and had a reputation for creating great Web sites." Luckily she knew someone who worked there, so getting an interview wasn't a problem. The tricky part was explaining why she was leaving a job after only six months. It didn't make her look so good. "I told the person interviewing me that I knew it didn't look too good, and that at my next job I'd have to stay there for a good year or two. If you tell them that you know you're leaving too soon and that at the next job you'll have to stay longer, they eat that up. You tell them what they want to hear, but I also meant it. I *knew* I had to stay at least a year or two."

Another tricky thing was getting them to commit. After nearly three weeks and two interviews, they finally did and offered Ronnie the job. But now Ronnie made *them* wait. "I wanted more money than what they offered, so I held out. But then I got scared and was going to call them and say I was flexible, but they called me and met my price."

Now, as a producer for Agency.Com, Ronnie is involved in creating Web sites for corporations such as Hitachi, GTE, and British Airways. She is the liaison between the account person, who is in constant contact with the client, and the creatives. "It's more of a product management position," she says. "I work with the schedules to make sure that all the project deadlines are met and make sure the content is in. Basically, you start the project, you launch it, and you carry it through."

Ronnie asked for life in the fast lane, and she got it. "I had absolutely no life the first six months. I'd go in at nine A.M. and leave at eleven P.M. and then go in on weekends." She's not complaining, however. "I absolutely love my job," she says. "You won't find someone who loves their job more than me." Why? "When someone gives you responsibility and that's what you want, then you run with it."

She admits that she might not be able to run at this pace forever. But then again, as long as there are chances for advancement, she'll keep it in high gear, Ronnie says. As she puts it, "You can't work at a job where there's not another job you want. There's nothing to look forward to, no reason to strive hard."

So, if you're thinking about entering the information superhighway workplace, you'd better be ready to merge with fast-paced speed freaks like Ronnie. If not, get the hell out of the way.

Chapter 13

FROM CONTACT TO A FACE–TO–FACE MEETING

You've schmoozed at a party and got the name and number of some guy who works at an accounting firm you would like to work at. You've spoken with your next-door neighbor, who has given you the name of his good friend who runs an advertising agency you'd love to work for.

You've dialed the phone; made your way past their assistants, voice mail, and endless rings; and you have them on the phone. You're there, they're there. What now?

You're thinking: "Give me a job."

They're thinking: "Damn. Another chump looking for a job. How do I get out of this one?"

THE BLOW–OFF

As mentioned at the end of the last chapter, this person you've called is probably going to try to blow you off by saying "Well, there's nothing available right now, but why don't you send your résumé." They're going to say it with such enthusiasm in their voice that they'll make you think, "Wow, cool! They're really interested in seeing my résumé."

Therefore, when you get them on the line, you can't mention the fact that you're interested in knowing if there are any jobs available. Ask this and not only do you sound greedy, but you're history. This is *not* what you want to know. This is what you want:

fact

The Twenty Fastest-Growing Occupations in the U.S. (in thousands)

Occupation	1992	2005	Change
Home health aides	347	827	138%
Human services	189	445	136
Personal and home-care aides	127	293	130
Computer engineers/scientists	211	447	112
Systems analysts	455	956	110
Physical-corrective assistants and aides	61	118	93
Physical therapists	90	170	88
Paralegals	95	176	86
Teachers, special education	358	625	74
Medical assistants	181	808	71
Detectives, except public	59	100	70
Corrections officers	282	479	70
Child-care workers	684	1,135	66
Travel agents	115	191	66
Radiologic technologists/ technicians	162	264	63
Nursery workers	72	116	62
Medical records technicians	76	123	61
Operations research analysts	45	72	61
Occupational therapists	40	64	60
Legal secretaries	280	439	57

—Bureau of Labor Statistics

"Five Minutes of Your Time," a.k.a. An Informational Interview

Whether this person is someone you know or someone who was referred to you, the first thing you want to do is ask to meet with them. Don't get into a conversation about their company or the industry in general, and don't ask if there are any jobs available. If you *do* ask if there are any jobs available, it enables them to blow you off by saying "No, but send your résumé."

The objective of the phone call is to hang up the phone with a scheduled "informational interview," as they're called. (You don't want to use the words *informational interview* with someone you're calling, but that's what it is.)

Your conversation with your contact will go in one of two ways. With each, here's how to avoid getting suckered into sending a résumé. (Remember, you got through the assistant, and now you're on the phone with your contact directly.)

Scenario 1: Your Contact Refers You to Someone Else at His Company

Me: Hi. This is Charlie Drozdyk. My mother went to school with your wife, and your wife said it would be all right if I called you. I hope I caught you at a decent time.

Him: Yes, right. How's your mother?

Me: She's great, thank you. Anyway, I don't know if your wife told you or not, but I'm looking to get into pharmaceutical sales, and I would love to come in and talk with you for five or ten minutes.

Him: The person you need to speak with is Barry Sheck. He's in charge of recruiting. Let me give you his number.

Me: That would be great. I really appreciate it. Do you think he would meet with me?

Him: Sure. Tell him I said to call him.

Me: Thanks a lot. I'll let you know how it goes.

Him: Okay. Take care.

Analysis: Now, this may *seem* like a blow-off, but it's actually not. He's cutting right to the chase and giving you the name of the person you need to meet. Sure, it would have been nice to meet this guy in person, but it would wind up going the same way as the phone call: he'd tell you that you need to speak with Barry Sheck.

What To Do: Call Barry Sheck and say the following:

> **quote**
>
> "Death is nature's way of saying 'Howdy.' "
>
> —Unknown

Me:	Hi, Mr. Sheck. I was speaking with Mr. Blow, and he suggested that I call you. I'm looking to get into pharmaceutical sales, and I would really appreciate it if I could come into the office and speak with you for five minutes.
Him:	Well, why don't you send me your résumé, and we'll go from there.
Me:	With all due respect, sir, I just graduated from college, and I don't have any real sales experience, but I am extremely motivated and eager to get into this field. That's why Mr. Blow suggested I meet with you in person. He thought that, since you recruit for the company, it would be better to meet with you instead of him.
Him:	Fine. Let me put you on with my assistant to schedule something.

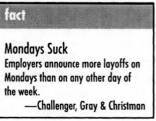

fact

Mondays Suck
Employers announce more layoffs on Mondays than on any other day of the week.
—Challenger, Gray & Christman

Analysis: This guy Sheck wanted to blow me off, but I wouldn't let him. Notice the part "Mr. Blow suggested I meet with you in person. He thought that, since you recruit for the company, it would be better to meet with you." This is bordering on putting words into someone's mouth. Even though he didn't *say* those words, that's why he passed you on to Sheck. That's what he meant. Sheck just needed a little nudge, a little reminder that he should do what Mr. Blow wishes. (We can assume that Mr. Blow is above Sheck in seniority or he never would have passed me on to him.)

definition

DIRECT DEPOSIT
The electronic transfer of food pellets from your work cage to a not-yet-defunct savings and loan.

Scenario 2: Your Contact Says "We're Not Hiring Right Now"

Whether this is a direct contact (someone you know) or someone you were referred to, there's a chance they're going to try to blow you off altogether, without even passing you off onto someone else. They'll say "Why don't you send in your résumé." They'll explain that they're not hiring right now.

Now, if this is someplace you really want to work, this is no good. Suppose a job does become available in, say, three weeks after you talk with this guy. Chances are:

• He will have completely forgotten who you are and won't even think about calling you.

• Someone else in the company will have heard about the job and will have suggested *their* friend for the job. The day the job becomes available, the guy who's responsible for filling the spot will already have a dozen calls from people in his company referring someone for the job. And since these people are recommended from within (whereas you were recommended from without), they're going to be considered likely candidates.

Now, if you had finagled an informal, informational interview with this guy, and if you guys hit it off, he will remember you and call you back in for another interview. This is why it is essential to meet with the people you want to work for, even if there's not a job available at that time.

Proceed to the next page and check out what to actually do once you're in the informational interview.

Chapter 14

THE INFORMATIONAL INTERVIEW: A PREVIEW

So, we've established that the informational interview is imperative because it gives the hiring person a chance to get to know you so when a job *does* become available, he'll think of you.

But—and this is important—this does not mean that when you meet someone for an informational interview, there *isn't* a job available. You think they're just doing you a favor by meeting you, but the truth is, they might actually be interviewing you for a job they haven't told you about. Let me say this again in case it didn't connect. They might be interviewing you for a job they haven't told you about.

This is actually pretty common. Why would they not tell you about the position in advance? you ask. Because they don't want to feel guilty about not offering you a job if they don't like you. Also, if you were referred to this person by someone else and they don't offer you the job they mentioned to you on the phone, they're going to feel like a jerk and their friend is going to be pissed at them.

So, you need to treat even the most casual of informational interviews as you would a regular interview where there's a job on the line—because there might be. Your preparation for the interview, how you connect with the interviewer, what you tell the interviewer, etc., should be the same as for a regular interview. (For this essential interviewing advice, turn to chapter 19, "The Tao of Interviewing.")

"CAN I USE INFORMATIONAL INTERVIEWS AS A WAY TO FIGURE OUT WHAT I WANT TO DO?"

Let's say you have a contact at International Paper. You've never thought about working at a papermaker, but now you're starting to think, "Hmm, maybe there are some interesting jobs there after all. Why don't I call my contact, get an informational interview, and ask him what jobs might interest me there."

Bad idea.

If you're going to ask someone to give you ten minutes of their time for an informational interview, then it's only fair that you go in there knowing what they do and what types of jobs and departments exist there. If you don't know, you're going to look like an idiot, and you'll piss the person off for wasting their time. You cannot call a contact and ask to meet with them without knowing what you want to do there. On the phone they're going to ask you what, at their company, you want to do. If you say, "I don't know. That's what I wanted to talk with you about," I can guarantee you you will never work at this person's company. The person is going to think you're an unfocused idiot. Also, if you have picked an area or two that interest you, it puts him in a better position to help you.

So, before you contact them:

• **Do some research on the company.** Look them up on the Internet. If they're a decent-sized company, Hoovers.com will probably have a profile on them. Or go directly to their corporate Web site if they have one. Learn things like how old the company is, where they make their money, their size, their billings, their plans for expansion, etc. Call the corporate affairs or personnel office and ask them to send you a copy of their annual report and 10K if they're a public company. If they're a private company, ask them to send you any literature they might have.

• **Pick a department.** Based on what you've read about the company, pick an area that most interests you. Remember, even a company that sounds like a real bore—like, say, AT&T—has many departments. There are advertising, marketing, sales, and graphic design, just to name a few. Pick one or two departments that interest you the most, set up your informational interview, and treat it exactly like a regular interview.

Part 4

FINDING THE JOB: THE GONZO APPROACH

Chapter 15

COLD CALLS

As I said in the last chapter, most people get their jobs through a contact. In part 3, I talked about how to make and how to use contacts to get yourself an interview. But what if there's basically only one or two companies you really want to work at, and you don't know anybody who knows anybody who works there?

Or worse, you have no contacts anywhere. You've made a list of all the people you could call (a mental list, at least), and you've come up with nothing. You have no neighbors, you have no friends, you don't know anybody. You're a veritable alien from another planet. You grew up in Hershey, Pennsylvania, went to Hershey University, and the only contacts you have are chocolate contacts. And you don't want to work in chocolate.

Are you screwed? Hell, no. You can send *anybody* a résumé, right? Do up a cover letter, send it to personnel along with your résumé, and hope for a response, right? Isn't this how it's done, after all? Unfortunately, this is how many people are told the job search is done. Not sur-

Something to Worry About
About 40 percent of workers aged fifty-one to sixty-five will not receive pensions from their jobs.
—National Institute on Aging

prisingly, not one person I've interviewed ever landed a job this way. I've spoken to a lot of young people who have made this the crux of their job search and who were amazed to find themselves without even one interview months later.

COLD–CALL BEFORE THE RÉSUMÉ

This is why I'm jumping right into this chapter on cold calls, not résumés. If you've racked your brain and have come up with no contacts at the companies you want to work for, the next step, step 2, is not "Okay, I'll send my résumé and a cover letter to the companies I want to work for."

---

definition

CHRISTMAS BONUS:
The large portion of an employee's salary withheld until year's end, thereby allowing employers to earn interest on it all year.

You got that? Do not send an unsolicited (meaning, something they didn't ask for and are not expecting) résumé and cover letter to a bunch of companies you want to work for. This is a last resort.

The purpose of the cold call is to make a connection, a contact at the company you want to work at, *before* you send your résumé.

Cold-Call Connecting

During her first year of graduate school, Kira cold-called the trading floor of a bank, looking for an internship. Somehow, she got the senior vice president on the phone, and incredibly, they were cracking jokes and laughing after fifteen minutes. Kira was psyched. The internship looked like it was in the bag.

When she told him that she was coming into town and asked to meet with him, he said, "First, send me a résumé and cover letter, and *then* I'll decide if I want to meet with you." As Kira says, "Since we had cracked jokes and everything, I knew I had to top the conversation. So I blew up my résumé and cover letter to poster size and sent them to him. We met and I got the internship."

THE HOW–TOS OF COLD CALLING

Get the Hiring Person's Name

Let's say you're interested in doing publicity at Company X. The first thing you have to do is find out who runs the publicity department. The boss at any company usually has a "Manager of" or "Director of" or "Vice President of" in front of the department name. Since you don't know which title they have, when you call the receptionist at Company X, simply ask the following: "Could you tell me who the head of publicity is, please?"

Now you have the name of the person who hires in the department you want to work for. At this point, you could just send your résumé to him as others would do. Don't. Why? You want to have as many personal encounters (phone calls are personal) with this person's office as possible—with the receptionist, with the assistant, and with the boss, if possible.

Call the Hiring Person's Office

> **quote**
>
> "Everybody likes a kidder, but nobody lends him money."
>
> —Arthur Miller

The next thing you do is contact this person's office. We'll call this person "Ms. Boss." When the receptionist tells you Ms. Boss's name, say, "Can you transfer me there, please?"

The receptionist will put you through to her office, and chances are, her assistant will answer the phone. We'll call the assistant "Bob." Bob will say, "Ms. Boss's office. This is Bob," or something like that. Now this is where the fun begins.

Bob is a gatekeeper. His job is to keep calls like yours from getting through to Ms. Boss. This doesn't mean, however, that you can't try to speak with Ms. Boss. Another thing about Bob—you want him on your side. You do not want to piss him off. He is essential—essential to your getting a job at that company—sometimes more so than Ms. Boss.

Ask to Speak with the Hiring Person

Say, "Hi, is Ms. Boss there?" Bob will ask you your name. You'll tell him. It won't sound familiar, so he'll say, "Will she know what it's regarding?" Now you can make up some lie, or you can tell the truth. I advise telling the truth. Tell him the following: you're interested in working in publicity at Company X, and you'd love to talk or meet with Ms. Boss. He'll probably tell you that they're not hiring. Ask him, then, if it would be all right to send your résumé. He'll say sure.

Send Your Résumé

Now you have a specific person to send your résumé to at Company X, instead of sending it to personnel. Plus, in your letter you can make it sound as if they requested your résumé by starting the cover letter this way:

> Dear Ms. Boss:
>
> I was speaking with your assistant, Bob, on the telephone today, and he said that even though you're not currently hiring, I could send in my résumé. . . .

The fact that you mention Bob's name in the first sentence gives your letter a big advantage over the hundreds of résumés that come in unsolicited. Your letter is now more familiar, and it's as if they're expecting it.

The Follow-Up Call. Circumventing "Bob"

Your résumé has been there for two weeks. It's now perfectly acceptable to call Ms. Boss to make sure she received it and to try to get an informational interview. Now that your résumé is there in Ms. Boss's office, it's an okay time to try to get her on the phone directly. How? By calling at a time when Bob may not be there, like at 7:30 or 8:00 P.M.

I don't recommend doing this on the first call, before you send your résumé. Why? Because the first thing she's going to say when you say "Hi, I'm so-and-so, and I'm really eager to work for Company X in your department and would love to meet with you" is "Why don't you send your résumé." Now you can say, "I spoke with Bob two weeks ago and sent it right away. I'm sure you must have received it by now." If you say this, you are showing yourself to be someone who is somehow familiar to her office. Now, while she is still a little off guard, do the following:

Nail It Home!

This is your moment. You have to know exactly what you're going to say. If you don't fumble but are friendly, articulate, and humble, there is a very good chance you'll end this conversation with an interview. Try something like this:

> Listen, I know you're really busy, and Bob told me that you're not hiring right now, but there is no company I'd rather work for than Company X. And since I don't know anybody there, I would be so grateful if I could meet with you so that when something does become available, you'll know who I am.

Ms. Boss Says, "No, I Won't Meet with You"

In the event that this heartless person says no, the game ain't over. It's just beginning. Getting a job at a company you want to work at is often a

---

fact

The Fastest-Growing Occupations Requiring a Bachelor's Degree

Marketing, advertising, public relations	36%
Personnel, labor relations specialists	36
Sports instructors, coaches, trainers	36
Vocational education	36
Secondary schoolteachers	37
Podiatrists	37
Recreation workers	38
Social workers	40
Recreational therapists	40
Management analysts	43
Construction managers	47
Psychologists	48
Speech-language pathologists; audiologists	48
Preschool, kindergarten teachers	54
Occupational therapists	60
Operations research analysis	61
Teachers, special education	74
Physical therapists	88
Systems analysts	110
Computer engineers/ scientists	112

—Occupational Outlook Quarterly

several-month process of slowly banging down someone's door, and prying open their heart.

If they say no they won't meet with you, try a letter like this:

Dear Ms. Boss,

It was a pleasure speaking with you the other day, even if it was for a quick second. As I told you on the phone, Company X is where I want to work more than anywhere else. I am an extremely hard worker and am not above doing anything. As I don't know anybody at the company, and since you head the department in which I want to work, I would love to meet with you, if just for five minutes. I don't want to bother you too much, but I do want you to know that there is someone out there dying for a break, ready to work their butt off for you.

Sincerely,
Charlie Drozdyk (212) 555-5555

If this elicits no response after two weeks, call them again when their assistant is gone (or whenever they pick up the phone themselves) and ask them if they received your note. If they say no, you need to use some humor. You have to say something like: "Well, it was just a quick note basically begging to meet with you and saying how I'd do anything to work there." If they say yes, they got it, say, "I don't want to drive you crazy. I just don't know what other course to take. I really, really want to work at Company X."

---

definition

FREELANCER:
Project-to-project serf unable to visit a physician.
CONSULTANT:
See Freelancer, only with gray hair.

If this doesn't get you anywhere, it may be time to give up on this person for a while. But not altogether. Every month send Ms. Boss a note telling her what you're up to and add that you're still very much interested in meeting with her to discuss how to get your foot in the door at Company X and that you haven't given up hope.

Stick-to-itiveness

"We had a guy working on Wall Street who used to send us Christmas cards. He used to send us weird, funny, crazy Christmas cards for two or three years, looking for work, and there *was* no work. Then one day something opened up, and we said, 'Remember that guy who sent those weird cards? He must have a great sense of humor. Let's get him in. Let's have him fill the job.' "

—Lloyd Kaufman, president, Troma Films

Should a job become available in her department, there's a very good chance she'll call you. Why? You've shown great interest in their company (employers love that), and you've shown determination and perseverance in the face of rejection—qualities any employer would love.

The Follow-Up Call. Dealing with the Assistant ("Bob")

You sent your résumé two weeks ago, and you've been calling after hours when Ms. Boss might answer the phone herself, but it's not happening. She won't answer her own phone. It's now time to deal with Bob.

The first thing you want to do is get Bob to sympathize with you and your cause. You need to be very nice and humble. You have to make him like you so he'll help you out. If you're any good at schmoozing at all, you should expect Bob to help you in at least one, if not all, of these ways:

· Set up an interview between you and his boss.
· Give you information about a job that might be opening somewhere else in the company.
· Give you a lead about a job at another company.

"Sorry, We're Just Not Interviewing"

If Bob says there is no way that his boss will meet with you, don't push it. If you're gracious and understanding, he might take pity on you and help you. Just get in a conversation with him. Ask him:

* Are there any other people at Company X who might be hiring?
* Has he heard of any other companies that might be hiring?
* What's the best way to get your foot in the door at Company X?

Making Friends with Strangers

I can't stress this enough. The job search is about building relationships with strangers over the phone. You're going to be calling and talking to people about jobs at their company. Chances are, they're going to tell you nothing is available. In this process of being blown off, however, your goal is to strike up a conversation with someone there. Make a phone pal. Be honest with the person. Say, "Listen, I really would love to work for you guys, but I don't know how to go about it." Ask them the following question:

"Can I Check in with You Every Few Weeks?"

This is one of the most important questions you can ask Bob, the assistant. Before you hang up the phone, say, "Listen, would it be all right if I checked in with you in a few weeks to see if anything has become available?" This question will catch them so off guard, they won't know what to say. Few people have the balls to say, "No, don't call me."

Why Am I Going On and On about Schmoozing an Assistant?

This is why. When you get hired at a company, it will probably go something like this. Bob, the assistant you've been talking with, hears that there's an entry-level position open answering phones or something. Bob's boss doesn't want to deal with filling the position. She's thinking something like, "Shit, our phone answerer is leaving. I can't waste my time looking for someone to do this basic function. Bob, you do it. Besides, it's such a shitty job, who would want it?" You, that's who. That's where Bob—who's always looking to be helpful (or should be)—pipes up, "You know, there's this guy Charlie who's been calling here every few weeks for the past six months looking for a job. Says he'll do anything. He's real persistent. Maybe I should give him a call. What do you think?" His boss replies, "Fine. Whatever. Get him in here." And that's a common scenario of how someone is hired.

BE A HAPPY CAMPER

None of this phone stuff will work for you if your phone manner isn't right. By right I mean you must be extremely pleasant and nonarrogant. A sense of humor doesn't hurt either. So don't call when you're in a pissy mood or when you have a cold or when you're feeling sorry for yourself. You must be smiling on the other end of the phone. Sounds stupid, but it's true. You must be cheerful. You cannot be a burdensome call like most of the others they receive on any given day.

A Receptionist Tells All!

Listen to these words about cold calling from a receptionist at Miramax Films (who is no longer there, by the way):

> Be really pleasant when you're speaking to the receptionist, because they take shit all day long, and speaking to a pleasant person on the phone always breaks my mood. I've had twenty-minute conversations with people on the phone just because they were really nice. I had a guy call a few weeks ago looking for a job, and he was really pleasant. So I told him that there were no jobs available and ended up giving him total inside information about [her company] and how we were doing mass firings and blah blah blah. And I said, "You might want to try an internship, because the turnover rate is high. You'd probably get hired really quickly."

I said, "What department are you interested in?" and he said, "I have no idea. I just want to work in film." And I said that I would suggest acquisitions because they're the nicest people in the whole company and it would be a really good place to get your feet wet. At that moment the head of acquisitions walked by, and I asked him if he wanted to pick up the phone and talk to a potential intern, and he said, "Yeah, sure." And the guy was in a half an hour later interviewing and started the next day. And then he got hired full-time soon after.

Why did you give him all this information and help?

Because he was nice, and I liked the sound of his voice.

What if people aren't nice—if you don't like the sound of their voice?

I've given out false information. I've hung up on people. I've spelled names wrong. They'll never even open up your letter if you've spelled their name wrong. So call a couple of times, a couple of different days, because receptionists take all the shit all day long. So it's worth it to find one who's in a good mood.

What should they say to you when they get you on the phone?

First off, when they call, they should immediately lower their status so that they know that I'm doing them a favor by giving them any information at all. That's always what opens me up and breaks my mood, for them to say, "I know you're incredibly busy, but I just graduated from college and I was just wondering if you could . . ." Just in a language that lowers your status. Not because I'm an egomaniac, but because I realize that you must know what I'm doing or that you're faking it really well.

Instant Gratification

"[Cold calls] are fine with me. Because I'm more likely to say 'Yeah, I'll meet with you' over the phone than I am to actually read a letter and make a response. Reading a letter is time-consuming."

—Robin Danielson, president, Mad Dogs and Englishmen Advertising

FEATURE INTERVIEW

Neal Justin
29 years old
Pop culture critic
Minneapolis Star Tribune
Northwestern University
Journalism major

Grades, schmades. While most of his peers at Northwestern were hunkered down with their books in the library every night, Neal was out getting a real education. "To be honest with you, my grades weren't that stellar. Some people bust their buns and get straight As, and that's great. But for me, doing other things, getting a variety of experiences, I thought, was more valuable. And quite frankly, more fun."

So while others were taking speech and television production classes, Neal was producing and hosting an entertainment cable access show. And while others were pulling all-nighters preparing for their film theory and journalism classes, Neal was out reviewing a movie for the college paper or working on a piece for the *Chicago Tribune*. His peers might have been out getting As, but Neal was out compiling published clips—something anybody wanting to get a journalism gig must have.

In fact, by the time he graduated, Neal was making a living as a journalist by doing freelance work and by writing regularly for the *Tribune*. Though he started out "making copies, stealing paper clips for editors, opening mail, and doing a lot of clerky things," after a few months they finally let him write a story. Why? "I just bugged people enough until they said, 'Just give the kid a story so he shuts up.' "

"Weren't you afraid of pissing them off?" I ask him.

"I think you have to needle people without driving them crazy. They have to like you first—before you start bugging them."

With all these clips and experience behind him, it's really no surprise that a Gannett-owned paper—the *Rockford Register Star*—came to his college and recruited him, offering him a full-time writing gig when he graduated. So Neal had a choice. He could either stick with the *Chicago Tribune*—one of the country's largest papers—or go with a smaller, way less prestigious paper, covering PTA meetings. He chose the latter.

"I didn't think I had gotten a lot of the basics," he explains. "I didn't think I had done my time as a reporter."

Well, with twenty-seven murders to cover in his first year, he got some of that time in he was looking for. And very much to his surprise, he ended up "loving it, and becoming a stronger reporter because of it." Sure, it had its drawbacks. Like getting called late at night Christmas Eve to go cover a murder only to find yourself outside in twenty below zero weather "for what seemed like ages" waiting for the detective to come out and talk to you. Or having to watch your speed and your ass whenever you drive through a certain town where you uncovered a story involving a chief of police and his household's 900-number calling habit paid for by the taxpayers. (The guy later resigned.)

This is what he left the bright lights of Chicago for?

"Listen, it's not for everybody," he says. "I talk to a lot of young people wanting to get into feature writing, and I tell them the best thing to do is to go cover cops and chicken dinners and PTA meetings in Palookaville for a year or two years. A lot of people go into this saying 'Oh, great. I get to write all the time.' If you come into it wanting to be a writer first and a reporter second, you're going to get screwed. Great writers don't always blossom in this job. It's too quick. It's too imperfect in terms of great writing. I see a lot of great writers struggle trying to do journalism. Good reporters understand the importance of being accurate and being fair, which is much more important [than] whether the writing's award-winning.

"Kids out of college ask me very often, 'I want to be a music critic. I want to be a movie critic. How do I get into it?' I tell them not to try to jump into a large paper right away. If you do get in, chances are, you're going to get swallowed. You're going to end up doing menial stuff. At a smaller paper you get a little more attention and more of a chance to get the front page. Then, you send those clips to a larger paper, and they go, 'Hey, that guy was a star there,' and you start off higher."

This is what happened with Neal. After three years in the rural trenches, he sent his clips to around ten larger papers and took an offer with the *Minneapolis Star Tribune* as their pop culture critic. Now, instead of exposing the local police chief and rushing to murder scenes, Neal has to contemplate things like whether or not he should interview Tom Jones.

"What do you think, should I interview him?" he asks me.

"Do you like him?" I ask.

"Yeah, he puts on a great show," he responds.

"Then you should probably interview him," I say.

"You might be right," he says, not seeming to miss those days of reporting PTA meetings and chicken dinners.

Not that everything's all cushy now with great stories falling into his lap or anything. He's still got that daily pressure of having to compete with radio and television and other newspapers. "There's pressure to get that story, but that's great. Having that competition makes you better," he says.

And even though it's great being "pretty much free to decide what I want to write about," he still has to do his homework. He reads five or six magazines a week and talks to people about what they're listening to and what they're watching and what they *want* to watch. "A lot of it is trying to pick what's going to be hot," Neal says.

"So your job doesn't suck because . . . ?" I ask him.

"My job doesn't suck because I get to deal with a lot of interesting people on a professional level, like Howard Stern and Bruce Springsteen and Kyra Sedgwick. Every day I'm dealing with very interesting, fascinating people that, you know, an idiot like me wouldn't have access to," he says, laughing. "The places I get to go and the people I get to meet—it's just great."

"So what sucks about it?" I ask.

"If you're somebody who likes set hours or a rhythm, it can pretty much suck. My schedule is different every day. Today I'll work from noon to 11:00 P.M., and the other day, because of Emmy nominations, I was here at 6:30 in the morning. I work a lot of weekends because a lot of entertainment stuff is going on. If you have a family or enjoy a set pattern, it would suck. When I was covering cops, I was on call twenty-four hours a day. For me that's a bonus. I like that topsy-turvy kind of schedule."

"Anything else about it that can suck?" I ask.

"If you screw up, 400,000 people might see it the next day—with your name on it."

Chapter 16

OTHER GONZO APPROACHES

SHOWING UP UNINVITED

If the idea of making a cold call intimidates you, then this next gonzo method of getting an interview will send fear through your veins. It's all about just showing up. Targeting a company you want to work at and simply strolling up to the front desk and asking to meet with someone.

It's a good idea to have a name to throw out to the receptionist instead of just saying "Can I talk to someone about a job?" This requires doing a little phone research to find out who manages the department you want to work in.

Before you go out and do this, realize that you will be judged as presumptuous and pushy. Some will be turned off by this, and some will be turned on by it. Although some peo-

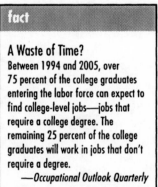

fact

A Waste of Time?
Between 1994 and 2005, over 75 percent of the college graduates entering the labor force can expect to find college-level jobs—jobs that require a college degree. The remaining 25 percent of the college graduates will work in jobs that don't require a degree.
—*Occupational Outlook Quarterly*

ple may say it's completely crazy, I disagree. I've heard of several people who have landed jobs by just showing up.

Put yourself in an employer's shoes. Imagine you're hanging out in your office. You're having a shitty day doing the same old shit, eating shit from the higher-ups. You're looking out the window and at the clock simultaneously, wondering if 6:00 will ever come. Just then the receptionist buzzes you and tells you that Joe Schmo is here to see you. "To see me?" you ask. "About what?" "About the possibility of working in your department," the receptionist says. "Are you kidding?" you ask. "Does he look normal, or is he a nut?" you ask. "Normal," the receptionist says.

Now, admit it. Aren't you a little curious about this person who's just shown up to meet you? Aren't you just a little bit flattered? Assuming you're not completely in the weeds,

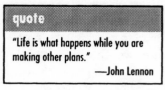

quote

"Life is what happens while you are making other plans."

—John Lennon

don't you think there'd be a fifty-fifty chance you'd say, "Sure, what the heck, I'll meet with the guy." If you're a guy and the person who has shown up to meet with you is a woman, well, I'd say there's a better than fifty-fifty chance you're going to meet with her. Why? Because men are dogs.

definition

RÉSUMÉ:
An 8.5" × 11" collection of lies with your name at the top.

HBO Human Resources VP Gets Accosted in Lobby

Listen to how one guy got the attention of the vice president of human resources and administration at HBO.

We were starting the Comedy Channel a few years ago, and this guy called a couple of times. I explained to him that we were still in start-up and I wasn't prepared to start seeing people. I said I would call him once we had a better idea what we were going to do organizationally. He understood. He was persistent—he'd leave messages saying "Just checking in"—but he wasn't obnoxious about it.

Then one day—I get to work early, around seven A.M.—I walk in, and this same guy is waiting in the lobby for me, and he says, "I just wanted to know if you had a minute to chat. I know you told me already that you guys don't know where you stand, but I just wanted you to know who I am." I invited him up, and he was a very nice guy. Of course, if this had not been a fit, he wouldn't have gotten the job.

WORKING FOR FREE

If you're looking to get into an industry where work is done in short projects—like film, commercials, photography, or design, to name a few—a great way to jump-start your career and to gain experience is by working for free.

For example, say you want to become a commercial film producer but don't know anybody who can give you a start. You know that the entry-level position on film shoots is production assistant, but all the production companies you've called have experienced production assistants they already work with. Offering to work for free on the next project will give you experience (something to put on your résumé) and an opportunity to prove yourself. If you do a great job, they will hire you on their next project, guaranteed.

A Cool Example

This is how Glen went from unpaid production assistant to producer in a few short months. He was volunteering on a commercial that involved filming a small twelve-foot sailboat. The shoot wasn't going too well, however, because the sailboat

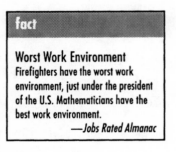

fact

Worst Work Environment
Firefighters have the worst work environment, just under the president of the U.S. Mathematicians have the best work environment.
—*Jobs Rated Almanac*

wouldn't hold still; it kept turning sideways in the water. Seeing an easy solution, Glen dove in the water and held the boat in place, basically saving the shoot. The director thought he was God after that and instantly put him on the payroll.

The Real Skinny with . . . Rob Slosberg, Advertising Creative Director

MAJORING IN ADVERTISING IS . . . ?

Stupid. I mean, there are people who have majored in advertising and made it into the business. But it's not good to have such tunnel vision. You need to draw on different stimuli.

Take philosophy, psychology. Be proud to be a liberal arts major. It lets you explore different areas of life, which, in turn, makes you a more creative person.

POLITICS:

Wherever there are people, there are politics. A boss will ask you to work on a commercial, and you'll come up with something you think is great. You'll show him and he'll say, "I don't like it. It's not working for me." Then two weeks later you find out that he presented your idea with a slight twist on it and put his name on it.

THE STRESS FACTOR:

It can be very stressful. Your boss will say, "We need an ad by tomorrow. It needs to be running by next week. We need a mechanical by Thursday. We need to shoot the ad Wednesday. And it needs to be great. Since we're on that schedule, you need to show concepts to me in an hour." And you're like, "Huh?"

REALITY CHECK:

I think the low point of advertising is after getting really, really excited about it, saying, "This is the most fun business, I love it, it's great," and then you wake up in the morning and you say, "It's just an ad." You know what I mean? Everyone in advertising has gotten that feeling at least once in their life, if not once a day. But some people can just go nine to five and not even give a second thought about selling somebody a douche.

Part 5

Résumés and Cover Letters

Chapter 17

RÉSUMÉS

Résumés suck. A résumé is simply a piece of paper that immediately finds its way into the trash or under a pile of junk in a corner. A résumé, sent with a cover letter, will not get you a job or an interview. A résumé is not a job-hunting tool. A résumé is the least important part about finding a job. So there.

As discussed, finding a job is about:

• Taking advantage of people you know and getting people you don't know to tell you about job openings and opportunities.
• Making a contact at a company and calling and calling and calling them until they tell you about an opening at their company or until they agree to meet with you.

Finding a job is not about sending résumés out to a hundred human resources departments at a hundred companies. A résumé should be sent only in response to a want ad or when someone at a company you're trying to get into has told you to send one. As said before, you do not send a résumé to a company until you have made contact with someone there and they are expecting it.

APPEARANCE

A résumé should be one page long, laser-printed on white paper. It should be easy to read, and it must be proofread by at least two people. It cannot have any typos. Even though I, and everybody else, say this, at least 25 percent of you will make a spelling blunder on your résumé. It's so common that human resources people actually scan the résumé first, looking for typos so they can throw it away before spending too much time on it. It saves them a lot of reading time.

```
definition

ASSISTANT:
A new-to-the-workplace college-educated pain sponge.
```

THE RÉSUMÉ'S THREE SECTIONS

A résumé has three sections: education, work experience, and skills. Activities, interests, languages, and travel are other acceptable categories that can be included. If you're just graduating from college and are looking for your first real job, you will probably want to put education at the top, unless you have, say, five good jobs and internships to list. And skills should always be listed at the bottom, after activities or interests, should you include such a category.

Education

List schools in reverse chronological order, beginning with the school you most recently attended (or are still attending). Include, in this order, the college, location, degree, major, and graduation year. If your GPA is above 3.2, list that as well. Also list any awards or honors. If your senior thesis is relevant to the position you're applying for, list that, too. Some people advise including your GPA in your major if it's real good. Personally, I don't think that says a lot for you. Why should I respect you for goofing off and doing shitty on 75 percent of your classes but doing well on those courses that interest you most? If you attended more than two colleges, I wouldn't list that on your résumé. Why make yourself look bad by including colleges that may not have been as good as the one you graduated from? Plus, three colleges makes you look flaky and noncommittal compared to one college.

Smart, Schmart

"I don't care to hear what your GPA is. I don't want it on the résumé. The fact that your GPA was high does not mean that you're a functional working person. And the expectation that it's going to wow me . . . You know, it takes hard work, tenacity, enthusiasm. It takes a good attitude. It takes a flexible personality to function in the workplace. The fact that you were an exceptional college student doesn't really hold that much weight."

—Personnel manager, Solomon R. Guggenheim Museum

Work Experience

Writing Your Experience with Power Verbs

The most difficult part of résumé writing is describing your experiences. You know, that stuff that explains what you did at each of your jobs. And although it may suck, it's actually very good for you. It's great practice for what lies ahead in your business career: the fine art of bullshitting. Not out-and-out lying, but truth stretching.

The best approach is to begin each job description with a power verb. *Improved*, *increased*, and *attained* are all examples of power verbs. They stress results, which are, after all, what employers care about most.

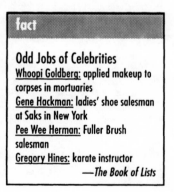

fact

Odd Jobs of Celebrities
Whoopi Goldberg: applied makeup to corpses in mortuaries
Gene Hackman: ladies' shoe salesman at Saks in New York
Pee Wee Herman: Fuller Brush salesman
Gregory Hines: karate instructor
—*The Book of Lists*

You can even string power verbs together. Examples:

- "Designed, developed, and implemented . . ."
- "Established, cultivated, and maintained . . ."

If you feel uncomfortable about inflating the importance of your position as an intern or a summer employee, well, get over it. It's become standard practice. Not that you should *lie* about your experience, however. They can bust you on this in an interview easily. But if you assisted on a project or task, go ahead and take coresponsibility for it. By saying you "Recruited and organized a group of volunteers to participate as focus groups" does not mean you did it all alone. You might have assisted on this duty. Saying, however, that you "Assisted in the recruiting of, and helped to organize . . ." is unnecessary.

For an exhaustive list of power verbs broken up into eight categories, turn to page 323.

Action Verbs and Bulleted Points

When writing what you did at a job—your experience—you want to use action verbs such as *increased, oversaw, implemented*, and *created*. Each duty or responsibility should be summed up in one sentence. The *Princeton Review* did a poll and found that the majority of recruiters preferred responsibilities listed in bulleted points as opposed to paragraphs. For example:

BOB'S ADVERTISING AGENCY
Intern, 1997
- Assembled list of 200 potential clients to solicit.
- Handled requests from the press for project photos and artwork.
- Recruited and organized a group of volunteers to participate as focus groups.

Recruiters claim that bulleted points are easier to read on the page. This approach also forces you, as the résumé writer, to be concise.

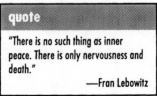

> quote
> "There is no such thing as inner peace. There is only nervousness and death."
> —Fran Lebowitz

Make It Interesting

Résumés are boring to read. When writing your experience, try to include something that might stand out and catch the reader's attention. Suppose you were an intern at Miramax Films, where you spent a summer making copies and answering the phone. And say one day you spoke with Jim Carrey for a second. I recommend putting this on your résumé somehow to spice it up. Here's an example:

MIRAMAX FILMS
Summer intern, 1997
* Answered vice president's phone, which involved assisting celebrities such as Jim Carrey.

The person reading your résumé will say to themselves, "Wow, they spoke with Jim Carrey. That's kinda neat."

Or say you helped your older brother coach his baseball team a couple of times. You can make this stand out by describing your experience like this:

PEEWEE LEAGUE BASEBALL
Assistant coach, spring 1997
* Coached a team of petulant, barely manageable eleven-year-olds. Developed patience and self-restraint while having a great time.

This gives a little personality to your résumé. It lets the reader know you have a sense of humor as well as a decent vocabulary (notice the word *petulant*).

Be Specific. Use Numbers

Try to use numbers or specifics whenever you can to illustrate an achievement. Instead of saying you were simply a short-order cook at Dairy Queen, add this: "Accomplishments:

Cooked over 200 burgers in a one-hour period with only one grill working."

Or say you worked on your college newspaper. Instead of saying "Oversaw distribution and advertising of paper. Worked with publisher to ensure timely deliveries," try to find an accomplishment. Maybe it's something like this: "Increased distribution of paper by 15 percent and advertising by 10 percent. Worked directly with publisher to ensure timely deliveries."

definition

SECRETARY:
What you actually are, as opposed to what you tell your friends and family.

What to Include

You know that stuff you'd just as soon put behind you or maybe even are embarrassed about? You know what? You might want to throw it on your résumé—even if you think it has absolutely nothing to do with the job you're applying for. Often these jobs or experiences can tell an employer more about you than time spent in an internship at Disney or Calvin Klein.

A crappy waitressing job or a job at a tollbooth can signal to an employer that you're someone who is not above doing the shitwork. That you are someone who knows what it's like to get your hands dirty and will therefore not complain when asked to do a crappy assignment.

Activities

This is where you list extracurricular, community, or school activities and sports. This is often one of the more entertaining and informative parts of a résumé. Or should be. It's where an employer says, "Okay, let's see if Joe Schmo is a well-rounded, interesting person or just a dweeb." I've spoken to employers who love to hire people who

Nanny Power

When Claire was in college, she was a nanny. Listen to how that experience *made* her résumé and helped to get her a job. "When the woman who hired me saw my résumé—more than other people who had, like, an internship at a major studio or something during college, which I didn't have—she thought it was really interesting that I was a nanny. Because somebody who was a nanny could really put up with a lot of bullshit work."

played on sports teams in college. They insist that the team-player mentality carries over to the workplace.

Travel

This can either be on its own or combined with activities—i.e., "Activities and Travel." If you spent a year studying in England, you can either put it here or in the education category. If you've bicycled across Europe, traveled through India or somewhere else unusual, or have ever lived overseas, you should definitely put that down. You might think it's no big deal, but employers know that someone who likes to travel is someone who is interested in the world and who brings different experiences to the table.

Skills

This is where you list all the computer programs you know, but it's also an opportunity for you to list any other interests that require skill or skills. For instance, you should include if you're a licensed scuba diver or pilot, competitive ballroom dancer or skateboarder. This is also an acceptable place to list any languages you speak fluently.

What *Really* Matters

Listen to how mentioning Italy on his résumé got John an interview and a job at Fox News. "I got a call from the news director's secretary, who is now a producer. She would get all the résumés and cover letters and never give them to her boss, because *she* wanted the job of production assistant herself, so she hoarded them. But she felt guilty and figured every now and then she had to give her boss a résumé—figured he was *expecting* them. She decided to give him *my* résumé because I had put on the bottom of it that I had studied in Florence. It turns out that the news director loved Italy, had gone there several times, loved Italian food, is just a real Italian lover. So she thought this guy will have something to talk about with me.

"Two weeks later I get a call. I go in for the interview and talk with this guy for about fifteen minutes, and all we talk about is Italy. The next day they called me and said, 'Can you start next Monday?' "

Career Objective?

Employers and "career experts" are divided about putting a career objective on your résumé. Personally, I don't think it's necessary. This is what a cover letter is for. If someone's looking at your résumé and needs to look at your career objective to figure out why they're looking at your résumé, then you're in trouble.

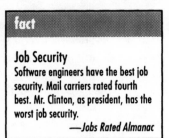

fact

Job Security
Software engineers have the best job security. Mail carriers rated fourth best. Mr. Clinton, as president, has the worst job security.
                    —*Jobs Rated Almanac*

References upon Request?

Employers assume you'll provide reference letters should they ask for them, so it's a waste of time to put this on your résumé. You'll find, however, that you will rarely be asked to provide a reference letter from an old professor or employer. But just in case, you might want to ask a professor to write one for you before you leave school. If you ask for one a year later, chances are, they won't remember who you are. If you decide to go to graduate school, this letter will prove to be very important for you. If you're worried about bugging a professor by asking them to write you a recommendation, don't worry about it. It's what they're paid for. They have a sample letter in their computer that they can adapt to fit you in two minutes.

A SAMPLE RÉSUMÉ

Let's pretend my brother just graduated from college and has interviews with Ballantine Books as an editorial assistant, and with Grey Advertising as an assistant account executive. Since he had no internships at any real companies through college, writing his résumé is going to be a challenge. And since his interviews are in two different industries, he needs to do two versions of his résumé. Let's start with his résumé for the publishing job.

Publishing Job Résumé

TATE DROZDYK
555 Peyton Place
Anywhere, NY 11111
(212) 555-5555
Tate@tnet.com

EDUCATION
University of Pennsylvania, Philadelphia, PA. BA, history, 1996. Received grade of A on senior thesis, which was published in the *Pennsylvania Historical Journal*.

EXPERIENCE
LONGSHORE SAILING SCHOOL
Sailing instructor, summers, 1992–95
- Taught sailing and windsurfing to beginners, intermediates, and advanced students.
- Developed patience and leadership skills.
- Voted "Instructor of the Summer" three consecutive years.

UNIVERSITY OF PENNSYLVANIA SAILING TEAM
Vice president/treasurer, 1995–96
- Spearheaded fund-raising efforts that exceeded previous budgets by 25 percent.
- Organized spring sailing trip, which included chartering ten boats, netting $5,000.
- Wrote all promotional materials and radio advertisements for spring trip.

FIVE GRAPES BOOKSTORE
Clerk, 10/94–5/95
- Responsible for informing buyer on new fiction titles to add to shelves as well as for choosing the "New Fiction Pick of the Week."
- Installed computerized inventory tracking system.

MARIO'S RESTAURANT
Waiter/busboy, summers, 1993–95
- Served food at high-priced, jacket-only restaurant.
- Learned how to deal with demanding customers and stressed-out owners.

ACTIVITIES
Competitive windsurfing on national level (Long Island Sound Champion). Traveled Europe and the U.S. with various soccer teams. Performed in three university plays.

---

definition

WANT AD:
Society's pose that one can gain a decent job without nepotism.

Explanation

Since this is for a publishing job, we thought they might be interested in the fact that he can write, so we added the fact that he received an A on his senior thesis and that he was published. The "Wrote all promotional materials and radio advertisements for spring trip" is somewhat embellished. Promotional materials consisted of some flyers, and radio advertisements consisted of announcements, basically. The whole thing about informing the buyer what new fiction titles to buy and choosing the "New Fiction Pick of the Week" were things that Tate volunteered to do but were not part of his real responsibilities. We felt he needed something that showed he was interested in reading. We made sure to add the "Performed in three university plays" because publishing people and theater people are cut from the same cloth (in my opinion, anyway).

Now, here's Tate's résumé skewed specifically for the assistant account executive job at Grey Advertising.

Advertising Job Résumé

TATE DROZDYK
555 Peyton Place
Anywhere, NY 11111
(212) 555-5555
Tate@tnet.com

EDUCATION
University of Pennsylvania, Philadelphia, PA. BA, history, 1996.

EXPERIENCE
LONGSHORE SAILING SCHOOL
Sailing instructor, summers, 1992–95
• Taught sailing and windsurfing to beginners, intermediates, and advanced students.
• Developed public speaking and leadership skills. (Classes had up to 25 people.)
• Voted "Instructor of the Summer" three consecutive years.

UNIVERSITY OF PENNSYLVANIA SAILING TEAM
Vice president/treasurer, 1995–96
• Spearheaded fund-raising efforts that exceeded previous budgets by 25 percent.
• Responsible for allocating funds appropriately and staying on budget.
• Organized spring sailing trip, which included chartering ten boats, netting $5,000.

FIVE GRAPES BOOKSTORE
Clerk, 10/94–5/95
- Installed computerized inventory tracking system.
- Developed "10 percent Saturday Nights," which increased weekly net profits by 2 percent.

MARIO'S RESTAURANT
Waiter/busboy, summers, 1993–95
- Served food at high-priced, jacket-only restaurant.
- Learned how to deal with demanding customers and stressed-out owners.

ACTIVITIES
Competitive windsurfing on national level (Long Island Sound Champion). Traveled Europe and the U.S. with various soccer teams. Performed in three university plays.

Explanation

A senior thesis, I think, is irrelevant to an advertising job, so we took it off. On the sailing job, we changed the line from "Developed patience and leadership skills" to "Developed public speaking and leadership skills" because, as an account executive, you're constantly dealing with groups of clients. I figured public speaking confidence would be more important than patience. On the sailing team area, we added "Responsible for allocating funds appropriately and staying on budget" because account executives are responsible for keeping their creative associates and projects on budget. In reality there weren't many funds to allocate or a real budget to stay on; they spent money when they had it. On the bookstore job, we added "Developed '10 percent Saturday Nights,' which increased weekly net profits by 2 percent" because it shows a concern and an aptitude for numbers, which an account person must have.

fact

Least Stress
Musical instrument repairers have the least stress. Advertising account executives scored very high on the stress meter—236 on the list out of 250. The president has the most stress.

—*Jobs Rated Almanac*

THE ALTERNATIVE BIO/RÉSUMÉ

It's my strong belief that a well-written cover letter or pleasant phone conversation is more likely to get you an interview than a good résumé.

> **quote**
>
> "Live life live."
>   —My friend Richard

People hire based on whether or not they like and respond to you as a person first and whether or not they see you as someone who has the skills to do the job second. For every job there are tons of people who would be qualified, but there aren't tons of people the hiring person would want to hire. Therefore, in order to even get an interview, you've got to somehow get this hiring person to like you, to respond to you.

One way of doing this is by making your presentation (what you send to this person in the mail) personal. Instead of sending a standard cover letter and résumé, you might want to think about combining the two—incorporating your résumé into the body of the cover letter. Here's an example, something I used several years ago:

Dear Ms. Executive:

As I mentioned to your assistant, Gary, Bryan S. suggested that I give you a call when I get out to L.A. I know Bryan from New York, where I was the assistant to Mr. Man, the producer of Bryan's off-Broadway musical *Spuds.*

Besides assisting Mr. Man on several Broadway and off-Broadway shows, I also served for two years as theater manager for the Criterion Center, which housed a Broadway theater as well as a three-hundred-seat cabaret. For all the shows that came into both theaters, I represented the house's interests. This included overseeing a staff of ten, being accountable for all monies that came into the box office, and generally doing anything and everything that needed doing—including going on the roof when it rained and finding the clogged drain responsible for causing embarrassing leaks on patrons.

Previous to that, I worked for a year at the Brooklyn Academy of Music as the assistant to the general manager. There I prepared contracts and budgets and was integrally involved in all aspects of mounting the many shows that came into one of the five theaters.

I'm making a bit of a career change and would greatly appreciate the opportunity to meet with you to discuss the TV industry in general as well as future entry-level positions at —— Productions.

Thanks for your time in reading this letter. I'll give you a call next week to see if we can set up a time to meet.

Warmest regards,
C.D.

This type of letter/résumé is so much more personal, besides being different, that it is a lot harder to throw in a pile and ignore. It's something you might want to think about using.

FEATURE INTERVIEW

Max Nahabit
29 years old
Fashion editor
***South China Morning Post*, Hong Kong**
USC, English literature and creative writing

When Max was getting out of college, she knew exactly what she'd be doing right now. "I would be living in the suburbs; married with three kids, giving chic little dinner parties on the patio with my husband, who had power tools and who wore golf pants," she says. "Really, I always thought that I would just get married because I wasn't really good at anything."

Actually, there was one thing she was good at—fashion. Putting outfits together. She had what's known in fashion terms as "an eye." In fact, by the time Max hit the seventh grade, she already had a reputation for being a "style maven." "That's how I got popular in junior high," she says. "The older girls used to ask to borrow my clothes, and I'd let them, of course. When Karen Johnson (captain of the cheerleading team) calls you and asks to borrow your Dolphin shorts and your Nike jacket, and you're a seventh-grade little scrub, you're like 'Yeah!' You were thrilled."

Even though everybody loved Max's fashion sense, she had no idea she could make a living with it. Sure, she knew there were these people called designers who made a living in fashion, but Max knew from an early age that that wasn't an option. "I knew I wasn't disciplined enough. I knew I was too lazy to be a designer," she says.

One thing Max thought she might want to be was a writer. That is, until she took a writing class with this hotshot professor who was touted as the new, hip contemporary American writer. "I always received outstanding marks in high school for my creative-writing efforts, but suddenly in this class *everyone* was brilliant and I became the C+ poster girl. Very disheartening!" An average grade wasn't the only thing that made Max consider fashion over writing, however. "I used to sit in his class and all I could think about was 'Oh, my God, I can't believe he's wearing those gray leather shoes; and look at that jacket—it's not even leather . . . it's *pleather.*' I couldn't concentrate on what he was saying. I'd just look at his pretend 'clip-on' earring in morbid fascination."

That experience, and mediocre grade, dissuaded Max from pursuing writing. And that sucked, because now she didn't have an answer to that question everyone was asking her— "What are you going to do when you graduate?" So in order to placate the masses—or at least her friends and family—Max started telling people she was going to be a fashion editor. "I only had a vague idea of what a fashion editor was," she says. "I had been reading *Vogue* since I was nine years old, and this was a term you'd always see."

When Max got back from a year bumming around Europe after graduation, she forgot about that fashion editor thing and got a job at a hot L.A. publicity company answering phones. "I didn't have a firm grasp on the fashion business," she explains. "I thought I could just be a fashionable publicist or something." So Max spent six months at the front desk answering phones, looking good in her Gucci platforms, and was then promoted to junior publicist—a job she hated. "I didn't want to spend the rest of my life perpetuating celebrities in the media," she says. "It's boring. It wasn't my scene at all."

Her scene, of course, was fashion. But not knowing much about the business—other than having worked on a few photo shoots during her publicist days—she didn't know where to look. So she didn't; she just showed up. "I just put on a great outfit, a confident face, and walked into *Sportswear International*'s offices [a fashion trade magazine] and said to the receptionist, 'I'll work for free. I can write, and I think I can style if you let me try.' " The receptionist told Max that nothing was available but told her to try upstairs at *Apparel News*, another fashion trade magazine. Their fashion editor had just quit, and they were looking for somebody, she told Max.

So without an appointment, without any publishing, writing, or styling experience, and *no* portfolio! Max walked upstairs. As Max explains it, "It never occurred to me that there might be a million other girls in Los Angeles that would die for that job and who were ten times more competent and experienced than I was." Incredibly, *Apparel News* was going through massive changes; everybody had basically walked out, and they were desperate for people. So they gave Max a shot. "I had convinced myself that I could do it, so it was easy for me to convince *them*," she says.

Next thing she knew, Max was going to fashion shoots, finding locations, booking models, hiring photographers, and meeting with designers—things she had never done before. Maybe you're wondering how she knew she wouldn't fall flat on her face. "It never occurred to me that I couldn't do it," Max says. "I just thought, why not?"

And when she found out that writing was a part of the job, it concerned her, but only for a minute. "Writing for fashion is not like writing prose or even news articles. It sounds corny but you have to have a firm grasp of clichés. There is a specialized jargon reserved for fashion writing. It's almost like rapping. Alliteration is a favorite tool of the trade." And while many fashion people take it so seriously, as if they were saving lives or something, Max seems to have put things in perspective. "They're not think pieces. No one's going to write a think piece over hemlines or Christy Turlington's bum," she says.

The most challenging part of the job was not the writing, it was the pressure of having to predict what was going to be hot. Whereas the fashion magazines—*Vogue, Cosmopolitan*, etc.—were three months ahead of season, *Apparel News*, being a trade magazine, was six months ahead of season. Luckily, Max had a knack for predicting what was going to be the "Next Big Thing." "I was never good at anything in my entire life," says Max. "But fashion, I had a natural knack for."

Then, after going to Hong Kong on business, Max quit *Apparel News* and moved there, hoping to land a job as easily as she had in L.A. two years earlier. And incredibly, she did. Having heard that a fashion editor at a major magazine had been fired, Max showed up with her portfolio on a Monday and asked to see the editor. When the receptionist said, "No, no, no, she's very busy," Max pushed her portfolio at her and said, "Please just show her this book, have her look at it, and *then* tell me if she wants to see me." Fifteen minutes later Max was offered the job of fashion and beauty editor.

But as quickly as she was hired, she was fired. Four days into the job, she was let go for disagreeing with her boss in front of a few others. Arguing a point with your boss might be standard practice in America, but in Hong Kong it doesn't fly. "Hong Kong lesson number one: Respect their sense of 'face' above all else no matter what. So if you disagree, you don't say so," says Max. "Obedience is more important than talent in Asia."

After always getting what she wanted pretty easily, getting fired was definitely a humbling experience for Max. And more. "It was devastating. I'd never been fired before. While all my friends were busy working until eleven at night, I'm sitting there watching Oprah and eating fried rice in my pajamas at three o'clock in the afternoon."

So after three months of nothing, Max started to plan her move out of Hong Kong. But at the eleventh hour, she heard through a friend that the fashion editor of the *South China Morning Post* had suddenly quit, leaving the paper with a huge hole. Luckily for Max, they knew who she was from the freelance work she had done for them. Freelance work she begged for, by the way. "I would hound them every day for freelance assignments. I was willing to style office supplies, kids, luggage . . . anything so long as my name got in the paper!" So after being

fired from a great job, Max landed an even better one. "I seem to always 'fail upwards,' "
Max says.

Even though Max is one of those people who annoy you for getting everything they want, it
doesn't mean she doesn't appreciate it. "Sometimes I walk down the street and go, wow, here I
am, this little girl from Valencia is having lunch with some of the biggest fashion people in the
world. I do pinch myself at times and go, my God, this is a cool job."

P.S.: Max Nahabit (now Max Kater) now lives and works as a freelance fashion editor in Singa-
pore, where she throws chic little dinner parties with her husband, Peter (who does have power
tools, by the way).

Chapter 18

COVER LETTERS

As discussed in the chapters on cold calls and connections, sending a cover letter with a résumé is a last resort. If possible, you want to get an interview without even sending a cover letter and résumé by getting the hiring person on the line directly, schmoozing them a little, and setting up an appointment to see them. If the person who hires tells you to send in a résumé before they agree to meet with you, then you have no choice.

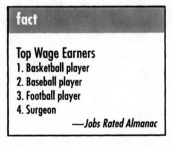

fact

Top Wage Earners
1. Basketball player
2. Baseball player
3. Football player
4. Surgeon
—*Jobs Rated Almanac*

Now the fact that you are going for this job means that, in your opinion, your résumé qualifies you (at least a little) for the job in question. So assuming that your résumé is decent, the only thing that will keep you from meeting with this person face-to-face is your cover letter. Your cover letter is going to be the thing that gets you into the room or not.

The thing about cover letters is, 90 percent of them suck. I was recently working at this company where I looked through a huge stack of cover letters to see what people were doing these days, and I absolutely could not believe what I read. I swear, 90 percent of them were crap. They were written in this strange gibberish that I've never seen before. But don't take my word for it. Robin Danielson, president of Mad Dogs and Englishmen Advertising, agrees. She says:

> I hate when people try to impress me. I hate cover letters that are full of catchphrases. I mean, I think the people who are starting

out trying to get jobs make the mistake of believing that there's this language that they have to use. Letters that don't use normal language really piss me off. You know, "As a marketing executive, you're aware of the need for brilliant solutions. . . ." Or, "I can bring the power of . . ." It's just like, fuck off, you stupid wanker! Kids forget that grown-ups are people. You get all intimidated and think that it's all so fucking complicated, and it's really not.

---

definition

HIRING FREEZE:
The time period in which you lack the juice to get friends jobs in your organization.

In all those cover letters I went through, I'd read crap like "Attached heretofore is my résumé for your perusal" and "I am henceforth enclosing my résumé with the interest of procuring an interview with your establishment." Who the hell talks like this? I don't know anybody who talks like this. I swear, it's as if, whenever someone has to write a cover letter, they all of a sudden become an idiot.

SOME GOOFY SENTENCES

Here are a few blunderous examples so you'll know what I'm talking about:

1. "Strong analytical skills coupled with excellent work ethic have further enabled me to develop my computer literacy, economic, and organizational skills."
2. "I have the ability to write and communicate effectively on many different levels."
3. "I would like to have an opportunity to discuss a possible mutual interest at your convenience."
4. "I am writing at this time . . ."

Critique: (1) *Coupled?* Who uses that word? Also, "coupled with excellent work ethic" is missing an *an*. (2) What levels could this person be referring to? (3) "A possible mutual interest?" Come on. (4) Writing at this time as opposed to another time?

So how *do* you write a decent cover letter? Good question.

WRITING A GOOD COVER LETTER

In this paragraph-by-paragraph walk-through of how to write a cover letter, I've given three different versions, depending upon whether you're (A) responding to a want ad, (B) sending it out of the blue, or (C) sending it after speaking with someone. A and B are both unsolicited responses, meaning you're either sending it out of the blue or you're responding to a want ad. C is the solicited response, meaning you've spoken with someone before you've sent it and they are therefore expecting it.

Paragraph 1: State the Position You Are Interested In

A. *Unsolicited—responding to ad:* "I am writing in response to the position of ＿＿ listed in the *Daily Journal* on September 5, 1997."

B. *Unsolicited—sent out of the blue:* "I am extremely interested in exploring ＿＿ positions at ＿＿ Company and am sending along a copy of my résumé in the hope of meeting with you."

C. *Solicited:* "As discussed with ＿＿, I am sending you my résumé with respect to the position of ＿＿."

If you are sending your cover letter at the suggestion of someone who knows the person you're sending it to (a referral), then mention this person's name in the very first sentence. People love referrals.

Paragraph 2: Explain What You Are Currently Doing

A. *Unsolicited—responding to ad:* "I am currently working as a ＿＿ at the ＿＿ Company, where I am responsible for [list no more than three things you do]. Though I enjoy the work that I am doing,

I feel it is time to start exploring my options. The opportunity described at your company is of great interest to me and is something I would love to be considered for."

B. *Unsolicited—sent out of the blue:* "I am currently working as a _____ at the _____ Company, where I am responsible for [list no more than three things you do]. I am very excited about the work that _____ [company you're applying to] is doing and would love to share with you how I can contribute to its success."

C. *Solicited:* "I am currently working as a _____ at the _____ Company, where I am responsible for [list no more than three things you do]. _____ thought that the position of _____ sounded like something I might be interested in, and he is absolutely right. I would love to explore how I might take my skills and contribute to _____'s success."

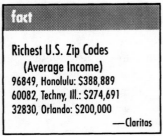

fact

Richest U.S. Zip Codes (Average Income)
96849, Honolulu: $388,889
60082, Techny, Ill.: $274,691
32830, Orlando: $200,000
—Claritas

Paragraph 3: Wrap It Up

All: "Thank you very much for taking the time to consider my résumé. I will call you in a week to see if we can set up a time to meet in person to discuss the position."

A Cover Letter Conversation with Freddy Gamble, Director of Personnel, Condé Nast

WHAT DO YOU LOOK FOR IN A COVER LETTER AND RÉSUMÉ?

I look for something that's going to stand out of the crowd. If someone is looking for a graphics position—well, how does their résumé look? How is it laid out? Is there an interesting typeface used? If someone is looking for a job as a copywriter, well, the cover letter is probably going to be as important as the résumé.

I remember one case where someone wrote in, someone right out of school. The letter started off, "Words, words, words." And it talked about how he enjoyed words and what they could do on a page. The letter was simple. We called the person in.

The objective is to make your application stand out of a crowd. And I think with a large organization of this sort, I would probably suggest stopping by, leaving a résumé and a letter, who knows, with a velvet ribbon wrapped around it. I'm not saying that that's the approach for everyone, but something to make it personal. Something that says, "I really want to work here, and it will be worth your time to talk to me because I'm a little different in a good way. And I care about your company."

DO YOU RECEIVE MANY COVER LETTERS WITH TYPOS?

It is shocking, shocking, how many résumés and letters we get with typos in them. And that is not a plus in a publishing company. Are they stupid, careless, or both? If you can't spell, pay a friend. And you might want to say that *liaison*, I've come to believe, is the most frequently misspelled word which almost always appears on a résumé. You could do your readers a big service if you remind them how to spell that word.

HOW DO YOU GO THROUGH THE RÉSUMÉS AND COVER LETTERS?

You develop an eye. Things sort of pop up at you. Some things are really basic, such as, are things spelled right? Or where does someone live? Alabama? If they come from out of town, they should put some explanation of how they're planning to live here.

One encouragement I have for young people regarding cover letters is, write them in English, not in personnel-ese or job-letter-speak. That's going to make someone stand out. A letter that starts off "Help! I really want to get a job, and I'd love to work at your company." That's going to capture my attention much more than "Attached hereto is the blah blah blah."

CREATIVE COVER LETTERS

The résumé that I just walked you through is conservative. If you've already made contact with the person who hires, or their assistant, this is the cover letter to use. If, however, you've been unable to have a decent phone conversation with someone there, or are replying to a want ad, you should seriously consider taking a more bold, creative approach.

"Yeah, So?"

"You have to separate yourself from the pack. I can't tell you how many people just send a letter saying, 'I will be graduating in May from the Darden School at the University of Virginia. I majored in marketing, my GPA is 3.78, and I would appreciate a response or an interview.' There are 8 million people writing that same letter. Why are you any different from anyone else? We would like to see everyone who's interested in working at HBO, but it is impossible."

—Vice president of human resources and administration, HBO

I didn't know what the hell I was doing a year and a half after I graduated from college and started looking for a job. I didn't take advantage of the many connections I had that I didn't even know I had. I had no idea how to network. I never thought about cold-calling companies I wanted to work for. I did realize, however, that sending a boring cover letter and résumé to the twenty top public relations companies I wanted to work for would most likely bear no fruit. They got thousands of résumés in the mail from people with more work experience than me. I knew I needed to do something that stood out a little bit. Something that showed I was creative, had a sense of humor, and had personality. This is what I sent:

fact

Whoa! Pay Cut
For the first time in recent memory, the average salary of a major league baseball player actually went down. On opening day 1994, the average major leaguer was making $1.19 million. In 1996 that went down to a piddling $1.07 million. (In 1990 the average was $587,930.)
—Associated Press

definition

DOWNSIZING:
You're fired.
RIGHTSIZING:
Someone else is fired.

Creative Cover Letter 1

To whom it may concern:

At dinner last night, a friend of mine told me that a cover letter should tell a little bit about you that a résumé doesn't. So here goes.

Getting to know Charlie in "quotations" and (parentheses):

- "Crazy, mixed-up kid. He's totally lost."
—Dad (Wanted me to join IBM like him.)
- "He's too short. His shots get blocked every time. Helluva kid, though. Writes pretty good."
—Junior high school basketball coach/English teacher (Explaining to my mom why I went the whole season on the bench and, inadvertently, why he lists "basketball coach" in title before "English teacher.")
- "He's cute, but I can't imagine *dating* him."
—First girlfriend in college (Overheard her saying to a friend at a large dinner party. Obviously had more imagination than she gave herself credit for.)

So that's a little about me. I'm very, very interested in discussing entry-level copywriting opportunities at your company. Please give me a call at (212) 555-5555, or I'll call you in a week or so.

Thanks so much for your time.
Warmest regards,
Charlie Drozdyk

I sent this cover letter to "Personnel" at around twenty companies as well as to an ad in the *New York Times* that listed a job for a "public relations copywriter." Incredibly, I received calls and interviews from three of the twenty companies as well as from the company that placed the ad in the *Times*.

Here are a few more examples of creative cover letters that you might want to adapt to fit you.

Creative Cover Letter 2

Dear Mr. Parker:

In response to your ad in the *New York Times* on September 7, 1997, please consider the following:

Why You Should Hire Me	*Why You Shouldn't Hire Me*
1. I'm creative.	1. I talk during movies. I know it's wrong, but I just can't help it.
2. I started a magazine while I was in college called *Burp*, which I was editor and publisher of for three years. It won a few awards and taught me a lot about editing, deadlines, and hard work.	2. I've never sent my mother a Valentine's Day card.
3. I've had two internships with great magazines, *Spin* and *Rolling Stone*, where I researched articles, wrote reviews, and did a lot of grunt work.	3. I hate Hootie and the Blowfish. (Actually, maybe this is in the wrong column.)
4. I'm a hard worker, not a dilettante. While I was doing my summer internships, I also waited tables forty hours a week to help pay my way through school.	4. If given the chance, I'd sleep ten hours a day.
5. I'm not an idiot, and I won't embarrass you at social functions.	5. I caused a five-car accident on the Long Island Expressway.

6. I know Lotus Notes, Microsoft Word, Excel, HTML, and Photoshop.

6. I love ABBA.

Thanks a lot for your time, and please call me—(212) 555-5555—if you're interested in meeting with me. If not, I'll call you every week until you tell me to get lost.

Sincerely,
Charlie D.

Creative Cover Letter 3

January 4, 1997
Re: *Boston Globe* ad / January 3 / Internet Copy Editor

To whom it may concern:

On the left, I have listed your requirements for the above-mentioned position as stated in your ad. And on the right, I have listed my qualifications. I trust you will find that I am well suited for this position.

Strong writer

I have written for the *Boston Globe* and *Travel* magazine and am currently a freelance editor for Little, Brown publishers.

Self-starter

As a freelancer, I either "just do it" or I don't eat.

Knowledgeable about the film business

I am a film buff, have subscribed to *Variety* for the past five years, and used to work in Hollywood.

Familiar with the Web

I have been on the Web for the past two years and can "surf" with the best of them.

Thanks very much for your time. I can be reached at _____. I'll call you next week to see if there's a time we can meet in person.

Sincerely,
Pete G.

A COVER LETTER CONVERSATION

In closing, here is a conversation I had with the director of personnel at Chiat/Day Advertising about cover letters:

HOW MANY RÉSUMÉS DO YOU GET?

In the spring I get more, probably fifty a week. The rest of the year I probably get like thirty a week.

WHAT DO YOU DO WITH THEM?

I look at all of them. With the college students, I'll read the cover letter first. If the cover letter is any good at all, I'll put it in one stack. And if the cover letter isn't good, I don't even look at the résumé.

WHAT ARE YOU LOOKING FOR IN A COVER LETTER?

I'm looking for complete sentences that aren't run-ons. I'm looking for somebody who's writing Chiat/Day and not sending the same letter over and over again. So I'm looking for somebody who reads the trades and can say something intelligent about the company. Such as "Gee, you just got this account. That must be very exciting." We're not talking about comparative research, but somebody who's just aware of the marketplace.

HOW ABOUT WIT IN A COVER LETTER?

It helps. Absolutely. But you don't have to be terrifically clever, because it's hard to figure out what kind of creative thing to say but not sound stupid. A lot of the cover letters are very boring. They're form letters. They'll say, "I believe that my skills can match those in your company," and then they don't say what their skills are and why they think they would match the company.

WHAT ELSE?

If my name is misspelled . . . [She shakes her head. Forget it.] That sounds really egotistical, but it shows they don't pay attention to details. They can call the desk and get the spelling of any name.

DOES THAT HAPPEN A LOT?

All the time. And they misspell the company's name.

Part 6

INTERVIEWING

MADNESS

Chapter 19

THE TAO OF INTERVIEWING

Interviews are sacred things and should be treated as such. I remember when I was young I treated interviews very lightly, thinking, "Yeah, I have an interview. No big deal. If I don't get an offer, I'll get the next one." I was an idiot. You need to treat each interview as if your life depended on it. If you want to land a job, then you have to treat each interview as if it were your last chance of ever getting a job. Why? Because if you don't treat each interview as if it were your last opportunity, then you're not going to say and do the things in the interview that will land you the job. If you treat an interview as if it were one of several, then you will never get an offer. Why? The person interviewing will be able to tell how much you want the job.

This chapter is about preparing you for the interview—telling you what the employer is expecting and hoping you'll say so he can

---

Embellishment

A few years out of law school, Lisa moved to England and interviewed with an entertainment law firm she really wanted to work at. She told them that she was from Hollywood—which she wasn't—and that she "knew everything there was to know about film law," which was also "a total lie." Says Lisa, "I basically got hired by a firm and had to learn very quickly everything there was to learn about film law." How? She got a book about film contracts and read it. Quickly. "You just fake it. You just do it. I knew I could do it given the chance to do it, so I embellished. You have to go out there and do whatever it takes to get the job."

make you an offer and stop interviewing a bunch of idiots who consider this one of several interviews.

BOSSES HATE HIRING

I guess this is the first thing you should know about people who interview job candidates: they don't enjoy it. A lot of young people think that people who hire, bosses, get off on the whole interviewing thing. It isn't true. In most cases they hate it. Put yourself in their shoes. The person you hired, trained, and learned to depend on has gone and quit on

> **fact**
>
> ## Odd Jobs of Celebrities
> Allen Ginsberg: merchant seaman, accountant
> Ralph Lauren: tie salesman at Brooks Brothers
> Frank Zappa: greeting card designer, encyclopedia salesman
> Agatha Christie: dispenser in pharmacy
> —*The Book of Lists*

> **definition**
>
> RAISE:
> 1. A yearly, adjusted-for-inflation bribe that prevents you from following your dreams. 2. A monetary reward for pathologically aggressive behavior in the workplace.

you, and now you have to hire someone else. But the thing is, you still have your job to do. You don't have time to go through tons of résumés and interview a bunch of people. So realize that the person who is interviewing you wants you to be the last person he interviews. He *wants* you to work out. He wants to get on with his job and put all this interviewing nonsense behind him.

> **quote**
>
> "Don't be humble. You're not that great."
> —Golda Meir

EMPLOYERS ARE PEOPLE, TOO

Another thing to realize is that bosses—people who hire—can be, and in most cases *are*, people, too. They're not your parents. If they're in their thirties, that means they graduated in the eighties, which means they didn't protest Vietnam, are too young to have seen the Doors in concert, probably started doing ecstasy in college, and have probably been to at least one rave in their life. So the point is, you don't have to be all stuffy with them when you meet them. Don't act like they're your parents' best friends. Relax. Don't be afraid to laugh and have fun in interviews. The candidate who does this—relates the best, not acting all stuffy and "grown-up" and formal—will get the job.

FEATURE INTERVIEW

Amy Guenther
Talent manager, Industry Entertainment
27 years old
USC—Film School

Amy had it all planned out. She was going to be a lawyer. She had wanted to be one her entire life. While a sophomore at USC, she was already thinking, "Okay, what can I do to get myself into law school?" That's why she applied to and entered the film school at USC her junior year. Her rationale: "I thought going to what most consider to be the number one film school in the country would be an interesting highlight on my résumé. I'd be somebody other than a history or political science major."

Though she was occasionally tempted to pursue a career in her new major—after all, she did "love" movies—she was dissuaded by her film teachers. One professor told her that the chances of making a decent living in the film business were about one in fifty.

When Amy got a paid internship after graduation with Addis/Weschler, a hot L.A. talent management company, she wasn't out to prove her teachers wrong and be that one in fifty. She just figured she'd "do something related to what my parents spent $100,000 on." But only for a year while she applied to law school and prepared for the LSATs.

It wasn't even supposed to become a full-time job. She was going to do it part-time and keep her job at Guess Jeans at the mall on weekends as well as her job at her alma mater's law school ("That was my foot in the door at USC law school," Amy says). But between all three gigs,

Amy was putting in over seventy hours a week and wasn't getting much studying done. That's when she kicked it into high gear and tried to make herself invaluable at Addis/Weschler "so they might catch on and hire me full-time so I wouldn't have to work at the mall and the law center."

In other words, it was a practical decision. Not "Oh, my God, I've *got* to work in film." She didn't even know what a talent manager *did*. "I wanted a full-time job with one company with medical benefits, a dental plan, the works," she says.

So Amy scoped out the situation at Addis/Weschler. Kept her eye open for a hole to fill. After around three weeks she noticed that the owner's second assistant would never work out. The owner was so busy, he had two assistants, and the "second assistant," as the person was known, was constantly getting fired.

So when this guy's first assistant asked Amy what she thought about giving the second assistant job a shot, she wasn't too psyched. If she failed like all the others did before her, then she'd lose her internship. Therefore, she'd also lose a shot at getting a job at Addis/Weschler she might actually have a chance of succeeding at. That's why Amy and the first assistant came up with this plan: Amy would work a few hours a day for a week or two in the job. If it didn't work out, then she could go back to being an intern "stuffing envelopes and typing labels" and wait for another position to open up.

Now you're probably thinking, what can be so hard about being an assistant? Well, having worked in the business myself, I can tell you this—a lot. First of all, when you're dealing with clients like Ray Liotta, Steve Buscemi, Sam Jackson, Jeff Goldblum, Leonardo DiCaprio, Clare Danes, and Cameron Diaz, there's a lot of pressure involved. You're talking about stars with little time and big egos—even if they do happen to be really cool. So one false move and you're fired. There's no such thing as "Oh, sorry, I forgot to tell you Cameron Diaz called." There's no such thing as giving Steve Buscemi the wrong appointment time for a reading—even if you do have four people on hold and if two new lines are ringing. There's no such thing as Ray Liotta calling and being put on hold for more than five seconds—even if you *are* giving Steve Buscemi an appointment time. Any of this can piss off a client and send them packing.

As second assistant, it was Amy's job to make sure none of this stuff happened. But besides juggling up to five incoming calls at a time, she was also in charge of placing all the outgoing calls. This is called "rolling calls"—which, as far as I know, is strictly a Hollywood thing.

Here's Amy on "rolling calls":

"I was asked to sit across the desk from my future boss at a chair with a little table and a phone. I would place a call to someone and say, 'I have Keith Addis calling for Joe Schmo.' And they would say, 'Okay, it's me. I'm here,' in which case I would put them on hold, and my boss would pick it up and start his conversation."

"In the meantime, I would start getting somebody else on the phone, anticipating him ending that phone call. The idea is that you time it so one call rolls right into the next, which is very difficult. Meanwhile, you've got four calls coming in at the same time."

In other words, Amy was in *assistant hell.*

"I was hanging up right and left on really important people. People would get pissed off and would call back and say to my boss 'Who *is* this person?' Then my boss would say to me, 'What are you doing? Why don't you know this?' He was under a lot of pressure and was used to having really intelligent assistants who could run his office smoothly. And here I come, this kid right out of film school who doesn't understand how important these people are and how important these calls are, or what I'm doing. I was really messing up his life right and left."

So much so that, at the end of the first day, her boss told her he didn't think it was going to work out.

If Amy needed a kick in the ass, this was it. "Here I was being told it probably wasn't going to work out—that I was going to be fired. I'd never been fired from a job. I always had good recommendations. I was like, 'Hell if I'm going to get fired from this job.' So I went into overdrive. I was determined not to get fired and not to mess up and basically be perfect, which was what the job demanded."

At the end of the first week, confident she had been close enough to perfect, Amy did something that was so completely ballsy, naive, or maybe a mixture of both. She walked into her boss's office and said, "I'm going to quit my other two jobs, and I can start full-time on Monday if that's okay with you."

The idea that this intern, this kid, would go ahead and hire *herself* caught her future boss completely off guard. "He looked at me with this weird expression on his face like, 'Who is this person?' " Amy recounts. Apparently he wasn't *too* offended, though. Instead of telling Amy that it was *his* call whether or not she would go full-time, he simply said, "Fine." After all, if she didn't work out, he'd simply fire her like the others.

Sure, Amy had a full-time gig with health insurance and the whole thing. It wasn't until many months later, however, that she stopped having nightmares every night about "messing up and going 'What am I going to do? How am I going to cover this up?' " It was also many months before she felt fairly comfortable that she might not be fired at any given moment for screwing something up.

Take, for instance, the "last-name debacle."

"I had to use first and last names," Amy says. "I couldn't say 'Joe is on line two' because there are a lot of Joes in this business. But I kept forgetting and [would] say, 'John is on line two.' And he'd say, 'John who?' It was obvious to me which John it was, but for him it wasn't. So I forgot a couple of times. Finally it was like, 'Look, the next time you forget someone's last name, we're just going to have to end this.' And I thought, 'I can't possibly get fired for forgetting somebody's last name.' I had little note cards on my desk of first and last names right by the phone so I would remember."

So what did she do the first time Sting called? "I was a little panicked at first, but then I was like, 'I'm just going with it,' " Amy says.

Most assistants would be like, "Screw it. I'm outta here" if they got yelled at as much as Amy did those first six months. But Amy had a way of keeping it in perspective. "I tried as hard as I could to take everything as constructive criticism because I think one of the ways that people really learn this business is by fucking up." But even though she had put the abuse thing in perspective, there were still those days when she'd question her sanity and say, "What am I doing to myself? I'm like a glutton for punishment here."

Ironically, it was after one of those moments of reflection on the abuse and punishment that Amy started to reconsider going to law school. After a year of this crap, Amy said to herself, "Do I want to put myself through that again?"—meaning law school. She figured that in another year or so she would probably make it to manager level, so why go backward? "Why would I build myself up only to start over again at ground zero? I sort of felt that I had done my graduate work," she says.

Law school was now out. Becoming a manager was in. To accomplish this, Amy had to learn one thing—everything. Luckily, her boss was behind her on this. One thing he'd do for Amy was have her take home a contract of one of their clients and highlight everything she didn't understand. Then, the next day they would go over it line by line. But don't think he took the time to do this because he's simply a nice guy. He had his own interests in mind, too. "He has a real strong belief in promoting from within. I guess he was preparing me for that," Amy says.

So by the time Amy finished her second year at Addis/Weschler, she pretty much knew enough to be a manager. Now it was simply a matter of her boss's saying "Okay, you're promoted. You're a manager."

Or not. Just as she had done over two years earlier, the way Amy got promoted was by promoting herself. How? "Little by little I lessened up on my assistant responsibilities and increased my managerial responsibilities."

But this alone wasn't enough, she realized. "Finally I realized that if I were to get promoted, there would have to be somebody to replace me. And that's what I did. I found a really strong second assistant who could replace me as first assistant."

It wasn't until Amy read the announcement in *Daily Variety* that Addis/Weschler had promoted a new manager—her—that she learned she was no longer an assistant.

But with the title change came lifestyle changes as well. "You have to give up a lot of yourself and your personal life. I spend half my weekend reading scripts for work. I can't go to happy hour at 5:00 because I don't get out until around 7:30, and then I go out and meet someone in the business for a drink."

Besides the change in her schedule, another thing Amy had to get used to was the politics. "There's very few people that you can trust," Amy says. "You have to be very careful. It can be very backstabbing. But it's not a tea party, it's business."

RESEARCH

You need to find out as much as you possibly can about the company you're interviewing with before the interview. They are going to expect this from you. If they're a public company, you should have read their annual report backward and forward. You should have read any printed literature they have issued about themselves. You should have done searches in the library or on the Internet for articles written about the company. You should have been looking through the trade magazines and newspapers for any mention of the company.

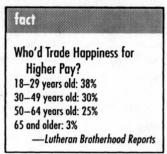

fact

Who'd Trade Happiness for Higher Pay?
18–29 years old: 38%
30–49 years old: 30%
50–64 years old: 25%
65 and older: 3%
—*Lutheran Brotherhood Reports*

You have to know what the company does before going in to meet them. Find out who owns the company. Make sure you know what all of their products and services are and who their clients are.

Say you're interviewing for a job with a small film production company. When you go for the interview, you should know the names of all the films that company has produced. Hopefully, you've rented and watched them all. Therefore, you should know what *kinds* of films the company makes so you can answer the question "What kinds of films do you like?" correctly.

If you have an interview with *CBS This Morning*, it goes without saying that you should watch as many episodes of the show as possible. You should get *Variety* magazine and check out its ratings and

---

Personality, Please

"[When I interview people,] I just see if they get it. Not about music, but about life. Are they quick and witty? Do they say things that make me furl my brow and say 'That's interesting. That's an interesting way to put that'? Or 'That's an interesting string of words.' "

—*Michael Meisel, music manager, Gold Mountain Entertainment*

share. You should watch the other morning shows so you can talk with insight about what makes *CBS This Morning* different from, better than, or the same as the other shows.

A Personal Story of Failure and Sloppiness

I'll tell you a quick story of how I blew an interview and a great job so that you don't do the same stupid thing. Remember, you don't get that many chances. At the time I didn't know this. I thought interviews were a dime a dozen.

First off, I had never heard of this company. They were small. I was like, "No big deal, a small, unimportant company; no big loss if I don't get the job." Well, it turns out they're one of the most successful companies out there in their field.

I knew that the company made movies for TV, but I hadn't bothered to find out what kind. Turns out they do movies based on tabloid news stories like Amy Fisher and kids who are switched at birth. I didn't know this, so when the hiring person asked me what magazines and papers I read, instead of saying *People, USA Today*, the *New York Post*, I said the *New York Times* and *Esquire*. Then she asked me what TV shows I liked. I could only name two shows on TV, period: *Seinfeld* and *Roseanne*. "What books have you read recently?" she asked me. "I just finished *The Sun Also Rises*, by Hemingway," I replied.

If I'd been interviewing at the *New Yorker* or PBS, they might have hired me and made me vice president. But here, they were not impressed. I buried myself. Here's a company that makes sensationalist movies of the week and I'm talking Hemingway and *Esquire*. She gave me some advice: "Go home and turn on the TV."

Apply this to whatever industry you're going after. A record company: what kind of music do they put out? An advertising agency: what kind of ads do they make? Fun, irreverent stuff, or conservative? Who are their accounts? Nike? Gerber? Just do a little homework so you don't look like an idiot. So there you go. You've learned from my mistake.

Corny but Cute

"I had to hire a writer's assistant right away for a sitcom that was beginning the following week," says Linda. "So this woman shows up, comes into my office, and before she sits down, she hands me a piece of paper. I look at the paper and it says, 'As I sit here opposite you, I want you to know that I really want this job. I am funny, I am honest, and I am hardworking.' After I finished reading it, I looked up and I noticed she was smiling at me. I just thought this was very clever. I hired her on the spot."

THE ON-DECK CIRCLE

You're there, at the company for the interview. You're in the lobby, in the reception area. Walk in the door five to ten minutes ahead of time. Sure, get to the building a half hour beforehand, but just sit in your car or hang out outside the building. Go easy on the coffee. The stuff will make you nervous and your hands clammy.

When you tell the receptionist you're there to see Joe Blow, for God's sake be nice and charming. If you rub them wrong, and if they're at all friendly with the person you're interviewing with, then you're history. If you're nice—and I don't mean, "Oh, what a nice bracelet you're wearing," but just nice—then they'll probably say, "Yeah, he was all right," instead of saying, "He was an asshole."

definition

VOICE MAIL:
A means for delivering excuses without the burning shame of face-to-face contact.

"Coffee?"

A lot of times the boss will send their assistant out to meet you and offer you something to drink, per their boss's order. All assistants I've ever known resent this ritual and resent the jerk who takes them up on it. If you say, "Sure, I'll have a Diet Coke," you're not scoring any points there. Go to the bathroom and get some water if you're thirsty.

The moment of truth is upon you. In twenty minutes you're either going to have a job and be happy, or not. Securing happiness through employment is the topic of the next chapter. Turn and learn.

The Real Skinny with . . . Laurie Wedemeyer, Fashion Buyer

WHO GETS HIRED:
I think the biggest factor is enthusiasm more than anything. People who are self-confident, not cocky necessarily, but believe that they're qualified and that this company would want *them* for the job.

> **fact**
>
> "Become a Mail Carrier. Get Bitten Less!"
> Number of bites:
> 1983: 7,000
> 1994: 2,782
> —Humane Society of the United States, U.S. Postal Service

PAYING YOUR DUES:
You feel like, "Somebody ought to give me responsibility," so you can show you know what you're doing. You want to be king of the world, and you're at the bottom again. So it's important to realize that it's not going to last forever, but it's a matter of paying your dues, however long it takes.

PROMOTING YOURSELF:
If you want to go forward in the company, it's important not to just sit and wait for them to come to you. I wasn't under the impression that somebody, someday, would knock on my door and say, "You're a buyer." I knocked on *their* door and asked for the position. Basically, every time I changed positions within the company, it's been because I asked for the job.

GARNERING SUPPORT:
I went up the ranks. I didn't go directly to the head of the department and say, "I want to be promoted." I went to my boss, got his support; I went to his boss, got her support; and went on, all the way up to the top.

GETTING POLITICAL:
I'd say the hardest part of my job so far has been trying to decide what the politics of the company are. A lot of what happens with your career has less to do with your ability to do

the job than with your ability to be political. How to act within different situations. Know who to talk to, know what to say, know what not to say, know how to dress.

ON BURNING BRIDGES:

The thing about this industry is that it's very close-knit—very small, in a way. The players remain the same. And you never know who you know who might become somebody important. You never want to burn any bridges.

Chapter 20

EIGHT THINGS YOU MUST DO AND SAY IN THE INTERVIEW

1. BE UPBEAT AND ENERGETIC

First impressions are everything. You will set the tone of the interview in the first five seconds. A lot of young people, because they're nervous, walk into the interview like they're going into church or a funeral home. You must remember, you're not going to be hired on how qualified you might be for the job. You're going to be hired based on your ability to sell yourself and on whether or not the person interviewing you likes you as a person.

In almost every job you're going to interview for, people are going to be looking for a self-starter—someone who can come in and hit the ground running. This means they're looking for someone who feels comfortable enough with themselves to ask questions and get to know people in the company on their own. The person interviewing you is going to make the judgment about you in the first few seconds whether or not you're outgoing and confident enough to adapt to new situations and environments. Therefore, you must walk into the room relaxed, confident, and with a smile on your face.

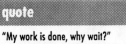

"My work is done, why wait?"
—Suicide note left by Kodak founder George Eastman

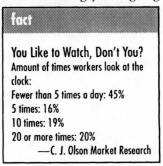

You Like to Watch, Don't You?
Amount of times workers look at the clock:
Fewer than 5 times a day: 45%
5 times: 16%
10 times: 19%
20 or more times: 20%
—C. J. Olson Market Research

Honesty Sucks

After graduating in the top five from an Ivy League law school, Mark had as many interviews as he wanted and was confident he'd receive at least a few great offers. So in one interview, when the interviewer asked him what his worst characteristics were, for some reason, he decided to be honest. "Instead of giving the stock answer, 'Well, I'm a perfectionist,' and so forth, I was really honest. I said, 'I have a big head. I can't delegate. I'm hard to work with. I think I know more than anyone else,' and went on a little bit along these lines. After that there was not a lot of discussion. The interview pretty much ended. I think they thought I must have been goofing on them because I was so honest. I'm certain that's why I didn't get an offer."

So what got into him? "I don't know what it was. For some reason, I decided to be honest. I had prepared answers for all questions including this one. I thought for a change I'd try honesty, and it turns out, I was wrong. Honesty is not the best policy."

2. BREAK THE ICE: GETTING THE INTERVIEWER TO LIKE YOU

The fact that you are in the room means that the person interviewing you considers you qualified for the job. If getting a job were about hiring the most qualified person, interviews wouldn't be necessary. But it's not. Hiring someone is about meeting all the people who are qualified to do the job and hiring the person you like the most, the person you feel most comfortable with. The person you connect with.

Nobody is going to hire someone they don't like or feel comfortable with. Why would they? They're thinking, "I've got to spend ten hours a day, five days a week with this person. Fifty hours a week." That's a lot of time to spend with someone. Therefore, they're going to offer the job to the person they like the most.

Listen to how Claire, a public relations executive, broke the ice in one of her first interviews:

Once you're in the interview, just act confident. Act confident and not stuffy. Make it fun. I met with this woman I'd be

working for and there were pictures on her desk of her grand-
children or whoever. And I was like, "Oh, who are those kids?"
And we started talking about kids, and it was something that was
bonding. Latch on to anything you can, you know? Something
that can bond you with these people.

3. TELL THEM YOU WANT THE JOB

You have to make it clear to the interviewer that you want the job.
How? Tell them. They might think your mother made you go on
the interview or that it's just one in fifty that you're going on, just
sussing things out.

You've got to realize where they're coming from. They've got a
bunch of people interviewing for the job. They know that the job is
demanding. Some bosses might think that the job they're trying to
fill is *so* demanding and crappy that they can't imagine why *anyone*
would want it. They know the long hours, the stress, the low pay,
the bullshit. They know the person who is going to last in the job is
someone who really, really wants it. You have to show them that
you're this person.

---

definition

DOWNTIME:
Playing Solitaire® on your PC's operating system.

I actually went on an interview where the interviewer told me in
no uncertain terms that the job available was a total headache. He
told me he couldn't imagine why anyone would want to deal with it.
He said, "You don't want this job. It really sucks. This is why it
sucks. . . ." He said, "Why don't you get back to me. Think about
it." I told him, "I don't need to think about it. I know I want the job.
I know it's going to be difficult and it might suck, but it's a great opportunity for me. At least I won't be bored." He told me three
months later, after I was hired, that he had been testing me. He
wanted to make sure that I really wanted it badly enough, and that
if I had had any hesitation, then forget it, he would have looked for
someone hungrier.

Remember Claire, the public relations executive mentioned a couple of pages back? In another interview she had to convince the interviewer how much she wanted the job. As she says, "I interviewed four times. Every time I went in—and I think this has a lot to do with it—I told him how much I wanted the job. I wasn't just passive. I mean, every time I went in, I said, 'I really want this job. This is the direction I want to go.' "

Brian Johnson, co-owner of the Dogwater Café, a fast-growing restaurant chain in Florida, agrees with my little "tell them you want it" advice. He says, "When I'm interviewing, I'm looking for someone with a lot of energy who wants this job more than anything. I want them to basically beg me not to interview someone else—that this is *their* job."

> **fact**
>
> **Average Workday in Minutes for Men and Women**
>
> | Country | Women | Men |
> | --- | --- | --- |
> | United States | 453 | 428 |
> | Industrial countries | 430 | 408 |
> | Developing countries | 544 | 483 |
>
> Not counted is the amount of time spent on taking care of the home, children, garden, and pets, too.
>
> —*Human Development Report*, 1995

4. LIE IF YOU HAVE TO

What I'm going to tell you next is actually pretty common. Through the years I've heard this applied to success over and over again in getting jobs. That is, sometimes you have to lie. What I mean is, there are certain things that shouldn't bar you from getting a job, things that have to do with experience. I'll give you an example.

I was interviewing for a job with a Broadway producer/general manager. I knew he was looking for someone a little older, a little more experienced than myself. So when he asked me, "Are you familiar with Actors Equity contracts for the larger-size venues?" I said that I was. The truth is that I didn't even know what one *looked* like, but I knew it was something that I could teach myself over a weekend. I knew of a place where I could get the different contracts and read them over and over until I knew them better than he did.

He also asked me if I knew Lotus. "Sure," I said. Not. I'd never used it. But I'd be damned if some stupid computer program that I could learn in a few hours should keep me from getting the job. Well, I got the job and then did my homework and taught myself the stuff I said I knew. No big deal. After a couple of days these were no longer lies.

Look at David Geffen, arguably one of the most successful entertainment businessmen in the world. Mr. Geffen got his start in the mailroom at the William Morris Agency, a job that required a college degree, even though it was completely menial. So Mr. Geffen, as the story goes, forged a letter from UCLA indicating that he was, in fact, a graduate.

When Ray Rogers, now an editor at *Interview* magazine, first heard about a job opening there, he was told that he needed to know desktop publishing. He said, " 'Of course I know it.' I sort of knew it. If I could teach myself to type from eighteen to thirty-eight words per minute in a week, I figured why not? I learned it over the weekend. I got the manual and stayed at the computer while no one was here for like ten hours a day over the weekend. And then I went home and read the book. I just made myself learn how to do it. I came in after the weekend and said, 'Oh, I learned QuarkXPress.' And everyone was like, 'You what?' I mean, I needed the job."

5. "I'll Do Anything"

If it's an entry-level job you're interviewing for, you've got to tell the interviewer in no uncertain terms that you are not above doing any-

---

Closing the Interview Deal

"I had to totally rework and rethink my approach to interviewing," says Kira. "I realized that I had to convince people that that particular job was the job I always wanted. I'd pursue like five jobs and make each of them think I was only interested in working for them. A lot of it was body language: leaning forward, not leaning back and being casual. I also took an aggressive sales approach. I said to them at the end of the interview, "Is there any reason I wouldn't be considered for the job, because I'd like to address that now." It was the big deal clincher. What you're doing is basically getting a commitment from them. You have to close the deal at the end of the interview."

thing. Entry-level jobs are about paying your dues. You're going to be doing the shitwork. Employers want to know that *you* know that you're going to be doing some boring, mindless stuff. If they get the impression somehow that you think you're above doing the crap-work, they're going to keep interviewing until they find the person who says, "Listen, I just want you to know that I'm not above doing anything."

The vice president of personnel at Liz Claiborne makes this point well:

> We're looking for people who have a passion for the apparel business. This business is crazy. And there's no question in my mind that you *have* to love it, because you're going to be working at it fourteen to sixteen hours a day. You're going to be asked to do everything from sweep the floors to rack the line, and you can't have somebody who says, "It's not my job." As I tell them, "That's interesting, because I haven't been able to figure out what *isn't* my job." If my boss asks me to do it, it becomes my job— whatever *it* happens to be. So you look for somebody who doesn't have an elitist attitude—somebody who's willing to do the mundane, stupid little jobs. Someone who has a passion for the business and who has a high energy level. Someone who is not looking for a nine-to-five.

"Tell Me What I Want to Hear"

"The people I hire are the people who tell me, 'I'll do anything.' The person who says 'I'll do windows, floors. I'll do anything. I just really want to be here.' In an interview I'm really looking for that excitement. You know, 'I want this job above anything else. This is what I want.' It's their passion I want because it's the passion that's going to keep them here, certainly not money. I want people who are dying to work here."

—Personnel manager, Solomon R. Guggenheim Museum

---

6. HAVE SOME GOOD QUESTIONS PREPARED

Have at least a few questions ready for the interviewer. Don't try to wing it once you're in the room. Your questions have to be smart and informed. They have to relate to something the company is doing or has done. They have to show that you're a critical thinker.

Remember what the vice president of personnel at Liz Claiborne said about passion in an interview? Well, here's what she looks for in the interview with regard to questions:

What I normally do—and I don't think it's atypical of most interviewers—is I ask all my questions and then I'll say to them, "Do you have any questions for me?" If the first thing they say to me is, "What does Liz Claiborne do?" I say, no. Not that I won't deal with them. I'll tell them, but that is the end of that

> **fact**
>
> **Bosses Who Say They Have the Right to Read Employees' E-mail**
>
> No: 23%
> Yes: 75%
> Unsure: 2%
> Nearly 80 percent of executives say their companies use E-mail, and 36 percent say they actually peek at employees' mail in the company's electronic communication system.
> —Society for Human Resource Management

person. Now, the person that comes in and says, "That green man's T-shirt that you had on the floor in the group called Nautical Express just really didn't fit with that group. Now, if *I* had been doing it, I would have made it a long-sleeve or short-sleeve or whatever...." You say, "That's the person who knows the business. *That's* the person who's going to be successful. That's the one who took the time to go to the store to look at the product, to formulate an opinion, to have something intelligent to say." And even if your opinion is wrong, we don't care—as long as you have one. If somebody's main thrust is, "How often am I reviewed, and what's the percentage of my increase, and when can I expect to be promoted?" then forget it. I think somebody *tells* them that those are good questions to ask because it's amazing how routinely they're asked. That's not the person we're looking for. The person we're looking for is the person who would *kill* to work for this company.

definition

SECRETARIES' DAY:
An eight-hour period in which those on career paths feign egalitarian feelings for their inferiors.

7. DON'T BRING UP MONEY

Save all salary issues, pay increases, 401(k) plans, insurance, etc., for after you get an offer or until you're certain they're going to make you an offer. If you ask about money in the first interview, the interviewer will think you care about money more than the job itself. So don't think it's going to make you seem all grown-up and tough, because it won't. They'll be put off.

As the vice president of human resources and administration at HBO says, "Don't ask about money until you're pretty far along in the process. It gives the impression to the interviewer that money is the issue and not the job. You should have a rough idea of what jobs will pay, especially if you're coming out of school. You should do that research before you show up."

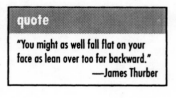

quote

"You might as well fall flat on your face as lean over too far backward."
—James Thurber

8. "WHERE DO WE GO FROM HERE?"

At the end of the interview, you should ask the interviewer something like, "So, what happens from here?" They'll probably say something like, "Well, we're interviewing more people, but we'll be in touch." At this point I think it's important to say, "Listen, I'm really excited about the prospect of working here, and I'll work my butt off. Is there anything I can do to increase my chances of getting an offer? Is there anybody else you'd like me to meet, or is there anybody you'd like to talk to—a reference?" This might seem a little forward and pushy, but it's not. It shows your enthusiasm and desire to work there. Who knows, maybe they'll take you up on your offer and have you meet with more people.

Chapter 21

THINGS TO AVOID, THINGS TO ASK

SOME STUPID THINGS TO AVOID

• Never ask "How late do you work?" or "What time do most people come in in the morning?"

• Never say anything bad about a former employer, even if they were an abusive ass. You can get your point across by saying "He was fine. I respect him." If you trash someone, the interviewer will think that *you* have a problem with authority, not that you worked for a jerk.

• Don't get too personal. You *want* the interview to turn into a conversation, a hanging-out session, but don't get *too* casual. Don't start talking about your sex life and using the occasional swearword. When I used to interview people at one job I had, I liked to have fun. I'd get real casual and prop my feet up. Two people thought, wrongly, that this gave them the freedom to tell me stuff that I didn't really need to know—one person about drugs, the other person about how they got arrested once when they were a kid.

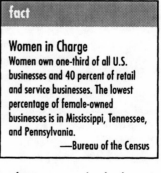

fact

Women in Charge
Women own one-third of all U.S. businesses and 40 percent of retail and service businesses. The lowest percentage of female-owned businesses is in Mississippi, Tennessee, and Pennsylvania.
—Bureau of the Census

• Boogers and stuff. This might sound stupid and obvious, but please, please go to the bathroom when you arrive at the interview and check for boogers or nose hairs that are trying to escape, lipstick on the teeth, ear hairs, and crap like this. One personnel person told me about a young guy who had something stuck in his teeth. She spent the whole interview fixated on it, not hearing a word he said.

"I Want to Hire You, But ... "

The person you're interviewing with might have reservations about hiring you. Maybe you lack the experience. Maybe he was looking for someone older or a woman or a man. Whatever. If you can tell that the person is reluctant, you can do what I've done before—offer them a trial period. (This is only for small companies, not large corporations that couldn't get away with doing this.) Tell the person, "Listen, I know you have some reservations about my experience or whatever. Therefore, how about if we do a three-week trial period? At the end of three weeks, if you're not happy with the way things are working out, then just let me go." This way, if they're reluctant to hire you, maybe they'll give you a chance, knowing you won't go crazy if it doesn't work out. It also shows that you are confident about your abilities to pick things up and that you'll do whatever it takes to get the job.

A Personnel Coordinator Speaks Out

Electronic devices: "If someone brings a beeper or a cell phone into an interview with me and it goes off, I won't even consider them. I don't even want to see them. It just says to me that something else is more important than them being there."

Perfume: "Wear very little. Please."

Eye contact: "Very important. It's something you notice right off the bat. If someone's not looking into your eyes, it's actually very unnerving and distracting. I won't even consider them."

Handshakes: "I hate it when women shake with their fingertips. A good firm handshake is very important with me."

—Chelsea Anderson, personnel coordinator, Durham, North Carolina

---

"I'LL WORK FOR FREE"

Again, if you're interviewing for a job at a small company of, say, seventy-five or fewer or are looking for freelance work, you have the freedom of taking a "do whatever it takes" approach to landing a job. Listen to how Becky, a freelance commercial and music video producer, did it:

> When I started working freelance, I would go to companies and say, "I'll work for you for free on the next job." I would do that, and then I would get hired over and over again. They're little investments that you have to make. You have to be able just to be a slave and accept that you have to grovel a little bit. I mean, who's going to say "No, I don't want you to work for free"? They'll say, "Okay, we'll give you stuff to do."
>
> Just to get in the door of some companies you have to say, "I've really wanted to work here forever." You just kiss ass. I *begged* to work for them for free. You've got to stroke these companies and say, "I'll do anything to work here. I'll do whatever it takes. I'll work for free." You have to literally *say* these things. If you do that, you are *going* to get hired. It's a guarantee.

---

definition

HMO:
1. Collection of graduate-educated butchers who hold themselves out to the public as "health care providers." 2. *Your* doctor.

INTERVIEW QUESTIONS TO WATCH OUT FOR

- Tell me about yourself.
- Why do you want to work for us?
- Why should we hire you over someone else?
- What are you looking for in a job?
- How long would you stay with us?
- I'm afraid you might be overqualified for this position.

- What are your strengths?
- What are your weaknesses?
- Do you like working in a team or alone?
- Where do you think our industry is going?
- Why are you interested in leaving your current job? Or, why did you leave your last job?
- What did you like least about your last job?
- What did you get out of college?
- What's your biggest accomplishment to date?
- In your last job, what were a few of your most significant accomplishments?
- How long have you been looking for a job now?
- What other jobs or companies are you considering?
- How much money are you looking for?
- What was the last book you read?
- What do you like to do in your free time?
- What are your future goals?

QUESTIONS, LIES, AND VIDEOTAPE

Something you might want to con-sider doing—seriously consider do-ing—is setting up a video camera and having a friend pose as the inter-viewer, asking you the questions listed in the preceding section. This will give you great practice at answering questions on the spot. It's an excellent way to get used to talking about yourself. I think it's a great idea to practice in front of a video camera rather than using your first few interviews as practice and possibly losing out on jobs you might have really wanted.

> **fact**
>
> **"Wanted: Loyal Pets"**
> Favorable traits in employees according to bosses:
> Dependability: 35%
> Honesty: 27%
> Good attitude: 19%
> Competence: 19%
> —Padgett Business School

FEATURE INTERVIEW

Julie Stern
Vice president, Malia Mills Swimwear
29 years old
Cornell
Communications, Hotel School

You can plan all you want, but by the time you're thirty, chances are, you're going to be do-ing something with your life you never imagined. Though this is almost always the case, we fight against it. "Not me," we say. We don't like living in limbo. We don't like uncertainty. We want to know exactly what we're going to be doing. We want to know exactly what we're going to be.

Julie felt the same way when she was in college. "I felt desperate to have a career lined up when I left college," she says. That's why she transferred into the Hotel School while at Cornell—because they're known for successfully placing graduates.

And Julie was one of them. In the spring of her senior year, a small corporate catering com-pany in New York offered Julie a job upon graduation. Julie's plan had worked. Kind of.

Julie showed up for work—having moved her life to the big city—and was instantly "bummed out." This was Julie's job: somebody would call and place an order for food; Julie would write the order down and pass it on to somebody else. "I was nothing more than a glori-fied order taker and order passer in a really small room," Julie says. "It wasn't at all what I had imagined."

What she had imagined was something more "real," something more "glamorous." Not a mom-and-pop operation in which she would have to fight for her health insurance. Not a hostile environment where, on her first day, she had to witness a fight between the owner and the man-ager. Not a situation in which, on that first day, the owner would throw the keys in her hands, lit-erally, and say "Congratulations, you're the new manager."

Even though Julie hated the job from the get-go, she stuck it out for seven months before throwing the keys back to the owner. She didn't even have another job lined up. She just had to get out. Not just out of that company, but out of the food business as well.

Another thing Julie was interested in besides the business of food was magazines. In no time and through the help of a friend, she quickly snagged a job as a temp with Time Warner, work-ing for all of their magazines. "One week I would work at Life or Time, the next at Sports Illus-trated or Entertainment Weekly. It's a great way to slip into the back door of the magazine world that most people don't know about," Julie says.

While it was a great introduction to magazines, it wasn't always exciting. One of Julie's temp assignments involved photocopying every single Time article that had ever been written about the Olympics. Probably not a bad assignment had the magazine not been in print since 1920. "I did this for two straight weeks," Julie says.

Finally, after eight months of being shuffled from magazine to magazine, photocopying junk for anybody and everybody, Julie got her big break. While she was temping for the head of marketing at *Fortune*—a real jerk who would send her out to get his lunch and who would yell at Julie if his phone messages weren't perfect—a friend of Julie's who was also temping at Time Warner called her with a hot tip. The senior editor who did the *Sports Illustrated* swimsuit issue was having trouble. She was about to go on a shoot, and one of her assistants was getting married and the other one had the measles. In other words, she needed help.

Unfortunately, the jerk Julie was working for at *Fortune* wouldn't let her out of her temp assignment. And instead of going "Oh, well, can't do it," Julie did both jobs. "I would go in to *Fortune* from seven to nine in the morning, go up to *Sports Illustrated*, go back to *Fortune* during lunch, go back to *Sports Illustrated*. . . . So I was working from seven in the morning to one in the morning. No joke."

It all paid off, though, when the senior editor at *Sports Illustrated* invited Julie to the French West Indies for three weeks to shoot the swimsuit issue. Sure, it was partly out of desperation because both of her assistants couldn't go. But as Julie says, "She wouldn't have asked me if she hadn't seen that I was a hard worker. Really, I was the temp that would not give up."

A hard worker or not, when they got back from the three-week shoot, Julie found herself back in the temp pool at Time Warner. Even though the senior editor at *Sports Illustrated* loved Julie and wanted to hire her, she already had two assistants.

That didn't stop Julie, however. She was determined to work there. With that in mind, she would take the editor's two assistants to lunch every once in a while to pump them for information. And she "constantly" wrote the editor notes telling her what she was up to. And just in case that wasn't enough, for Christmas Julie made her a gingerbread person dressed in a bikini.

But as determined as she was to get that gig, when a staff job as an editorial assistant at *Entertainment Weekly* became available, Julie went for it and nabbed it. "All I wanted was a Time Warner ID, health insurance, and a salary," she explains. Two months into that job, however, the senior editor at *Sports Illustrated* called and offered her a job as "fashion reporter."

So for three and a half years, Julie traveled to exotic islands organizing shoots, finding locations, and dealing with models for the annual *Sports Illustrated* swimsuit issue. And even though it was, in her words, "an incredible job," it still wasn't enough. It wasn't what she really wanted to do. It wasn't her. As Julie says, "I'm someone who finds a lot of my identity through my career. It's a big part of what makes me happy or unhappy. I think that when you graduate from college, you think that having a yuppie lifestyle is what it's all about—your boyfriend, going out to dinner with friends, all that."

Maybe for other people, but not for Julie. She knew there had to be the right career for her out there; she just didn't know what it was. So she quit *Sports Illustrated* to find it—again, quitting with nothing else lined up. As it turns out, the answer, the career, had been staring her right in the face without her knowing it. It took leaving *Sports Illustrated,* however, to find it. Actually, for "it" to find her.

You see, when Julie was at *Sports Illustrated,* she showed her boss a few swimsuits that her sorority sister from Cornell had designed. Julie's boss loved the suits, and with that encouragement Malia Mills decided to move to New York to become a designer. When Julie told Malia she was wondering what to do next, having quit *Sports Illustrated,* Malia suggested she become a partner in the business. After all, who knew the swimsuit business better than the person who had put together the *Sports Illustrated* swimsuit issue for the past three years?

Though her title sounds glamorous on paper—vice president, Malia Mills Swimwear—the first two years were anything but. "The last two years have been the hardest two years of my life in every way," Julie says. Not having enough money to pay people to do the most basic things, all the work—including the manual labor—fell on Julie and Malia's backs.

And not drawing a salary the first two years made matters worse. "One of the biggest mistakes we made was not taking a salary from the start," says Julie. "It almost led to the breakdown of the business and to my breakdown. I think we suffered more than we had to." The lowest point, she says, was hand-dyeing two thousand yards of satin in a pot in Malia's tiny kitchen with no fan and no air-conditioning.

Along with the bad came the good, however. A good she had never experienced before—not even at *Sports Illustrated.* "At *Sports Illustrated,* nothing ever really pushed me over the edge," Julie says. "Now, a bad day can be the worst day: it can push me close to a breakdown. But when good things happen, there's a pride that I've never experienced before."

And she's got some stuff to be proud about. Malia Mills swimsuits are now sold in over 110 stores, including Barneys New York *and* Tokyo. Malia Mills suits graced the cover of the 1996 *Sports Illustrated* swimsuit issue—the highest honor for a swimsuit designer—and also nabbed the cover of the 1997 *Victoria's Secret Swimsuit* catalog. In addition, Malia Mills suits have appeared and been featured in MTV's *House of Style, Entertainment Tonight,* CNN, and every single fashion magazine you can think of.

But even though they've gotten tons of great press, they can't quite relax yet. "It's definitely fame before fortune," Julie says. But hopefully not for long. "I'd be lying if I said I didn't want to make a lot of money," says Julie. "But that's because I work extremely hard and I want to enjoy the rewards of it. It's not about the money; it's about the success and accomplishment."

Chapter 22

THE THANK–YOU LETTER

The thank-you letter is more than just a formality you have to deal with. It can cost you a job offer you *should* have had, and it can get you a job offer you *wouldn't* have gotten as a result of the interview.

Now, the way it can cost you a job offer is if you don't write one. I've spoken to people who never sent thank-you letters and who got offers anyway. I've also spoken to employers who tell me that if they don't receive a thank-you letter from an applicant, then he's history. One interviewer lamented to me that there was this one woman she wanted to hire, whom she loved, but didn't hire because she never sent her a thank-you letter.

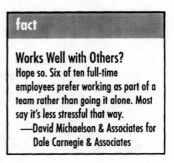

fact

Works Well with Others?
Hope so. Six of ten full-time employees prefer working as part of a team rather than going it alone. Most say it's less stressful that way.
—David Michaelson & Associates for Dale Carnegie & Associates

definition

REFERENCE:
1. Any living relative with a different last name. 2. Former lover whom you're still speaking to.

As Lauren Marino, editor at Broadway Books, says, "If people don't write a thank-you note, it means they don't want the job. It's their way of saying 'Who gives a fuck?' That's how you tell who wants the job and who doesn't. And since you're often trying to make a decision very quickly, if your letter gets there after the fact, it's too little too late."

In fact, a good thank-you letter is how Lauren got her first job in publishing. In one of her interviews, the interviewer asked her, "If you could publish any book, what would it be?" "I didn't really have an answer in the interview," Lauren says. "So in the thank-you note, I told him how I would love to do Madonna's biography. He told me later that it was the thank-you letter that got me the job. It was between me and another person, and the other person didn't write a thank-you letter and I did."

SUCKY INTERVIEW, GREAT COVER LETTER, "THE JOB'S YOURS"

> **quote**
>
> "I hate to advocate drugs, alcohol, violence, or insanity to anyone, but they've always worked for me."
> —Hunter S. Thompson

As mentioned, a good cover letter can change an interviewer's mind about you and get you a job offer you weren't going to get. Here's proof:

> We hired a guy who sucked in the interviews, frankly. But that day he had thank-you letters to everybody he saw. And they were personalized. It wasn't just "Thank you very much for seeing me." It was, "Thank you very much for seeing me. The next time you're at So-and-so Bar, we'll have to get together." To me it was, "Thanks for seeing me. It was really interesting to talk about Planning [her job]. I didn't really understand it before, but now I do, and I think I'd really enjoy working with you."
>
> After the interview write down a note to yourself about a way to make your note personal. It showed initiative, and it also showed that he had writing skills, which I hadn't expected because he wasn't that articulate. There's no way we would have hired him if he hadn't written such good thank-you letters.
>
> —Robin Danielson, president,
> Mad Dogs and Englishmen Advertising

WRITING A DECENT THANK-YOU LETTER

Example 1: Safe but Good

Dear So-and-so:

I just wanted to thank you for meeting with me yesterday. I enjoyed speaking with you about the position and learning more about [company name]. I hope I adequately expressed my interest to you in the interview, because I would be thrilled to be part of the [company name] family and contribute to its ongoing success.

If there's anything at all that I can do to convince you that I am the right person for this position, please let me know. I'd be more than happy to provide you with references and/or writing samples and would love to come in to meet with you again or any of your associates.

Again, thanks so much for your consideration.

Warmest regards,
Joe T.

Example 2: A Little More Animated

Dear So-and-so:

Thank you very much for the opportunity to meet with you yesterday. I was very excited to hear about your ambitious plans for the agency. On a more personal level, I especially enjoyed hearing how you rose up the ranks from receptionist to vice president. I hope that I can follow in your footsteps.

In case I wasn't clear in the interview, [company name] is without a doubt my first choice. I respect the work that you all produce, and I would love to have the opportunity to be a part of it. As I said in the interview, I'll do anything to get my foot in the door. If it means starting as receptionist or in the mailroom, I'll do it. Whatever it takes!!

Hope I'm not being too pushy; I just want you to know how badly I want this.

Sincerely,
Jane F.

P.S. I remember where I got my pin. It was Lani's on 6th and Bleecker. I'm glad you liked it.

Example 3: A Little Different

Dear So-and-so:

It was great meeting with you yesterday. I know you're considering many people for the sales position, so I thought I'd give one last sell on why you should hire me:

I'm persuasive.	I convinced six of my college friends to take a last-minute, two-day road trip to Mexico that was a bust.
I'm a hard worker.	I worked thirty hours a week throughout college while maintaining a 3.5 GPA.
People seem to like me.	I was president of my high school and college senior classes.
I'm a Yankees fan like you.	It doesn't make me more qualified, but it *does* make me a better person.

That's it. I hope you give me the opportunity to help make [company name] an even more successful company than it is today.
I hope to hear from you soon.

Best,
Carla G.

---

definition

HUMAN RESOURCES DEPARTMENT:
Individuals excused from the profit-making function of a company and charged with the responsibility for generating an internal police-state apparatus as well as proactively maintaining a chilling climate of fear.

NO WORD? FIND OUT WHAT'S GOING ON

People are busy. People are indecisive. People are lazy. Maybe they're waiting for the final budget approval to hire another person. So if you haven't heard from the people you interviewed with after about two weeks, go ahead and call them, and call them, and call them, until you get either a no or a yes.

After Claire's interview with a film production company, she recalls, "I didn't hear anything, so I kept calling and calling and calling. I called every day. I felt really comfortable there, and I wanted to work there. So I was calling every day, and finally the guy said, 'Okay, I'll let you meet with the woman who has the final say.' "

fact

I'm Sick!
Since 1992, workplace absenteeism is up 14 percent and costs U.S. companies an average of $668 per employee annually. These are the top reasons for blowing off work:
Illness: 45%
Stress: 6%
Feel entitled: 9%
Personal needs: 13%
Family issues: 27%

—CCH survey

Chapter 23

GETTING A JOB OFFER

Getting your first job offer is like having sex for the first time. You can't believe it. It's just too incredible. You've waited for it your whole life. So before you shout out in your excitement "I'll take it!" do the following:

ASK FOR SOME TIME

Whether you're in the room and the person interviewing you says, "Well, the job's yours," or whether they call you at home to offer you the job, thank them very much for the offer, tell them you think it's great and you're very excited, but that you would like a day or two to think about it. Two days is usually an all right amount of time. A week is pushing it.

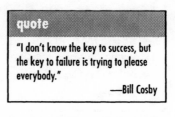

quote

"I don't know the key to success, but the key to failure is trying to please everybody."

—Bill Cosby

CONSULT SOME PEOPLE

Immediately call one or two people you trust and get their input. Try to find someone who knows the industry and maybe even the company that has offered you the job. They might know something about that company or industry that you were not aware of.

For instance, some guy E-mailed me about a job offer he had just received. It was a sales job with an Internet company that wanted to charge subscription fees to look at its Web site. The company was very young and small and had no track record at all. I told him that his chances of failing at the job were great because people expect to get information from the Web for free and that there are only a few sports sites that are successful at it and *they're* not even turning a profit. Now, if this were the *only* opportunity he had, the only offer he had received in many months, I might have told him to take it. It wasn't. He had other interviews lined up and felt confident that he would get a job offer in a few months.

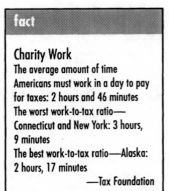

fact

Charity Work
The average amount of time Americans must work in a day to pay for taxes: 2 hours and 46 minutes
The worst work-to-tax ratio—Connecticut and New York: 3 hours, 9 minutes
The best work-to-tax ratio—Alaska: 2 hours, 17 minutes
—Tax Foundation

She's Got Balls

Jillian is an actress. She's also a little crazy. She auditioned for a part that wasn't due to start rehearsing for six months. Meanwhile, she was about to leave for Europe, where she was going to be for five months. She wanted to know if she had the part or not before she left. She wanted to know that she had a paying gig waiting for her upon her return.

So the day before she was leaving for Europe, she sent the director a note thanking him and accepting the job offer he never made, and asked him to forward the contracts to her agent. Two weeks later she called her agent from Europe. Turns out, she got the job. Her agent told her that the director said she had "balls." "He said he liked that," says Jillian.

SAY NO IF IT DOESN'T FEEL RIGHT

Although a job offer might seem like the answer to your prayers, it might also be the work of the devil. When you really, really need a job so you can, like, eat and stuff, it's hard to think about whether the offer you just received is something you really want. I would encourage you to really look at what the job is. A lot of young people wind up taking a job they *thought* was one thing but turned out to be another. They do the job for a few weeks and realize, "Wait a second, *this* is what I'm going to be doing fifty hours a week?"

One of the biggest problems with taking a job that sucks is that it takes you out of consideration for a job that doesn't suck. You'll have no time to interview and network. You'll come home from your crappy job in a shitty mood, turn on the TV, and sulk about your miserable life. It will suck the life and optimism from your body. This is a bad thing. So if your gut is telling you that you wouldn't be happy in that job, listen to your gut and turn it down. You don't want to start off your working life on such a destructive, negative note.

How do you know if your gut is telling you not to take the job? Easy. Are you really excited to start working in that job, and can you imagine being happy doing it every day for a year? If you say "I'm not sure" because you're not completely sure what the job entails, then you haven't done your homework and you didn't ask the person interviewing you the right questions. The only way you can know if you'll be happy, and therefore successful, in a job before you start it is to learn as much about the job as you possibly can. Many, many people fail to do this, wind up hating their job, and consequently wind up sucking at it.

GET THE OFFER IN WRITING

It might seem a little pushy, and it may catch the person making you the offer a little off guard, but it's a very good idea to ask if they wouldn't mind giving you an offer in writing. Make sure the letter includes the start date, the position, and what the salary and benefits are.

My life would probably be a lot different if I had asked for a particular offer in writing. I was working at a TV production company as a temp and after two months was offered a full-time job as the owners' second assistant. (I had been interviewing at other companies and was actually being considered for a job at one of them but told them to take me out of the running because I had gotten another offer.) Then, two days later, the first assistant (who is considered by everyone who works there a first-class bitch on wheels in serious need of mental care) and I were talking about my new position, and I told her how her boss (one of the owners of the company) had met with me personally to convince me to take the job. When she heard this, she freaked out. She was so threatened by my relationship with her boss and insisted that my offer be rescinded. So on Sunday the director of human resources called me at home and told me not to come in on Monday. Not liking the first assistant either, she told me exactly why I wasn't getting the job. "But you made me an offer," I said. "Not officially," she said. Not sure what kind of legal case I had, I agreed to accept a $2,000 restitution fee. If I had gotten the offer in writing, I would have gone after a lot more.

So before you give notice at your current job (if you have one), or turn down that second interview somewhere else, make sure you have a written offer in your hands.

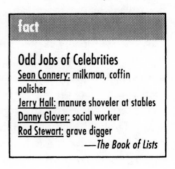

fact

Odd Jobs of Celebrities
Sean Connery: milkman, coffin polisher
Jerry Hall: manure shoveler at stables
Danny Glover: social worker
Rod Stewart: grave digger
—*The Book of Lists*

GOT ONE JOB OFFER, WAITING ON ANOTHER

Suppose you've been offered a job at one company but are waiting to hear back from the company you'd *really* like to work for. This first company is waiting for your answer, but you don't want to give it to them until you know if you've gotten the other job or not. What you have to do is call the company you're waiting to hear from and tell them you've been offered a job somewhere else and you need to give them an answer very soon. Tell them you're sorry to inconvenience them, but you need to know their decision by a certain date. Make sure you come across as humble as you can. Don't give them the impression that you're trying to force them into making an offer. They might get pissy and change their minds.

TURNING DOWN AN OFFER

If you're in the enviable position of having to turn down an offer, it's important to do so properly. You want to leave the door open at the company you're rejecting in case the job you *do* take turns out to suck. Don't feel guilty about turning down an offer; it happens all the time. Call and tell them that you received an offer elsewhere that you're going to take but that you really appreciate their offer. Try not to go into too much detail about the other job or company. Then, write the person a very nice thank-you note telling them how much you appreciate their offer and how hard a decision it was. This will impress the hell out of them and will leave the door open for you should the other job not work out.

NEGOTIATING YOUR DEAL

If this is your first job out of college, you don't have much leverage to negotiate. Your salary is pretty much whatever they offer. Some people might say that everything is negotiable and that you should ask for more than they offer you. Considering you have no real experience to offer them and that your first few months are going to be spent just learning what you're doing, I don't think you're in a position to do this.

However, provided you have a good rapport with the person making you the offer, you may want to ask if that number they're offering you is at all negotiable or flexible. If it's not, they'll tell you flat out. If it is, they'll say something like, "Why, what were you looking for?" If you get asked this and your offer is $25,000, then say, "I don't know. I was hoping maybe $30,000." Now, since you're really in no position to negotiate at all (in my opinion), I would add a caveat like, "If that's all you have in the budget, then I understand. I don't want to make this an issue on whether or not I accept the offer." You'll be surprised at what people will do out of kindness. You also don't know what's on their minds. They might be thinking to themselves, "He's right to ask for $30,000. See, I knew $25,000 was too little. Who can survive on $25,000? I'm going to try to get him $27,500."

Things You Can Ask For

If you're relocating, you *can* ask for moving money, although a lot of companies are starting to hold off on reimbursing moving costs until the employee has worked there an entire year. If it's a sales job that requires a lot of driving, then you should expect either a company car or, at the least, reimbursement for mileage. Also, if you already have a vacation planned, make sure you bring this up before you accept the offer. Once you start working, you're not in a good position to say, "Um, I kinda had this vacation planned before I started working here. Is there any way . . ."

NEGOTIATING YOUR SECOND JOB

When you're going on to your second job (and thereafter), you are now in a position to do some negotiating. Here are some tips:

Get *Them* to Make an Offer

Some interviewers will ask you, "So, what are you looking for?" If you're asked this, try to turn it around on them by asking, "Well, what were you thinking about offering?" What they're willing to offer you might be more than you had expected. You don't want to give a number lower than what they were going to offer. If they insist on your giving a figure, start high. If you want $40,000, ask for $45,000. You'll probably wind up settling at $42,500.

Don't Start Too High

The problem with starting too high is that it's hard to come down real far without looking like an idiot. For example, a friend of mine interviewed with this small company. The guy asked her how much she wanted, and she said $50,000. He told her that she was, by far, his first choice and that he would talk to his partner and try to get it for her. (Meanwhile, she had been making only around $30,000 at her last job.) When the guy she interviewed with told his partner she wanted $50,000, he nearly fell off his chair. He was expecting to pay around $30,000. The truth is, my friend would have taken $35,000 (she really wanted the job), but she thought she might as well go for a lot since this company was doing really well.

Well, it seems to have backfired. He called her back and said he was sorry but he couldn't offer more than $30,000. She said she would take less than $50,000. He said $30,000 was all they could afford. So she dropped her asking price from $50,000 to $35,000, at which point he said he'd get back to her. In my opinion, it made her look ridiculous. He never called her back. She kept calling to see what their decision was, but she never got a straight answer. Eventually, they told her that they'd hired someone else.

> **fact**
>
> **A Man's World**
> Although women make up 46 percent of the workforce, only 10 percent of corporate officers at the five hundred largest U.S. companies in 1996 were women. In 1994 it was 8.7 percent.
> —Findings of Catalyst survey

FEATURE INTERVIEW

Anibal Escobar
Mutual fund manager
B.A., Cornell, Engineering
M.B.A., Columbia

Introduction: This interview is different. It's not about how Anibal got a job and moved up the ladder in the financial industry. Rather, it's all about work behavior in the financial world. Though he now works independently as a mutual fund manager, this advice comes from his five years working for one of the largest financial institutions in New York City.

How come everybody on Wall Street looks miserable? And they all look and talk the same. It's so damn serious.

A lot of corporate settings are very unnatural. You can see it in the contorted expressions on people's faces. Your face has to stay in this position that's completely unnatural. I think this is why people's faces age really quickly in the financial industries. It shows on your face. It's just one of these weird modern facts.

So you *have* to look serious all the time. It's an act?

Most corporate settings are about self-control. You're not supposed to show any sort of feelings or emotions. For example, hand motions are completely taboo. You never see people moving their hands. You're supposed to hold them very close to your body. You're also not supposed to move your face or your body. Everything has to be so perfectly controlled.

The corporate world is very restrained and constrained. If you want to move up, you have to learn to play the game.

A friend of mine said he went to lunch with one of the principals of his company for the first time in the three years he's worked there and was terrified of ordering the wrong thing. What lunching advice would you give to young corporate turks?

If you go to a business lunch, do not drink. Your boss will not have a drink, and if for some weird reason he does, you will not. Everybody just has mineral water and a very light lunch, like a salad.

How about the bill?

If you are at lunch with your boss, it is understood that the most senior guy at the table pays. Do not reach for your wallet. If you reach to try to pay like some hotshot, you are going to look like an idiot.

Why salads? What's the significance of that?

All the bigwigs are thin. You rarely see fat people in the upper echelons of the corporate world. The upper-echelon guys are thin. Most of them are runners who don't drink. Looks matter a whole lot. If you're fat, it creates this impression that you're not in control—not in control of your body.

I've got this friend who lost his company millions of dollars and was just hired by another company for even *more* money. What's with that?

You're taught in school that profits matter and the bottom line matters, but it really doesn't. Being smart and being successful with the money is not that important. There are guys who are at the top of the totem pole who have lost millions and millions of dollars. They may have made money once, but even if it's all downhill after that, people keep coming back to them because they're confident and are great talkers.

Small family-run businesses are different. A small business is very concerned with the bottom line. A big business's bottom line goes up and down, and no one knows who to give the credit or blame to.

So being successful is about giving off a certain impression, not about performance?

The people who get ahead are the people who create the impression about themselves that they're moving and shaking—that they're people who are really on the go. It's completely an impression; it has nothing to do with the reality of what they're actually doing.

How come people wind up following them?

You can never overestimate the level and degree of insecurity the average corporate employee has about everything. About their position in the organization, about their knowledge and judgment, and about their opinions in general. The average corporate Joe is a very insecure person. So whoever can portray themselves with extreme, unrealistic, and extraordinary security is the one who everybody winds up flocking to and following.

Anibal's eight easy steps to giving the "right" impression:

1. Never lose an opportunity to express your importance to others. If there's a project where there're other people involved, always express an opinion, even if you don't have any expertise in it. You always have to have a say. You have to exert your view even if it's random or tangential. You just have to introduce yourself into the process a lot, and early on.

2. Take advantage of every opportunity to show yourself in a positive light in front of superiors. You don't have to be burdened by the truth. If somebody else did something and you were part of it, highlight the fact that you were there and part of it.

3. Your dress has to be expensive but understated.

Guys: An English suit with a shirt with French cuffs. Understated, elegant, and rich-looking. Very subtle. Solid colors. Thin lapels, single-breasted, never double-breasted. Pinstripe is okay, but it has to be very subtle. Suspenders are good. Lace-up cap-toe shoes. No facial hair, no jewelry.

Women: Nondescript suits. Never pants.

4. Don't have any photos of children in your office. In finance jobs you get little mementos—Lucite blocks—from prior transactions. The more of those you can stack in your office, the better. Big executives will have forty or fifty of them.

5. Never mention anything about your personal life. Never mention roommate or relationship problems. Never mention you got drunk.

6. Never let on that you have failings or the fact that you have blemishes in your past. No way; you are infallible.

7. You cannot let on that you have doubts. You cannot say "Maybe this or maybe that." You cannot share doubts with people. You have to remember the formula: 100 percent self-confidence. Even if you have the wrong opinion, it doesn't matter—as long as you have complete security about it.

8. The later you stay, the better—even if you have nothing to do. Play solitaire on your computer or something. You have to give the impression that you're working really, really hard. Arriving early is critical. More so than staying late. The power guys have an earlier schedule. They get in earlier. When you're in a corporate job in your twenties, you want to go out and party, but you can't. You should definitely be there by eight A.M. The real highflyers are usually in their office by seven A.M.

Do you have to watch your ass all the time?

The backstabbing in the corporate world is more subtle. It's done over a period of time. It's not like you're immediately aware that you are on somebody's bad list, but over time you realize that you are. Outwardly everybody is very diplomatic, very supportive; you're part of the team. Even if you're not and they want you gone, they won't let you know. Little by little you'll be left out. Your input and opinions won't be sought any longer.

So instead of firing you, they freeze you out.

Exactly. That person won't be included anymore. Their opinion won't be sought anymore. And eventually they'll realize it's time to leave.

Now, why would this happen?

This would happen because you've created a bad impression on somebody. Not because of the work. Maybe you came in to work too late too many times, or you came in disheveled too many times. People notice this, and they do not like it. Or maybe you had "unprofessional behavior." People notice. They won't say anything, but they'll notice.

Why are they such jerks?

They want people to give up their lives like they did. It's like fraternity hazing. The corporate world just wants to re-create this image in everybody, so everybody has to toe that line. And if you don't, you're gone.

So it's all about impressions and acting, isn't it?

Impressions are everything. You can *highlight* that and put it in CAPS. It's everything.

Chapter 24

DEALING WITH REJECTION

This is a fact. You're going to go on an interview, and it's going to go great. You're going to connect with the person. You're going to tell each other jokes. You're going to sit there for two hours having a great time, and at the end of the interview, the interviewer is going to say to you, "It was great meeting you. You will hear from us *real* soon." They've basically told you that you are going to get the job. Hell, you *know* you've got the job.

One week goes by and you call, just checking in. You ask if you can call back again in five days if you haven't heard from them. They say sure, absolutely, but that you proba- bly will hear from them sooner than that. You call back in five days and the assistant tells you that you didn't get the job. Sorry.

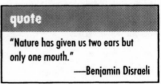

quote

"Nature has given us two ears but only one mouth."
—Benjamin Disraeli

You're stunned. You're pissed. It's impossible. That job was *yours*. They all but said it was yours. The truth is, they probably *were* going to hire you but something happened. Maybe they were forced to hire the president's daughter or a client's son. Maybe their budget got cut. Maybe the person who wanted to hire you got fired and the new person decided to hire someone *they* found.

definition

CAFETERIA:
Depressing area where employees consume drugged meals prepared by hate-filled workers in the name of convenience.

This happens to everybody at least once, but usually more. So when it happens to you, remember that I said it would happen and don't get suicidal. Move on. Whatever you do, don't dwell on it and let it get you down. It's hard to say, "Be positive and optimistic and happy," but you must be. You can't go into your next interview pessimistic, still hurt from your last rejection. Remember, people hire optimistic people with positive outlooks. If an employer senses your negative energy or self-doubt, you will definitely not get the job.

fact

You Suck!
Here's the winning entry (creatively submitted by an employee) for the 1996 Worst Boss Award: "Most Wanted List: Office manager. Successful candidate must be able to: Schedule fake business trips to spend time with another woman. Forcibly kiss secretary on the lips. Wear the same clothes all week. Cough in employees' faces, and pass gas and act as though this is normal behavior. Rig company raffles and keep merchandise for yourself. Rub against employees whenever possible. Separate a fast food order to the correct employees by taking a bite out of each sandwich to determine its contents. Lie or cheat as long as yourself and ONLY yourself will benefit."
—Jim Miller, *Best Boss, Worst Boss*

Part 7

ON THE JOB

Chapter 25

YOUR FIRST DAY AND REAL-WORLD RULES

Your first day on the job is a big deal. To you. Sadly, nobody else is going to give a shit. Sure, there might be one person who actually goes out of their way to introduce themselves and offer help if you need it. But don't expect it.

This actually drives me crazy. Why are people such unfriendly weasels? I mean, why do otherwise decent people become jerks once they hit the workplace? Why? Because people are insecure; they might consider you to be a threat. You're just another person to compete with on the way up the company ladder.

So, what do you do? Well, if nobody has introduced you to the people around you, go up and introduce yourself. Don't walk around the whole floor introducing yourself like you're running for mayor. Do it slowly and inconspicuously. If you're a naturally friendly, outgoing person, you may want to tone it down a bit. If you go in introducing yourself to everybody, people are going to look at you funny. In the workplace, people feel threatened by outgoing, confident people.

I'm not saying you have to change

fact

"Give Me Your Bummed Out"
Study: Depressed workers do better work. A study by a professor of psychology at the Norwegian College of Business in Oslo concluded that unhappy people do better work than cheerful ones. Surprised by his own findings, he said that cheerful test subjects overestimated their own ability, underestimated the complexity of problems presented to them, and tended to opt for answers that seemed easy or obvious. The glum were less confident, looked deeper, and found far more creative solutions. "There is a lot of anecdotal evidence of people doing their best work while depressed," said Dr. Kaufmann. "Einstein has said he was in a sad mood the day he came up with the basis of his theory of relativity."

"Honestly?"

Sometimes you're going to be asked to work on a project you're not interested in. You have two choices: (1) Be a good guy and say, "Sure," and wind up being miserable. Or (2) say, "No thanks," risk being the bad guy, but probably be a lot happier.

This is the situation that faced Brian as a second-year associate at a top law firm in New York. The partners were trying to transfer associates from litigation to corporate because there was more work to be done in corporate. But nobody wanted to move. So they went around to the associates and said, "How would you feel about spending some time in the corporate department?" When they got to Brian, he said, "Point-blank, I'd rather blow my brains out." It worked. They moved on to the next guy, and Brian was saved from working in a department he didn't want to work in.

---

your whole personality. Not at all. Just be mellow and do your job without attracting too much attention in the beginning. Let people get to know you over time. Let people get to know you at their own pace. But don't be surprised if it takes a long time to happen.

REAL-WORLD RULES

People find all sorts of ways to show their boss and coworkers what utter morons they are. And usually in the first few weeks. Each office and each industry has its own set of rules. Before you start assuming the place is a certain way—liberal, conservative, honest— take a good look around to see what's really going on. For instance, maybe it's uncool to take a full hour off for lunch. Or maybe it's uncool to wear a tie. Or maybe it's uncool to have a drink at lunch, even though the boss is.

Here are a few basic things to keep in mind:

Your E-Mail Is Not Your Own

Companies have the ability and the right to screen your E-mail. And more and more are starting to do it. So make sure you don't send or receive any E-mail that could in any way offend anybody or make you look like an idiot.

I just read in the *New York Times* how six junior executives at a large advertising agency got canned for sending an E-mail that contained racially offensive jokes. They didn't send it to anybody who was offended by it. It was just a case of management thinking these guys were bigoted idiots—which they were—and didn't want them working for the company.

Companies can also monitor what you're downloading. A friend recently told me about her friend who had just taken a big-time banking job, making over $200,000 a year. On his first week, after hours, he was browsing the Web and went to a few porno sites. The next day he was called into the president's office and canned. Even though downloading pornography on the Web is legal, this particular boss was against it and, for whatever reason, fired the guy.

---

definition

OFFICE PARTY:
Oxymoron describing ritual cake-eating ceremony with paper plates and plastic forks, accompanied by gloomy atmosphere and a mild sense of dread.

Alcoholism Isn't Cool

Depending on where you work, there might be many occasions where there is alcohol. And since I've heard from more than two people how people they know have made total assholes of themselves, I thought maybe it was necessary to remind you that, unlike college and with your friends, having more than a drink or two at a work-related function is not cool.

This is an unbelievably pathetic little story that happens to be true. This guy I know—we'll call him Bob—got this great job with this investing company making over $100,000 plus perks at age twenty-five. He was a hotshot. Well, one night at 6:00 his boss says come on, let's get a drink, so he goes. They get in the limo (this boss apparently took a limo everywhere), hit one bar and then another. Bob tells his boss, meanwhile, that he's got to get some food in him 'cause he hasn't eaten all day. "Yeah, yeah, yeah, later, don't worry about it," his boss replies. So Bob proceeds to get shit-faced and doesn't remember what he said. It must have been bad because, in the middle of the highway, Bob's boss tells the driver to pull over and he kicks Bob out of the car and tells him he's fired. Moral of the story? Don't be an idiot and don't let your boss tell you when you need to eat.

---

fact

The World's Richest People

Name	Net Worth (billions)	Company	Country
Bill Gates	$18.0	Microsoft	United States
Warren Buffett	$15.3	Stock market	United States
Paul Sacher	$13.1	Pharmaceuticals	Switzerland
Lee Shau Kee	$12.7	Real estate	Hong Kong
Tsai Wan-lin	$12.2	Insurance, finance	Taiwan
Li Ka-shing	$10.6	Diversified	Hong Kong
Yoshiaki Tsutsumi	$9.2	Real estate	Japan
Paul Allen	$7.5	Microsoft	United States
Kenneth Thomson	$7.4	Media, real estate	Canada
Tan Yu	$7.0	Real estate	Philippines

—Forbes

The Office Is Not a Singles Bar

Another mistake among rookies is using the office as a place to get laid. Now, I could say to you "You should never, under any circumstances, have sex with someone you work with," but that would be ridiculous. If you're horny and hot for someone in your office who is hot for you, you're not going to listen to my stupid advice; you're going to go for it. So I guess the only advice I can give is this:

Never Sleep with Your Boss

Sure, it might seem like a good career move at first, but when you decide to dump this person's ass, kiss your own good-bye. Imagine working for an ex-girlfriend or -boyfriend whom you dumped. Think of the opportunities for retribution they have—how they can make your life a living hell.

If you are a woman (and for some guys), you are inevitably going to have at least one boss who is going to want to have sex with you. Therefore, know ahead of time (like now) what you're going to do when they ask you out for a drink or to dinner.

Women, if your boss asks you out to dinner, there is a chance that he considers it a date, not a business meeting. So be very careful here. If he starts getting too personal, asking about boyfriends and stuff, then he considers it a date. If you go out to dinner with this person again, you are accepting a date and will therefore start the process of leading this person on. If you don't give in to his or her advances after a few dates, your ass is grass. This person is going to feel like an idiot and is going to be angry for your leading them on. Sure you never did anything to lead them on in *your* mind; these were business dinners. In their mind, however, they were more than business dinners.

---

definition

OFFICE KITCHEN:
Windowless, cheer-free room with microwave, sink, and filthy minifridge.

So have an answer ready for when you're asked out by your boss. Try this excuse: "You know what? My boyfriend/girlfriend gets jealous when I go out to dinner with people I work *with*, but since I work *for* you, he/she can't get jealous, right?" This way you're letting them know you're not available (even if you are), but you're not rejecting them either. Hopefully they'll lose interest and say something like, "Well, we better not, then. We don't want him/her getting jealous." If he says this, you know his intentions weren't business-related.

If you happen to be out at a late meeting or out of town on business and both of you need to eat anyway, then go ahead and have dinner with your boss. But don't have an after-dinner drink or go to another bar, for God's sake. Say good night.

Have Sex Only with Coworkers You Would Consider Marrying

(This is assuming you believe in sex before marriage.) The point here is that you shouldn't use your office as a place to get laid. Why not? Because it's not the seventies; it's just not cool anymore.

Guys: People are basically looking for any reason to hate you and talk behind your back in most offices around the world. Being known as the guy who had sex with two women in the company, neither of whom you're now dating, will make you look like a

---

The Image Factor

After Sam graduated from George Washington University, he moved to New York City and got a job with the PBS affiliate WNET. Knowing that the station had an air of elitism about it, he figured the less he told people about himself, the better. After all, he wasn't some famous person's son or stepson. He was just some kid from Pennsylvania. Let them imagine what they want was his attitude.

After he'd been on the job one week, a bunch of Sam's coworkers were going out on a yacht on a Saturday and asked him to join them. He didn't know how to sail real well but knew it would be politically incorrect to blow it off. After sailing, the ten of them decided to go to a popular actor hangout restaurant in the theater district. But they forgot that it was Saturday. You couldn't get into this place on a Saturday night without a reservation. So when they got there, the maître d' said, no way, impossible, and started to send them on their way.

Then, out of nowhere, the maître d' said, "Well, why didn't you say you were with Sam," and whisked them to the back table that had been reserved for someone else. As it turns out, Sam had gone to college with the maître d'. And while the others were lamenting about where else to go eat, Sam slid up to him and said, "It's me, Sam. Make me look good."

Sam didn't tell any of them how he knew the maître d', and nobody asked. They just assumed Sam either knew everyone or actually was someone important. Either way, it gave Sam instant clout and respectability among his impressionable coworkers.

scumbag, even if you're not. You can tell all the people you want that it was consensual, casual sex, but no one will believe you. Yes, this will probably hurt your chances of getting laid a third time, but it's worse than that. Bosses generally consider people who use the office as a place to get laid as stupid.

Gals: People are basically looking for any reason to hate you and talk behind your back in most offices around the world. Having sex with more than one guy in your office will mark you as a "slut," even if you're not. Nobody likes or wants to promote a slut.

Trust No One

In the workplace there is no such thing as "Just between you and me, okay?" Whatever you tell an office mate, assume they're going to tell others, including your boss. At my last job at this medium-sized company, there was this really, really nice, fun, outgoing, very popular young woman whom I happened to

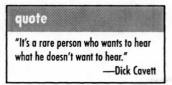

fact

Work Can So Kill You
There were 1,071 Americans murdered and 160,000 physically assaulted at work in 1994. Eighty-five percent of assaults and 55 percent of homicides are committed at retail trade or service industry work sites. Taxi drivers suffer the greatest risk of being killed.
—*USA Today*

sit next to. (Hello, in case you're reading this.) She was a lot of people's friend. She was also good friends with the owner of the company. Well, I'll tell you, people (the people who thought they were good friends with her) would be shocked at the disparaging things she would say about them as soon as they walked away. It absolutely blew me away. *This,* from *her?* I couldn't believe it. People she pretended to be best friends with, she maneuvered to get fired. So be very careful whom

quote

"It's a rare person who wants to hear what he doesn't want to hear."
—Dick Cavett

you decide to open up to. Unless this person is one of your best friends whom you go out with at least once a week, keep your mouth shut.

Be Fake and Dishonest

In the beginning things are going to suck. You're going to be completely lost. Nobody is going to offer you help. You'll think every day is going to be your last. Meanwhile, everyone—from the mailman to the VP—is going to ask you "How's it going?" Your answer? "Great! Thanks for asking." The point is, never show your weak side. Don't be vulnerable and don't be honest. If somebody you don't know really well asks you "How do you like your job?" even if you hate it, you must say, "Oh, it's great. I love it."

Chapter 26

YOU AND YOUR COWORKERS

PERSONALITY DEFICIENCIES OF THE WORKINGMAN

The working world is a weird place. There's nothing else like it. It creates and breeds monsters. It turns otherwise decent, nice people into greedy, selfish jerks. To me, it explains why we think our parents are so weird. They used to be normal, but years in the working world have made them uptight and rigid. The dog-eat-dog-ness, the pressure of pulling your own weight and of being fired, of office politics, of aging and not being where you thought you would be by now. It can all loom large and weigh heavily on an insecure person with a short fuse, creating a psychotic, abusive, backstabbing idiot. (Watch out. It could happen to you.)

So get ready to walk into a world where the rules of conduct you were brought up to follow—modesty is good, lying is bad, etc.—are, in a lot of places, scoffed at. In business, the only rule is profit and performance. As long as someone contributes to the company's profit and as long as they are producing good work, it doesn't matter how they treat their fellow workers.

fact

Joblessness Wreaks Havoc
For every 1 percent rise in the jobless rate, homicides increase by 6.7 percent, violent crimes rise by 3.4 percent, crimes against property go up 2.4 percent, and deaths from heart disease and stroke rise by 5.6 and 3.1 percent, respectively.
—Michael Moore, *Downsize This!*

---

definition

DIVERSITY IN THE WORKPLACE:
People of various races, creeds, colors, and sexual orientations who all possess an identical lust for money and will do absolutely anything to get more.

So, what am I saying? To go in to your new job, cheat, steal, and lie and step over the bodies on your way to the top? Nope. I think success can be achieved by being honest and decent. Some may disagree.

DEALING WITH CLIQUES

On my last job at this Web development company, people, in general, were very unfriendly. First of all, it wasn't a huge company, around sixty employees. You'd think someone would have taken me around and introduced me to people. No one did. You'd think people would have come up to me and introduced themselves. One, maybe two, did. You'd think someone would have come up to me and said, "Hey, you want to join us for lunch?" No one did. Everybody had their own cliques, and they weren't interested in having someone new break into their circle. They wanted to keep the company their own. They didn't want me to feel like the place was my home, too. If this happens to you, all I can say is, don't take it personally. Just be as nice to everybody as you can. Maybe they'll invite you along, maybe they won't.

PICKING YOUR COWORKER FRIENDS

A huge factor in being successful is your ability to swim in the shark-infested office waters. And the basic no-drown doggie paddle won't cut it. You've got to be able to switch from backstroke to crawl to butterfly effortlessly. You have to gain the respect of the hotshot who would sell their own mother to close a deal, without selling your soul. You have to laugh at some idiot's jokes and pretend you really like them, when in fact you don't. You have to go out for drinks with a bunch of knuckleheads so they don't think you think you're better than they are, even though you are.

HANG OUT WITH THE HOTSHOTS—THE UP–AND–COMERS

I don't want to sound like an opportunistic jerk, but try to make friends with people who are going someplace in the company. Don't get sucked in by some idiot with a bad attitude. Unfortunately, someone with a bad attitude is the person most likely to reach out to you—looking for a convert or an ally, as it were. My advice: stay away. People are going to judge you by the company you keep. If you start hanging out with some bitter, low-level guy who has made it known to others that he's unhappy, people are naturally going to assume that you're a whining loser also. Avoid these people like the plague.

What you want to do is make friends with the optimistic, overtime-working stars at the company. The people who are on the fast track who are a little higher up than you, as well as people in more senior levels in other departments. I'm not saying you have to become their personal friend; they've probably got all the friends they need. But you do have to become their "office friend." Why?

Political Monsters

"If you have any ambition at all, you're going to have to deal with politics. And you better learn how to *play* politics. I know a lot of people with mediocre talent skills who have moved up quickly because they just play the politics so well."

—Neal Justin, pop culture critic, *Minneapolis Star Tribune*

Playing the Game: Some Ideas

- Attending the Halloween party at the boss's house. (And getting dressed up for it.)
- Finding out what club the president plays tennis at and joining.
- Being *for* something and *against* something at the same time, depending on whom you're talking to.
- Smiling all the time, even when you're miserable.
- Getting invited to the Friday night poker game.
- Making everybody think you're their best friend, even though you hate them all.

Three Reasons to Suck Up to Up–and–Comers

1. **Up-and-comers wield power.** They may not have the authority to fire you or get you promoted, but they very often have the ear of the top brass and are often asked their opinion of their coworkers.

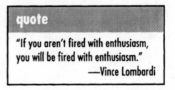

"If you aren't fired with enthusiasm, you will be fired with enthusiasm."
—Vince Lombardi

At one job I had, I was considered an up-and-comer, a real hard worker who was concerned about the company's success and all that. Though I had no real power in the office, the people above me liked me a lot and respected my opinion. I was that person whom, if you were new (and even if you weren't), you wanted to become friends with and impress. One of the heads of the company used to regularly ask me, "What do you think of so-and-so?" And I'd tell him. There were a couple of coworkers whom I didn't respect and frankly didn't like. When my boss asked me about them, I told him that I thought they were basically useless and had bad attitudes. I think he thought this already, but I had confirmed his suspicions. The next day both of them were fired.

2. **Up-and-comers are tomorrow's bosses.** Another reason you want to suck up to the up-and-comers is because of where they're going. These people are soon going to be in a position of power and will therefore have the influence to get you promoted—or fire you.

3. **They're your contacts for tomorrow.** The people whom you

work with today are going to be essential for your career tomorrow. I can't stress enough how true this is. Your peers—your hotshot peers—are going to go to different companies where they will either have the authority to offer you a job or, at the least, be in a position to tell you about a job opening and *refer* you for a job.

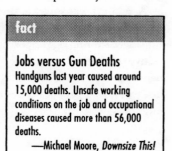

fact

Jobs versus Gun Deaths
Handguns last year caused around 15,000 deaths. Unsafe working conditions on the job and occupational diseases caused more than 56,000 deaths.
—Michael Moore, *Downsize This!*

How to Suck Up to the Up-and-Comers

Make Sure They Know Who You Are

Say hello to them every morning, even if they don't say hi to you and don't remember your name. If you keep saying "Hi, Susan," Susan will eventually learn your name out of sheer embarrassment.

Compliment Them on Their Work

Have they recently landed an account or made a big sale or gotten some of their work approved? If so, make it a point to go up to them and congratulate them. You don't have to get on your knees and kiss their ass. Just say, "By the way, congratulations on the Dreyfuss account. That's great." Everybody loves to be complimented.

When I was working at this talent agency, there was a young woman assistant who had been there for like four years and was about to be made an agent. I didn't like her. She was very pushy. We'd had it out more than once. Knowing that she would probably be made an agent shortly, I knew I had better make nice with her. Why? You aren't made an agent if the other agents don't like you. So after overhearing a conversation/negotiation she was having with a producer regarding a client, I said to her, "Damn, I'd hate to be that guy." It was a subtle way of saying, "You're a good, tough agent," something all agents get off on being. She smiled and went on to tell me about the deal she was negotiating on behalf of her boss. She was happy to have the opportunity to brag about what she was doing—everybody loves to talk about themselves—and I was glad to listen.

Actually, I was smart to listen. In that five minutes I had turned a probable enemy into an ally. Had I stayed there long enough to be considered for an agent position, she and the other agents I had effectively brownnosed or made friends with would prove to be essential in my becoming one. And even though I left shortly afterward, this was now a person I could tap for information regarding jobs she might know about.

Ask Them for Their Advice on Something

Find an occasion to ask them for their advice. Even if you're smarter than they are and know more than they do, find something to ask them. Make sure that it's not something dumb, though. If, however, this person is really busy and hates all distractions, then skip this.

Feed Them Information

There are a bunch of great, inspiring quotes about information—how it is one of the keys to business success and so forth. Unfortunately, I can't remember any of them. They basically say that he who has information has the power. Information about competitors, about technology that will affect your business, about how to do something more cheaply, etc.

---

definition

POWER PISSING:
Effortless, witty banter with a significant higher-up situated at an adjacent urinal.

Say you're working as an assistant account executive at an advertising agency. You've scoped out the landscape and have identified a senior-level account person in another department whose ass you want to kiss. (We'll get to kissing your boss's ass later.) Find out what accounts this person works on—you know, Tide, Chrysler, Winn Dixie—and make it your business to learn everything about them.

Then, scour the newspapers for any and all articles that relate either directly or indirectly to his accounts. If there's an article in *Brand Week* about a competitor of one of his clients, cut it out and attach a note to it that says, "I thought you might be interested in seeing this," and put it in their in-box or mailbox. Don't leave it with their assistant if they have one. The assistant might throw the thing away. And if he doesn't throw it away, he's not going to like your barging into his territory.

The best way to get it into their hands would be to leave it on the side of your desk, and when you see them, jump up and hand it to them saying "Oh, I was just going to drop this off for you at your office." This is a great way to make small talk and for them to get to know you as a person who can actually speak, who has a brain, and who is ambitious.

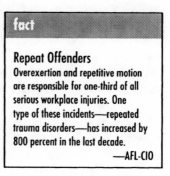

fact

Repeat Offenders
Overexertion and repetitive motion are responsible for one-third of all serious workplace injuries. One type of these incidents—repeated trauma disorders—has increased by 800 percent in the last decade.
—AFL-CIO

The Real Skinny with . . . John Verrilli, Associate News Director, Fox News

AVOIDING PERSONNEL:
Don't send your résumé to personnel. Especially in television, because personnel doesn't hire anybody except trainees and interns. The actual hiring is done by executive producers, news directors, and managing editors.

HOW TO GET RESPONSIBILITY:
If you take an active interest and know what's going on, people will always trust you to take responsibility—if you're good. And once they trust you, the more responsibility you get. [When I was starting out,] this one producer learned to count on me. So I took advantage of it and really worked hard. And I think he recognized that and gave me a shot to do other stuff.

MOVING UP THE LADDER:

After a year and a half of being a production assistant, I came in on my own time, on the weekends, to write. The next step from being a production assistant is to become a writer. So I would come in on the weekends and do that on my own. At first they weren't paying me, but after a while, when they started using my stuff, they said, "Okay, we'll pay you." And eventually they made me a writer on the weekends.

DEALING WITH BULLY BOSSES:

A lot of people in power like to have someone to punch. If you stand your ground, people start to respect you. If you let them stomp all over you, they'll stomp all over you.

THE REAL WORLD:

Producing a live news show is one of the most hectic things there is to do in life. I have a stomach condition because of it. So many people I know in the business have ulcers or are alcoholics. I'm not going to live the rest of my life worrying about whether I missed a story or not.

F E A T U R E   I N T E R V I E W

Diana LoGuzzo
Diesel USA Inc.
28 years old
Marketing and advertising manager

Question:

She is the VP of marketing for Diesel Clothing. What is her educational background?

Answer choices:

a. B.A. in romance languages with a master's in Italian. Did master's thesis on "The Image of Women in Early Renaissance Painting from 1450 to 1500 in Tuscany."
b. B.A. in design with a minor in communications. Did undergraduate thesis on "The Voice of Fashion in America from 1975 to 1995."
c. B.A. in English with an M.B.A.
d. None of the above.
If you're saying to yourself, "It's impossible. This question sucks," then you get an A+. You

see, "a" through "c" could wind up doing thousands of different things. And this is the point: liberal arts majors can do anything.

"I would never have guessed I'd be doing what I'm doing," says Diana, profile "a" above. She *thought* she'd either go into doing special events in a museum or would teach. What she wound up doing was packing her bags and moving to Italy.

Diana's first job in Italy was doing translation work for an advertising agency. Nothing thrilling, nothing long-term. But while she was there, she got to know people at one of the companies the agency did work for—a very successful specialty grocery store—and got a job with them.

Voilà! Diana was living and working in Montecatini, Italy. "The most beautiful place on earth," she says. What could be better? Well, there was one drawback. Since the town was so small, everybody knew your business. "You're the American girl with the blue Volkswagen Golf. Everybody knew my comings and goings. It started driving me nuts." And then there was the job itself. It sucked. If the owner hadn't been inclined toward screaming, turning over desks, and taking employees by the throat, maybe it would have been better. But he was. "That was my last job in Italy. I was like, 'See ya. I'm outta here,' " Diana says.

New York City, the home of anonymity (and the home of her alma mater, NYU), was the obvious relocation point for Diana. And the Italian Trade Commission was a natural place to get freelance work, considering her proficiency in Italian. It was there that Diana heard that the small but fast-growing, hip, Italian clothing company, Diesel, was looking for someone to take care of the advertising and media buying. Things Diana basically knew nothing about.

How do you prepare for an interview when the answer to the inevitable question "What makes you qualified for this job?" would have to be "Nothing in particular"? You don't. "I think the guy liked me because I was incredibly straightforward," Diana says. "I didn't try to mask the whole thing and say 'Oh, well, I'm an expert and can bring you all these things.' I laid it on the table that I would be learning. I said, 'If you teach me, I will learn it.' " The fact that Diana was telling them this in Italian, their native tongue, was a huge plus. "Understanding their mentality and speaking Italian was important. They wanted someone they could talk to and relate to."

Had Diesel been as large then as they are today, Diana would probably not have gotten the job. That's the advantage of going to a small company. The other advantage of starting with them when they were small was getting to see how everything worked. "This was so beneficial to me, it's unbelievable," she says. But as beneficial as it was, it also brought a lot of hard work. The fact that it *was* so small meant that everybody pitched in where needed, including answering the phones and signing for things from the FedEx guy. These were Diesel's prebureaucracy days.

Diana's immediate responsibilities included doing the media buying (deciding where to advertise and how much) and editorial (getting Diesel's clothes into magazine stories). She was the PR *and* marketing departments. Though she'd never done buying and editorial before, it was a perfect fit for Diana. As she says, "You have to read the magazines, you have to know what's going on, you have to know what new models are coming out and who is using what photographer." Stuff Diana knew some about but was eager to learn everything about. "There was a lot of educating that I needed to give myself in the beginning, so I just sucked it up and let it take over my life."

Now, Diana's life and her job have kind of become indistinguishable. "I'm a face for Diesel," she explains. "From a marketing standpoint, you want Diesel to be present at every event, at every hip, cool, edgy thing that exists on planet earth from Amsterdam to New York to everywhere. Me being at a party, I represent." In other words, wherever Diana is, Diesel is. "Everybody in my office is always out. We're seen at all the 'right' places. I'm constantly out going to film openings and art exhibitions and new restaurants and those kind of things. Our promotions person goes out every night to every club, every club opening, and every restaurant opening."

While free dinners, free tickets to shows, free music, and invitations to all the best parties are nice perks, they taught Diana that it *is* possible to have too much fun. Working all day and then having to go out six nights a week can be a drag no matter what you're doing. Especially when you're required to be fab at all times. So from January to March last year, she hibernated. "I didn't go out. I said to myself, 'That's it. I'm over it.' "

Knowing when to draw the line and say no is also the reason Diana has moved up at Diesel. "Having an opinion has definitely helped me. I'm not wishy-washy," she says. Whether it's challenging people in a meeting by saying "Hey, do you really believe that?" or "Isn't that price astronomical?" to making the decision to run hard with an advertisement that features two male sailors kissing.

Though it doesn't seem like a big deal, that one decision to put the kissing ad in major magazines like *Rolling Stone* and *Premiere* could have been a major career faux pas for Diana. "With the sailor ad, some people were really worried. You can get very negative backlash that you won't survive," says Diana. The ad *did* get some backlash from religious fanatics and the military, of course, but it garnered Diesel more publicity and talk than any other ad had ever done.

And this is Diana's job, as elusive and immeasurable as it sounds—to get people to associate Diesel with things Diesel believes in: "Freedom, choice, options, culture, and education." Part of Diesel's success is directly related to its quality and fit and fabric, but another part of its success comes from image. "That's what I deal with directly," says Diana. "That's what I cultivate."

And while image cultivation is everything in this image-crazed, consumed, and motivated culture, it's also something you can't really measure. "I represent a very costly part of the business that's hard to measure. I do not produce revenue directly," she says. "Dollars to cents, it's not like sales, where you can say 'Last year I sold ten, this season I sold twelve, next season I want to sell fifteen.' " And herein lies Diana's internal, political challenge. "You have to keep fighting for your budget and for your staff." And this is where Diana's Italian pays off for her. "When you need to support yourself, fight back, or be aggressive, it helps when it's in their language."

Question: "Diana, what sucks about your job?"
Answer: "Very, very little sucks about my job. I'm very lucky. I'm very happy. It's really rare."

Chapter 27

GAINING THE RESPECT OF YOUR COWORKERS

KEEP YOUR PERSONAL LIFE AT HOME

Your girlfriend just break up with you? Has the fact that your boyfriend is directing a commercial in Miami for Miller Beer with a bunch of bimbo bikini models got you near tears? Leave it at home. Hide it from your boss and your associates.

Even if you think your boss and associates are really cool, are on your side, and don't mind hearing about your roommate or boyfriend problems, they aren't and they do. Sure they'll listen to your tales of sorrow, and they might even be truly concerned and offer kind words of consolation. When they step away, however, they will think that you are weak and emotional and have personal problems. It may not even register consciously in their brain, but they will come to think of you as unprofessional, flaky, unconcerned with your image, and too consumed with personal issues and not your career.

Example 1

Recently I was in roommate hell. My two roommates hated each other and were trying to make the other's life miserable so they would move out. It wound up getting out of hand on a few occasions with the police actually being summoned. Every day was something new. I was working a nine-to-five job, and it was making my life hell.

Every other day I would get a call at work from one roommate or the landlord trying to figure out how we were going to evict this other person. I sat in an open office with no doors, so I made an effort to talk very quietly when a certain associate was around. Though she was not my boss, she was an incredibly hard worker whose respect I didn't want to lose. I knew she respected me as a hard worker, and this helped me to get my work done with her. She always made time to assist me on projects we were working on. Without her cooperation, my job would have been very hard. If she had heard this ongoing soap opera every day, I know she would think I was being unprofessional and slacking off, and I didn't want that.

My roommate, on the other hand, the one who was getting booted, bitched to me one day how this whole apartment thing was ruining her career. She wanted to get it settled because her boss and people in her office were sick of hearing about it. "That's your own fault," I told her. "You should never have let them know about it."

Example 2

Remember how I said that your coworkers will think you're flaky if you bring your problems into work, and how they'll give you no indication that they feel this way? Well, last night I was at a party, and I ran into a guy who works with a good friend of mine at a market research firm. I asked him how my friend Jane was doing, and it launched us into a discussion about her career and fate at that company. He told me how he thought she wasn't going to be promoted.

"Why?" I asked.

"Her head's just not in it," he said. He went on to tell me how she cries on the phone sometimes with her boyfriend, a guy who travels a lot. "She's smart and a hard worker and all, but you just can't do that," he said. Jane had basically taken herself out of the race by showing others that her relationship with her boyfriend was more important than her professional image and job.

DON'T BE TOUGH TO DEAL WITH

As an entry-level person (and even when you're beyond entry level), people in your company are going to bother you all day with requests for this and requests for that. It's a drag. You're trying to get your work done, and you keep getting interrupted. It's like trying to have sex in your dorm room while your roommates, one by one, start knocking on the door, ostensibly looking for something. It can drive you crazy. When you are asked for something from a fellow employee, your gut reaction might be to blow them off, give them attitude, and not give them what they've asked you for. I've seen this a lot. Believe me, a lot of people fall prey to this temptation and are assholes to their coworkers. If you do this, you'll get a reputation for being uncooperative. Not a reputation you want.

definition

EMPLOYEE OF THE MONTH:
1. Any worker voluntarily engaged in a sexual relationship with his or her head supervisor.
2. That employee who most successfully creates the appearance of actually liking their boss.

As Neal Justin at the *Minneapolis Star Tribune* says, "I've seen people who are continually hard to deal with get a reputation, and it only makes it harder for them to move up."

Again, if you cop an attitude because you can't handle the shit that's being thrown at you, all you're doing is telling people you're not smart enough to handle the pressure.

BE THE HAPPY/OPTIMISTIC PERSON

quote

"I don't want any yes-men around me. I want everybody to tell me the truth even if it costs them their jobs."
—Samuel Goldwyn

Moody people suck. That's all there is to it. Being moody is not okay. It's a sign of weakness. It's an announcement that, deep down, you're an unhappy person. People don't want to hear what a shitty night you had, and they don't want to see it on your face. People want to work with, want to promote, people who are consistently upbeat and happy.

Think again of the infomercial guy Tony Robbins. *This* is the guy you want on your team. *This* is the guy you want to see in the office every day. So if you're a moody, unhappy person, do yourself a favor and get some therapy.

Chapter 28

SOME MORE STUFF TO CONSIDER

THE BENEFITS OF BEING LIKED

Some people, I realize, might come off as being moody or unfriendly when actually they're not. It's just who they are. I know someone like this. She's extremely nice, but she's not fake. One way that she's managed to make herself more approachable to people is by always having candy and pretzels in bowls in her office. All day long people are walking in and out of her office. Not only is it a friendly gesture, but it also has the great effect of keeping her in the game, so to speak. People come into her office for candy, and usually, information and/or gossip is exchanged. If something is going on in the company, *she* is going to hear about it right away. As you'll find out, being included, being informed, having people tell you things, is crucial in any office. It's when people stop including you in things and stop telling you things that you are in trouble.

STAY IN TOUCH WITH THE DEPARTED

Make sure you keep in touch with coworker friends who leave your company for another one. Get together for drinks every other month and invite them to a dinner party once in a while. You never know when you're going to quit or get laid off and need this person. Plus,

> **fact**
>
> **"I'm soooo busy"**
> The average American worker complains about having less than twenty hours of free time a week, yet admits to watching twenty-one hours of TV.
> —*American Demographics* magazine, June 1996

this person will have made additional contacts that could also be beneficial to you in a future job search.

YOUR COWORKER THE HUMAN RESOURCES PERSON

Besides your more senior hotshot coworkers, you also need to suck up to at least one human resources person. Make it a point to become friends with them. They can prove invaluable to you in the future, so lay the groundwork of a friendship in the beginning, before you need them.

Anything can happen in your new job that will make you wish you had a friend in HR. For example:

Your Boss Could Be a Psycho Maniac

Your boss seemed like a somewhat normal guy in the interview and the first three weeks. What you didn't know was that he has a predilection for yelling and throwing his shoes at you. If you've made friends with an HR person and they like you and think you're a good guy, then they might support you in transferring to another department or another job. If they don't know who the hell you are, and you go to them and complain that your boss is being abusive, then they probably won't go out of their way to help you. People help people they know and like in life. Work is no different.

Your Boss Might Get Fired

If your boss is canned, and your job is dependent upon his being there, your company has no obligation to keep you. If, however, you've made an effort to show an HR person that you're an asset to the company, they will definitely go out of their way to find another job for you. If they just remember you as "that guy" they interviewed a few months past and have no idea of your worth, there's no reason for them to go out of their way to help keep you in the company.

You Might Want to Transfer

Say you go on vacation and fall in love with some woman who lives three thousand miles away, and you *have* to be near her or you'll die. Chances are, your boss isn't going to be very supportive about your leaving him high and dry to be near some girl who's probably going to dump you in a few months anyway.

For example, after seven months of working at Company X in Los Angeles, I decided I wanted to move back to New York. Company X, however, had an unwritten policy of not allowing assistants to transfer from one coast to the other. Why? I have no idea. I knew my boss wouldn't be supportive about the move, to say the least. She had wanted a two-year commitment from me, and here I was leaving after seven months. (If she hadn't been a total jerk to me, I would have stayed the two years, no problem.) There was no way she was going to help me out.

There was no one in HR for me to turn to, as I had never interviewed with them. So I called the HR person in the New York office directly and explained that for personal reasons I wanted to move back to New York. She was nice but told me they really don't allow it.

Not willing to take no for an answer, I asked an assistant friend who had been there a long time what she would do. She told me that I should talk to the executive assistant of one of the bigwigs in the L.A. office. We'll call this person Ralph. I was told that Ralph wielded a lot of power because he was friends with the New York HR person. There was one problem, though, my friend said. Ralph isn't very approachable. "How do I get to Ralph, then?" I asked. She told me that his friend Marjorie (name changed to protect the innocent) was friends with Ralph and that Ralph trusted Marjorie's opinion. I kind of knew Marjorie but not enough to ask her to recommend me to this Ralph guy. So over the next few weeks, I developed a friendship with Marjorie, not telling her about my planned move.

When I did confide in her that I wanted to transfer to New York, Marjorie said, "You should talk to Ralph. He's only an executive assistant, but he wields a lot of power and is friends with the HR person in New York." I told Marjorie that I didn't know Ralph, and she kindly offered to introduce us and to give me a good referral.

I met with Ralph and asked if there was any way he could help me in my quest to transfer. We spoke for ten minutes, and he said he'd see what he could do. After the meeting I ran to the store and bought him a card, thanking him for his time. A few days later he told me that the New York HR person was expecting my call.

In the meantime I had also asked agents whom I knew in the New York office to send E-mails to the HR person there saying what a good guy and hard worker I was. So when I called the HR person a few days later, she said, "Well, I've heard a lot of good things about you." It worked. They made an exception and let me transfer.

Chapter 29

NETWORKING OUTSIDE OF YOUR COMPANY

The last chapter was basically about sucking up to the right people at your job. This chapter is about making friends with people on the outside.

Remember how I said that getting hired was all about getting the person interviewing you to like you? Well, succeeding, becoming successful, requires the same thing—getting people to like you. And not just at your own company. The people you talk to on the phone all day from different companies are just as important for your career as your boss is. After a year or two on the job, the people whom you do business with at other companies are the first people you're going to call when you're looking to make a job change.

Again: After a year or two on the job, the people whom you do business with at other companies are the first people you're going to call when you're looking to make a job change.

So start making phone buddies with all the assistants and higher-ups who call for you and your boss. Ask

fact

Happy, Schmappy
An estimated 20 million Americans are staying in jobs they hate in order to keep their health insurance.

them their name and introduce yourself. If you're starting out as an assistant, it's probably not appropriate to ask someone out to lunch who is calling for your boss and who is on the same level as your boss. But it is a good idea to ask this person's assistant out to lunch.

You've got to start making friends with as many people as you can. You might be fired next week, you never know. Therefore, you want to have people lined up at different companies who know and like you, whom you can call and ask if there are any openings at their company.

START AN ASSISTANTS CLUB

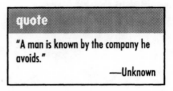

If you're an assistant, something you might consider doing is starting an assistants networking group. While I was working in Los Angeles in film, I had heard of this one group of assistants who would meet for breakfast every Friday at 7:30 A.M. A friend of mine in the group asked me to join them, but for whatever reason, I was too stupid and never showed.

The group consisted of assistants at talent agencies and at production companies. The production company assistants would mention what scripts they need directors and actors for, and the talent agent assistants would pitch their agencies' clients for the jobs. Then, the talent agency assistants would go to work and tell their boss that such and such production company is looking for a director for such and such script. If this is news to the boss, then this assistant gets a pat on the back and hopefully some recognition in a staff meeting or something. Likewise, the production company assistants would go back to their boss and suggest a couple of directors who might be appropriate for the movie they're producing.

Not only are these assistants bringing in information to their bosses, which can only help to make them look good, but those breakfast meetings are also a place where they all share information about what jobs are available, or will soon be available, at their companies. Assistant networks are great opportunities to form tight bonds with people whom you will know for the duration of your career. Remember, it's who you know.

GIVING THE RIGHT IMPRESSION

Knowing that the people you talk to on the phone all day are critical to your future, you have to make sure that you're making the right impression with them—that is, that you are a hardworking, conscientious, thorough workaholic. Doing this is simple, and amazingly, it's rare. Here's how it's done. When somebody calls you from a company you work with, it's generally because they need something. Numbers or information of one kind or another. The manner and speed with which you get the person calling the thing they need will determine how they think of you. Either you are slow and not very helpful, or you are fast and very helpful. Either you are competent in their eyes, or you are incompetent. Believe me, they will be judging you. The Bible says not to judge your fellow man, but you *will* be judged.

For instance, when I used to work at the William Morris Agency, part of my job was talking to casting directors and casting directors' assistants. They would call up and ask me for an actor's head shot or their work availability. As an assistant, this was my job; my boss was too busy negotiating deals to handle little things like this. So whenever a casting director would call, it was *my* job to make sure they got what they needed. Even if I was completely in the weeds, I would take the time to get them the information they needed as soon as humanly possible. Apparently, other assistants weren't nearly as helpful as I was, for I would constantly hear from casting people how much they appreciated the fact that I got them what they needed right away. On several occasions casting people said to me, "If you ever want to quit the agency and go into casting, then call me."

---

definition

CLIENT:
The individual you would suck up to even if it turned out they had a Nazi past or, say, delighted in killing endangered marine mammals.

GIVING THE WRONG IMPRESSION

I was in my book agent's office the other day hanging out. (Now, instead of working for an agent, I *have* one.) A call came from an assistant editor at a publishing house, a guy who is editing one of her clients' books. When she got off the phone with him, I could tell that she was annoyed. "What, bad call?" I asked. "Every call with this guy is bad," she said. She went on to tell me how unpleasant this guy was to deal with. Yeah, they were in the process of final negotiations for a book, something that is rarely ever pleasant, but this kid was just such a weasel, she hated dealing with him. In fact, she kind of vowed never to do business with him again—which, for him, is very bad news.

As an assistant editor, a wanna-be editor, he is dependent on agents. An editor's job is to have good relationships with all the agents around town so they send you books that you can, in turn, buy for your publishing house. Without agents, you don't have access to quality writers. The fact that this editor, in the beginning of his career, wasn't making a concerted effort to be liked by my agent might not kill his career, but it is definitely going to hurt it. You can be sure that my agent will tell her peers what a putz this guy is, what a pain in the ass he is to deal with, and they might not send books his way either.

So don't shoot yourself in the foot early in your career by being a hard-ass. People like to do business with people they like, not with jerks.

FEATURE INTERVIEW

Amy Cacciola
Assistant director of public relations
ESPN X-Games
Providence College, class of 1995
23 years old
French major, marketing minor

Going into her senior year at Providence College, Amy had no idea what she was going to do with her life. Nothing really grabbed her. "To be honest, I didn't want to do anything," she says. And then the circus showed up in town.

Well, maybe not the circus but pretty close to it. It was ESPN's X-Games—the Rollerblading, street luge, BMX bike freestyle, skateboarding, grunge Olympics that was taking place in Newport, right near Amy's college.

Sounds cool, thought Amy when she found out they were looking for unpaid interns for the spring semester. The only thing was, over a hundred other students thought the same thing. So how did Amy snag the nonpaying, highly sought after gig over all the others? Grades, you'd think, right?

Wrong. "My grades were okay. I'm not a school person. I don't like to study. I'd rather take pictures or write for the newspaper than study," she says. And that's exactly what she did her four years, as well as manage the volleyball team.

Ironically, it was these study-avoiding extracurricular activities that secured an internship spot with the games. That and her experience as a toll collector for the Massachusetts Turnpike Authority at Logan Airport, which Amy boldly included on her résumé.

You see, while Amy was collecting fares, Larry Bird came to her booth the day before he retired. So Amy had him sign a five-dollar bill. And as it turned out, the guy she interviewed with at the X-Games "happened to be the biggest Larry Bird fan on the planet," says Amy. "So I think that's what did it for me. He was jealous," she says, laughing.

You'd think she'd be reluctant to put the toll-collecting job on her résumé. You'd also think she'd be reluctant to include her high school job—five years at a supermarket. Not very impressive stuff. She didn't see it this way, however. "I wanted him to see that I wasn't afraid to work hard," she says.

And that's what she did during her internship. "I worked my butt off," she says. "I did absolutely everything. I always said, 'What else can I do? Give me more and more projects.' "

This is something that not all the interns did, however. "Some interns come in," says Amy, and "they think it's glamorous. They think, 'Oh, I'm going to work for ESPN.' They'll say, 'What else do you have to do? This isn't fun.' Yeah, it's not fun. You don't start out as the CEO."

Not even close. After graduation, while all her friends were making two hundred bucks a night waiting tables and lying on the beach all day, Amy stayed with the X-Games in a type of postinternship gig making two hundred dollars a week.

"I was completely jealous of those guys," she says. "I was working sixty hours a week for what they would make in one night. Plus, I was waitressing on weekends to pay the bills. So I was working seven days a week."

Her jealousy soon ended, however, when she walked away at the end of the summer with a full-time job as assistant director of public relations—a job each of the other five paid interns were vying for but Amy snagged. How come, you ask? Good question.

"I showed the greatest amount of interest and was willing to devote as much time as was needed," she says. "Plus, I had expressed interest to my boss from the very beginning." How? She was honest—and unintimidated. "I said to him, 'This is something I obviously enjoy and something I think I do a good job at. Would you consider hiring me as assistant director? Can you give me a chance?' "

Well, they were a little reluctant because she was so young and right out of school. In fact, it wouldn't have happened for Amy if her immediate boss (the Larry Bird fan) hadn't pulled for her. When Amy asked him a few months after she landed the gig why he *did* pull for her, he said, "I just knew that you would work your ass off."

When I ask Amy what sucks about her job, it takes her a minute, but then she answers, "I don't think this is a drawback, but my boyfriend does and my friends do. They seem to think that the long hours are a drawback 'cause they never get to see me. But if I could stay awake, I'd work twenty-four hours a day. Unfortunately, I need to sleep for about six of them."

Pretty annoying, huh? How can *anybody* like their job this much? Hang on, it gets worse. "When people ask me about my job, I say, I wake up every morning and go, 'Oh, I'm going to work. I'm so excited! It's fantastic!' My parents are jealous. They're like fifty years old, and they wake up and go 'Oh, we're going to work.' I can't wait. I'm not kidding you. I'm a freak of nature. I'm very lucky."

Chapter 30

PAYING YOUR DUES

WHAT ENTRY LEVEL IS

All right, say you're lucky and someone decides to give you money, a job, because the guy before you who used to answer the phone, type things, get coffee, pick up the boss's dry cleaning, water the plants, etc., got sick of it, decided it wasn't worth it, gave up, and went home.

Funny. When they hired you, you *thought* you heard them say, "We're looking for smart people who are ambitious, who will grow with the company, blah, blah, blah." Well, they're not going to attract you to the job by saying, "We want someone who's going to be content answering the phones and doing all the shitwork with no chance of advancement."

What am I getting at? It's this. The majority of entry-level jobs out there are just that—entry-level. They're low-responsibility, assistant-type jobs. How can they be much more? You just graduated from college. You have no real experience. What can you really offer an employer? They've hired you to provide assistance. They've dipped into their profits to hire someone to make their lives easier and to help them do their jobs better. They haven't hired you thinking, "Oh, won't he eventually be able to do my job great one day?"

THE SHITWORK

A lot of entry-level people are misguided. They're like, "I'm hot stuff. I'm a graduate." Wake up, baby. You're at the bottom. Yeah, maybe they've tossed you some bone of a title with the word *associate* in it. Truth is, you ain't much more than Alice from *The Brady Bunch*. You're there to do the crap that nobody else wants to do. Picking up your boss's dry cleaning or someone's mother at the airport. Getting coffee. Straightening your boss's desk.

Not fair? Not what you were hired for? Listen, if someone's given you a job, you're lucky. The only reason you're there is because someone with energy, guts, and endurance, the level of which you (or I) can't even fathom, created something from nothing and is now able to offer people like you money. So in my book, employers have the right to ask you to do anything when you're entry-level, even if you don't think it falls within the realm of your responsibility.

Really, give up the notion of being above anything right now. If your boss tells you to do the dishes and you do it grudgingly, you're being foolish. He's not doing it to punish you. In his mind, his money and human resources are being spent best by having you, rather than someone else, do it. Complaining isn't going to convince him to have someone else do the dishes. Demonstrating that your time is too valuable to do that crap will.

Pretty much everyone I've interviewed over the years has told me stories about how interns and assistants have blown their chances of advancement by copping an attitude about doing the shitwork. I think Greg Drebin from MTV says it best:

> A lot of people come in and are like, "Well, I'm making copies, but that's really beneath me." But if you're making copies, be damn good at making copies. If you're just going through the motions and it's obvious that you're sick of it and you want to get out, no one is going to let you do anything. Because then it's like, well, if I hire you, are you going to do the same thing to me? Are you going to say, "Well, yeah, he hired me to do this, but what I really want to do is this, so I'll just go through the motions here." Uh-uh. I want someone who's going to be 100 percent.

TIME TO GIVE UP YOUR LIFE

If your first job doesn't absolutely consume you, if you're not thinking about it twenty-four hours a day, then, in my opinion, you're not going to go anywhere. If there's one quality that all of the young successful people I've interviewed share—one thing that stands out so clearly as being the major reason why they advanced in their careers while others have stood still—it would have to be their enthusiasm to work. Just the willingness to do anything. As a producer at Fox News said to me, "You either establish yourself as a hard worker or you don't."

GOOD NEWS: NINE OUT OF TEN ENTRY–LEVELERS SUCK

> **quote**
> "Nothing succeeds like the appearance of success."
> —Christopher Lasch

Sure, you've got competition all around you. But the good news is that nine out of ten of your entry-level coworkers fail to present and establish themselves as hard workers—as stars. And it's only the stars who advance. Being good might have gotten you somewhere post-WWII, when things boomed for forty years. But now it just won't do.

Listen to what Becky, a commercial and music video producer, expects from entry-levelers:

> I'll do people favors and hire them if they really want to get in as a P.A. [production assistant—entry-level]. I'll open the door for them. But unless they really kick it in, I'll never ask them back. You know what I'm saying? You want people who are really hungry. And there just doesn't seem to be any of that anymore. I run into that so rarely nowadays. I want people who are like me, who just work like slaves to get where they want to go.

YOUR TWO OPTIONS

So you've got two options. You're either going to be that person who becomes so valuable, whom people cannot live without, or you're not. You'll work relatively hard. Hard enough. And then you'll start bitching about the person who sailed by you and got the position you wanted to get. That person being the former of the two types.

In every company there are two types of people: the rare, exceptional person who gets promoted, and the other kind—the whiner who bitches "Whose ass did they kiss to get that promotion?"

Part 8

Moving Up the Ladder: From Being an Assistant to Having One

Chapter 31

YOUR PREDICAMENT

WAITING FOR SOMEONE TO KICK THE BUCKET

Somebody dies. Somebody quits. Somebody retires. Somebody gets sent to jail. When you're an assistant and you don't want to be an assistant anymore—you want to be a real person—these occurrences never seem to happen. At least not often enough. You're just waiting for someone to keel over at their desk and be carted away down the service elevator.

What's worse, the people above you with the jobs you want are, in most cases, baby boomers. Those nowhere-near-retirement, healthy, Chinese-chicken-salad-eating, Stairmaster-climbing, mountain-biking, trying-to-make-up-for-all-the-drugs-they-did-in-the-seventies type of people. In other words, they ain't going nowhere—by death or by choice. They've got a mortgage, a kid, a Saab, stock options, alimony; they're there for life. There to make upstarts like yourself crazy.

fact

"Hey, Baby"
Forty-five percent of women in white-collar jobs experience sexual harassment. More than 10 percent report deliberate touching or cornering, and 10 percent say they are pressured for dates.
—Klein & Associates

NOBODY CARES ABOUT YOUR FUTURE

The sad truth is, nobody really cares if you move up the ladder or not. I know, it's a bummer. But it gets worse. Not only does no one care, there are actually people like yourself—competitive, power-hungry, ambitious overachievers—who don't want you to succeed, who would gladly step over your dead body to get ahead of you to get that promotion.

---

definition

BACHELOR OF ARTS DEGREE:
Paper certificate written in Latin costing tens of thousands of dollars that proves you had no idea what you wanted to do with your life at twenty-two.

Stop. Hold it. Back up. What I just said is probably the biggest fallacy a young person believes about the working world—that you get "promoted." Listen up, because this is important. Nobody is going to say to you, "Hey, you've been doing a great job. Here's your reward: You're promoted!" Get over that idea right now. I'm telling you, if you ever move up the ladder, you're not going to thank, or be grateful to, anybody but yourself.

So how do you go from being this low-life human coffeemaker to being a real person with a real job? It starts with this: you've got to want it. That's it. Whoever wants it the most gets it.

Fortunately, or unfortunately, this may go against how you thought it worked—sleeping with the boss, nepotism, being a kiss-ass, being really smart and charming, etc. A little of all of these won't hurt you and might be necessary (now, I'm not saying to jump in bed with your boss), but without that *je ne sais quoi*, that burning desire, the want, the need to prove yourself—you don't have a chance.

All the crap that follows, about how to behave and what to do in the workplace in order to move up the ladder, depends on your wanting "it" more than everybody else. So if you don't really want it, travel around the world, watch a lot of TV, and get really bored until you do. Because in order to do the stuff that I'm gonna lay out, it's absolutely necessary.

YOU AND YOUR BOSS

Whether you're starting a job as an entry-level assistant (secretary) or as an "associate" with actual responsibilities, your future, your chances of moving up the ladder at that company, is pretty much in the hands of your boss. He can, and will, make you or break you. He will either make your life a living hell (or merely be indifferent to your career), or he will become like a mentor and help you move up the ladder. Generally, there is no middle ground here. In the Bible, God says that you are either for him or against him. There is no middle ground. It's the same with your boss. If he's not for your success, actually doing things to help you move up the ladder, then he is against your success.

Think I'm exaggerating? Take Lauren Marino's (see interview on pages 61–64) word for it:

> As an assistant, your career is so dependent on your boss. Your boss is the person who is going to let you learn things and who is going to give you more responsibility. If your boss really likes you and trusts you and gives you work, you're in a really good position. Ultimately, they're the person that's going to fight on your behalf to get you a promotion and a raise and get you more responsibility so that your job is more interesting.

Scream, Beg, Plead

After Jenna had worked for a year and a half as an editorial assistant at a large publishing house, and another year and a half as an assistant editor, she finally became an associate editor—something without an *assistant* in the title. But it didn't come easy. "Basically my boss just yelled and screamed [to the higher-ups], and we begged and pleaded. He's like, 'Look, she's doing all this work, she's acquiring her own books, and she's doing my books [editing her boss's books].' I was also pretty pushy: 'It's time to promote me. I need more money. I need more money.' If I'd been like, *this* much pushier, I would have driven everyone insane and been fired," she says.

The problem is, your boss isn't inclined to really give a shit about you. He's got his own ass to look out for. He's probably so worried about losing his own job, he can't worry about you keeping yours— let alone worry about whether or not you move up the ladder.

In order to pull your boss out of his self-centeredness, you've got to stand out like no other person under him has stood out before. You've got to make his life and his job so much easier and stress-free that he will feel guilty if he doesn't make it his mission to help you succeed. In other words, you've got to get him to love you. The next chapter tells how to do this.

Chapter 32

GIVE YOUR BOSS THE IMPRESSION YOU GIVE A SHIT: GETTING YOUR BOSS TO LOVE YOU, PART I

Impressions are everything. Having your boss love you is crucial. Here's how to win his love by giving him the right impression.

THE BASICS

Arrive Early

If starting time is 9:00 A.M., get there by 8:30 A.M. Though bosses will never say anything, they are aware of what time you get to work. And though they might not seem to care, they do. The easiest way to say to your boss (and to others) "Hey, I'm here to kick some butt. I care about this company, and I care about my job" is to get there before everyone else.

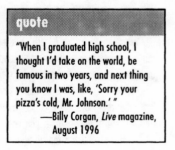

quote

"When I graduated high school, I thought I'd take on the world, be famous in two years, and next thing you know I was, like, 'Sorry your pizza's cold, Mr. Johnson.' "
—Billy Corgan, *Live* magazine, August 1996

Stay Late

Never, ever leave before your boss. Even if you have no work to do and have to *pretend* you're working, fine, do it. Not only will your boss be impressed by your willingness to work long hours, but it's a great opportunity to do some bonding with him, and with other people.

In addition, staying late is a great way to include yourself in projects you normally wouldn't be included in. For example, if a senior executive is staying late, it's probably because she's got a lot of crap to do. So if you're there at eight P.M. and she needs help, you're the person she's going to go to. But don't wait for her to approach you. Go to her office and say, "Here late, huh? Can I give you a hand with anything?"

Take Lunch at Your Desk

Even though you're given an hour for lunch, you might want to think about taking it at your desk. Your boss may not say to you, "You know, I'd really prefer it if you took lunch at your desk instead of acting like you're a government employee with your hour-long lunch breaks." However, if a bunch of your coworkers are going out for lunch and invite you, then by all means go. (And if they don't invite you, ask them if they wouldn't mind if you went with them.)

Setting Boundaries

It's ten P.M., you're at home chilling out after a long day at work, and your phone rings. It's your boss. "I can't believe you," she says. "You're senseless. What's wrong with you? You're not using your brain!" She yells some more and slams the phone in your ear.

What would *you* do? Here's what Gail did. "The next day I walked in and said, 'I think your behavior was extremely inappropriate. I don't accept it, and I think I deserve an apology.' She kind of brushed it off and said, 'Yeah, yeah, yeah.' "

Evan though Gail's boss didn't apologize for her behavior, sticking up for herself was what really mattered. "I had to tell her how I felt," Gail says. "You definitely have to set a line somewhere. If you want to feel good about where you're working and what you do, and not feel like you're swallowing your pride all the time, you have to set boundaries and limits to how much people can abuse you in your work area." Right on.

Come in on Weekends

If you just said to yourself, "Forget it. I'm not coming in on weekends unless they *pay* me to come in on weekends," then your attitude sucks. Try to get your money back for this book, because I don't even want to be in the same room with you. You're an idiot, and you should get a job at the post office (not that people who work for the post office are idiots by any means. Many people in my family were postal employees), where you *will* get paid for coming in on Saturdays.

You don't have to come in every Saturday for a year, only for the first few months. However, don't waste your Saturday unless someone is there to notice that you're wasting your Saturday. A nice trick to make people think you've worked all weekend is to send E-mails either from home or the office on the weekend. An E-mail that takes five minutes to write on a Saturday morning makes it look like you were working at least a good part of the day.

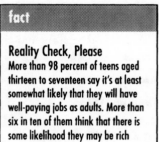

fact

Reality Check, Please
More than 98 percent of teens aged thirteen to seventeen say it's at least somewhat likely that they will have well-paying jobs as adults. More than six in ten of them think that there is some likelihood they may be rich someday.

—Gallup poll

Listen to what Becky, a freelance commercial and music video producer, did on her first job to prove herself:

When I first started, I didn't know anything. I didn't know how to type. I was a disaster at phones. Everyone wanted to fire me. Everyone treated me like shit. It was frowned upon when you left early. I got that right away. So even though I was making a pittance, I would go there two hours early and just type the dictionary or any document that was sitting around. Or even though I had nothing to do with a job—you know, all the grown-ups would be on the other side of the room freaking out over some problem—I would just stay. No one would give me any responsibility, but I was just there all the time until they left, *then* I would leave. I would just stay. I wanted a better job. I wanted to be one of them.

A QUICK SELF-EVALUATION

Wondering whether or not you're giving the impression that you give a shit? Ask yourself these questions about yourself:

- Do you welcome assignments, even the shitty ones, like when someone asks you to photocopy their Rolodex?
- Do you ask for additional work?
- Do you hide from additional work?
- Are you well groomed and presentable?
- Do you take yourself seriously?
- Are you pleasant and optimistic?
- Are you a complainer?

The Real Skinny with . . . Lance Fung, Art Gallery Owner

FROM INTERN TO ASSISTANT:
As an intern, I worked hard. I was probably the fastest label sticker. I didn't know a thing about the computer when I started. I didn't know how to turn one on. By the end of that first week, I knew every system backwards and forwards. I came in early; I stayed late. I came in every day with a happy face, and I left every day with a happy face, and I made people enjoy their jobs.

THAT AIN'T WORKING:
There's no such thing as a vacation, and there's no such thing as a day off. You eat, sleep, and live work seven days a week, twenty-four hours a day. I could be in Venice, Italy, taking a water taxi down the Grand Canal, and then I'm off to a gallery to see art. How can you call that work? You can't call that work.

AGEISM:
Being a twenty-seven-year-old dealer was a big challenge. The first year I wore suits. I thought that was a way to look older. That was an insecurity that I had, though I think it was valid. You don't spend a million dollars with someone who's younger than your son or daughter, except if they say something that a sixty-year-old would say, right? But now I don't give a shit. People have come to respect me even more because they understand that I don't give a shit and that I am telling them exactly what I believe in, take it or leave it.

BREAKING IN:

Within the employment portion of the art world, it's ruthless, it's brutal, it's backbiting, it's backstabbing, and I don't think it's necessarily the most pleasant environment. However, I really think if you're true, you're smart, you're aware, and people can see that you're sincere, then you can break in. I really do.

Chapter 33

Don't Suck: Getting Your Boss to Love You, Part II

All right, you're sending out the signals that you give a shit by doing the obvious stuff like getting there early and staying late. But this is just scratching the surface of getting your boss to love you. At this point, if you've done the above, maybe he's beginning to *like* you.

Love starts to develop in your boss's cold little heart when he begins to respect you. When he begins to realize that you don't suck. (Not simply because you're there early and late.) You see, even though he's hired you himself, he's naturally going to assume that you suck. Why? Because most new hires *do* suck. It's not until most young people's second or third job that they realize, "Wow, unless I really kick it into gear—unless I eat, breathe, and sleep work—I'm not going to get anywhere." Here are a few basics on how to prove to your boss (and your coworkers) that you don't suck.

Don't Suck

"Not screwing up is the main reason you do well at work. You just have to do your work, basically, and do it right. The thing is, most people are very mediocre at their jobs. So if you can be good at it, you're better than everybody else. And most people don't even like their jobs. So if you can find a job that you like, you're going to succeed."

—J. J. Fix, advertising executive

YOU MUST BE A PERFECTIONIST

It's the little things. If you want your boss to trust you to do more important things than photocopying and filing, then you have to prove that you can do those things—photocopying and filing—perfectly. People (your boss and other people over you) are afraid to give away even the slightest bit of responsibility for fear that you will screw it up. Your first few months on the job are going to be about their seeing whether or not they can trust you with the little things. If so, then you have a *chance* of being trusted with bigger things.

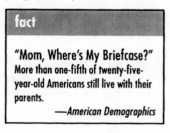

fact

"Mom, Where's My Briefcase?"
More than one-fifth of twenty-five-year-old Americans still live with their parents.
—American Demographics

So when anybody asks you to do what seems to be a very simple task, make sure you do it perfectly. When somebody says, "Hey, will you photocopy these articles and bring them back to me?" Believe me, they will look very closely at how good a job you did. Are the copies centered? Are they the right shade? Do they look great? If you've done a perfect job with them, as stupid as it sounds, they will notice and say, "Okay, this person is thorough. This person gives a shit." Then, you're in the running to be trusted with bigger, more important projects.

definition

RETIREMENT:
The state that attaches to you at the exact moment you are fired from the last job you'll ever have.

YOU MUST HAVE FOLLOW-THROUGH

Being a perfectionist (in my definition in the preceding section) has to do with being detail-oriented—typing a letter that is perfectly centered, with everybody's name spelled correctly, with perfect grammar, and with zero typos. Having good follow-through is about doing and completing something in a timely manner.

For example, if someone asks for a list of all potential donors or a list of the best hotels in San Francisco, make sure you get this to them as soon as humanly possible. Though this sounds so basic, more than half of you won't do it. It's true. Someone will ask you for something, you'll say "Sure," and you'll put it on the back burner until they ask for it again. Then, when they ask you again, that's when your brain says, "Oh, they asked for it again. I guess they really want it."

Don't Be Told Twice

A major complaint among bosses about their assistants (or associates) is, "I always have to ask for something twice. I ask them for something that I guess they don't think is very important, and they don't give it to me. A week later I'll be looking for that thing, assuming they've given it to me, and I won't be able to find it. Then all of a sudden it's *my* fault because I forgot to remind them to get it for me? I don't think so."

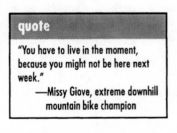

quote

"You have to live in the moment, because you might not be here next week."

—Missy Giove, extreme downhill mountain bike champion

Write It Down

I don't want to insult you, but when your boss asks you to do something, write it down. Don't assume you're going to remember; you won't. I swear, if you write down every little thing your boss asks you to do and you actually do it without her having to remind you, you are going to shock the hell out of her. I'd say that at least 90 percent of the entry-levelers out there do not do this. If you *do* do this, you can be sure that your boss will entrust you with more important things, knowing you can be trusted to follow through.

NEVER TAKE NO FOR AN ANSWER

People don't like to hear no. Bosses especially. Your boss is going to ask you for something—last week's sales numbers, reservations at the hottest restaurant, whatever—and people are very often going to tell you no. "No, those numbers aren't available yet." "No, there are absolutely no tables available." "No, Mr. Steinbrenner cannot be reached today. He is unavailable."

Well, this is unacceptable. In the business world *no* rarely ever means "no." You can't go back to your boss and say, "Sorry, he can't be reached. He's gone for the weekend," or whatever excuse you've been given why you can't get whomever on the phone. It's just not good enough. You have to *find* a way to get him on the phone. You have to *find* a way to *make* him available.

FEATURE   INTERVIEW

Michael Meisel
Artist manager (music), Gold Mountain Management
28 years old
University of Michigan, 1990

"Hello, Michael?"
"That's me."
"Hi, I left word on your machine. I'm the guy who's writing the book *Jobs That Don't Suck.*"
"Then you must have the wrong number." (Laughs.)
"I don't know, I thought managing bands for a living was a pretty unsucky thing to do."
"Yeah, it can occasionally not suck," he concedes.
"Do you have time to talk?" I ask him.
"Sure," he says as he tells his assistant to hold all calls.
Cool, I thought. He's going to pass on all his calls to talk to me . . . an uninterrupted interview. *Wrong.* To his credit—every twenty seconds he says to his assistant, "I'll call him back," when a call comes in, but about every other minute, he says, "I'm sorry, Charlie, . . . I've got to take this." Then, a few minutes later, he comes back with some explanation of why he *had* to take the call. Here was one such explanation: "That was a marketing director at a record label, and I have an album coming out on his label in two weeks. He's a very powerful guy and controls the money. *That's* the first rule of the music business (and life), you know: When the person who controls the purse strings calls, . . . you *always* take the call."
That might be the first rule of the record business for Michael now, but I doubt it was of much concern to him thirteen years ago when he got his first job—as a runner for the River-bend Music Center in Cincinnati, Ohio. Back then, the rules were simply "Get whatever the band

needs . . . and pass out these fliers." But it was the rule three years later when he signed his first client at age eighteen, someone he still represents today.

"I've been doing stuff in music—both as a performer and on the business side—since I was twelve," says Michael. "I've only had one job not in music, and that was as a junior salesperson in my father's furniture store one summer, which I really enjoyed." While he clearly likes what he does, Meisel is not without some second thoughts: "I will always regret not being able to work more with my father. . . . I learn more from watching him work than I do from anyone in the music business."

While in college, Meisel led what he now terms a "less than exemplary academic existence." "I never went to class. I remember telling my mother that I was learning more in college than I've ever learned in my life, but I was learning it all between the hours of twelve A.M. and four A.M. I was fortunate enough to have become friends with some of the smartest people I'd ever met. . . . I learned so much just by being around them. What's funny is that I keep in close touch with many of them . . . and they are still some of the smartest people I know." While many of these friends were more academically oriented, Meisel did not put too much effort into grades. "I'm a bachelor of general studies . . . a B.G.S. degree. . . . The 'G' was optional," Meisel says. "I'm basically educationally qualified to be, like, a talk show host."

Michael's remaining college summers—after the stint selling furniture—were spent involved in music. He promoted concerts in Cincinnati with his best friend since first grade (whom he still speaks to at least once a week) and went to Los Angeles to intern with a large management company. "I got the internship by sending a letter telling them I was a smart guy who was in school at the University of Michigan . . . and that I'd work for free for the entire summer."

It was that internship that led to Meisel's first job out of college—with Triad Artists in Los Angeles, a large talent agency that has since merged with the even larger William Morris Agency. Turning down a spot in their prestigious training program ("I had no interest in being validated by my ability to pick up dry cleaning"), Meisel managed instead to get a position as an assistant to an agent in the company's variety (i.e., shows your parents would go to) department. While 95 percent of such positions were filled by members of the training program, none of them were interested in the position, as it involved working with gaming territories (Las Vegas, Atlantic City), for clients like Johnny Mathis and Engelbert Humperdinck. Though it wasn't necessarily the "sexy" end of the music business, Meisel learned a great deal from the experience. "For starters, I learned that those acts make lots of money!"

Still, Meisel knew that he would eventually have to move from the department and start working on music that he actually liked. Eventually, the arrival of a new agent in the contemporary ("rock") department provided the opportunity. This wasn't without repercussions, however. Meisel's desire to switch departments upset the agent he'd been working with—who tried to have him fired. "It was the first time I'd experienced anyone proactively trying to have a negative effect on my career . . . and I've never forgotten it." If Michael hadn't made allies at the company who stuck up for him, he might have lost his job.

(For the record, Meisel was vindicated a few years later when, at the MTV Music Awards, he saw the agent who had tried to have him fired. "I was already working for Gold Mountain and was there with Nirvana," Michael remembers. Given the circumstances, Meisel had a pass that allowed him unrestricted access to all areas backstage—access that was denied to his former boss. "He saw me at the credentials gate and struck up a conversation. While I was polite, I had no problem walking through the gate while the security guards stopped him at the door." Looking back over his shoulder at the guy who had tried to impede the growth of his career, Meisel felt as if the score had been settled. "I have always sworn never to do anything to hurt anyone, ever. . . . The fact that fate allowed for that little moment was all the payback I could ever want.")

Now in the contemporary department, Meisel then had to work his way up the sometimes slippery political ladder toward the goal of being made an agent ("knighted" is how he put it). "Getting that promotion was like a never-ending search for the holy grail," Meisel muses. He finally ended up leaving the company before being made an agent. "I was fortunate in that my decision to attempt a move to artist management coincided with an opening at the most respected management company in the business."

While becoming an agent was important to him at the time, Meisel is now more circumspect about the position. "I got into the music business because I felt I possessed the ability to conceptualize what a band was about and what decisions should be made in all areas of their career: what kind of records they should be making, how they should be marketed, who they should tour with, what T-shirts should look like . . . everything." While Meisel is quick to point out how important agents are to the equation, he prefers management, in that "I like overseeing the whole pie and not just a slice."

On the recommendation of a friend from Triad, Meisel got an interview with Gold Mountain Entertainment for an assistant's job. "I was lucky, in that the guy who was leaving (who was also given the autonomy over hiring his own replacement) was a guy from Cincinnati—my hometown." Though they didn't know each other, members of their families were friends. "We'd never met, but we knew of each other for quite some time." After one interview, Meisel was offered the position.

Meisel then went to work as one of two assistants for John Silva, then a manager and now president of Gold Mountain. "It was crazy . . . *crazy*," Meisel remembers. "I went from issuing contracts for some hundred-seat club in Albuquerque to working on the entire careers of Nirvana and Sonic Youth (and later for Beck)." While he admits to wanting to strangle his new boss from time to time in the beginning (let's just say that John can be a little "high-strung"), there is no one whose instinct for the music business he respects more. "If I said something was blue and John said the same thing was red, . . . I'd stare at it for a few minutes and say, 'Well, . . . is it red?' . . . There aren't many people in whose opinion I'm that confident."

Now, after a few years working as an assistant, Michael has the freedom to sign and work with his own bands, though he does have strict criteria for these signings. "First off, they have to be great. Secondly, they have to be high-quality people. I have no desire to work with people that I wouldn't invite to my wedding. I would stand in front of a train for any one of my clients . . . and I know they'd do the same for me."

Basically, artist management can, in Meisel's estimation, be viewed in terms of a normal corporate structure. "If you look at a band as a corporate entity, there are different facets of the 'company.' The band's record label and merchandiser (T-shirts, etc.) can be equated with a production arm of a company. The band's lawyer is that company's legal affairs department. The band's business manager is the company's accounting department, etc. . . . Additionally, there are booking agents, publishers, publicists, concert promoters, and dozens of other integral players in any band's career. Viewed like that, the artist is the chairman of the board, and I'm the president of the company."

Though Michael enjoys what he does, it can be a bit draining. "Management is an eight-day-a-week, twenty-five-hour-a-day proposition." Meisel feels wholly responsible for the lives of his clients. While he thinks this trait makes him a more effective manager, he also realizes that it takes a great deal of energy to sustain. "Instead of having my own problems as a human being, I tend to absorb the problems of my clients . . . putting the problems of twenty people on my shoulders. I once had to end a relationship with a woman who always complained that I spent more time thinking about my 'kids' (clients) than I did thinking about her."

At the end of the day, however, Meisel takes a certain pride in what he does that is not at all unique to the music business. "Of all my friends from childhood, I'm the only one who had a particular goal from age twelve and is now doing exactly what he said he was going to do." Regardless of whether he has bad days, Meisel always remembers that he has lived up, at least in part, to ambitions he's held for sixteen years. "If I ever don't like what I'm doing, I have no one to blame but myself. . . . I did exactly what I said I was going to do."

"All right, last thing," I say. "How much cooler are people in the music business than the rest of us?" I ask Michael.

"Let's put it this way," Meisel says. "Ten years ago I would have thought I was *really* cool."

A Personal Story of Not Accepting No

I was house manager of this Broadway theater a few years ago. It was winter, it was raining, and water was leaking onto a few seats in the audience. The president of the theater happened to be in the audience at the time, spotted it, and came and told me. He told me to send one of the maintenance guys up there to find the problem, so I did. I told the guy to make sure all the drains were clear and so forth. He'd been there longer than I had, so he didn't need me to tell *him* what to do. Half an hour later there was still a leak. He said he couldn't find the problem. So I sent someone else up to the roof with him. Same thing. Couldn't find the leak. Instead of going to my boss and saying, "Sorry, we couldn't find it," I put on rain gear and boots and went up on the roof in the freezing rain with a flashlight and searched for about fifteen minutes until I located the problem. It was doing stupid little things like this that made my boss really appreciate me.

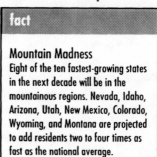

Mountain Madness
Eight of the ten fastest-growing states in the next decade will be in the mountainous regions. Nevada, Idaho, Arizona, Utah, New Mexico, Colorado, Wyoming, and Montana are projected to add residents two to four times as fast as the national average.
—*American Demographics*

NO WHINING

Here are some examples:

- "Do I *have* to?"
- "Isn't there someone *else* who can do it?"
- "You want me to come in on *Saturday?*"
- "You want me to type it *again?*"
- "You want me to finish that *tonight?* I'll be here until nine P.M."

Even if you think you have a good relationship with your boss and can jokingly whine about things, don't. The only thing your boss wants to hear when they give you a shitload of work and say, "Sorry, got more for you," is "No problem."

Watch out about whining to coworkers as well. Nobody wants to hear how busy you are or how much work you have. Though they might smile, nod, and agree with you, they'll be thinking, "What a

---

Be Thorough

"Before you tell someone, no, that it doesn't exist or it can't be done, you better be right. Because someone else will find it and make you look like an asshole."
—Becky Coleman, commercial and music video producer

wuss." And if they're friends with your boss, they'll probably tell him over drinks, "Oh, by the way, your assistant is a wuss."

DON'T BE DEFENSIVE

This is about accepting criticism. Before you blow this off, saying, "Oh, I can accept criticism fine," read the following conversation between a boss and their underling.

Boss: Here's the contract you wrote up. It's good except you forgot to add the rider about immunity.
Underling: I thought you told me not to add it.
Boss: I didn't say that.
Underling: Remember when I asked you the other day whether or not it was the same contract as the Harper contract, you said it was.
Boss: Yes, but I didn't say— Just add it, OK?

There is nothing more frustrating for a boss than an employee who feels the need to defend themselves at every turn. All this boss wanted to hear was, "OK, I'll add it." He didn't want to hear a defense. Even if he told you *not* to add it, he doesn't care. Proving that you were right and he was wrong is not going to make you look any better. It's only going to make you look worse. As I said above, you're probably saying to yourself, "I don't do this." Sorry, but most people do. I know *I* used to. What I finally realized was that my boss wasn't being critical and didn't think any less of me. He just wanted something changed.

"Lie to Me"

"Even if the world is falling down around you, keep your cool. When there's a crisis and you keep your cool, people know you're trying to fool them into thinking everything's okay. They *want* to be fooled, though."

—Mark P. Lawyer

Don't Suck Special Report: Giving Good Phone

1. First impressions are everything.
2. Most first impressions are made over the phone.

All the people you talk to on the phone at your new job are going to be judging you right off the bat. So will the people you deal with in person, obviously. The people you deal with on the phone, however, will most likely outnumber those you deal with in person. And though you think these people don't matter that much to your career because you can't see them, or because they aren't your boss, you are dead wrong.

People love to make instant judgments about the new guy, whether it be your boss's coworker who works on another floor whom you never see or one of your boss's clients or business associates he talks to a few times a week whom you also never see. In the first conversation they have with you, they are going to decide if you are lame or if you are on the ball—and therefore if they like you.

NOW, IF THEY THINK YOU'RE ON THE BALL AND IF THEY LIKE YOU, TWO THINGS WILL HAPPEN. THEY WILL:
1. Praise you to your boss the next time they speak with him. "Hey, that new guy you hired is real good. He's really on the ball. Good personality."
2. Think about stealing you away to their company sometime in the future. (This happens all the time.)

AND IF THEY THINK YOU'RE LAME, THEY WILL:
1. Not say anything good or bad about you out of politeness or say to your boss, "What's the deal with the new guy?"
2. Never consider stealing you away to their company.

Maybe you're saying to yourself, "Big deal, so I'll never work for their company. I *have* a job." It is a big deal. Your second job is most likely to come from someone you've talked to on the phone a lot as an assistant. Someone you've maybe even never met.

Maybe you're saying to yourself, "This writer is full of it. What do they care how you work? You're not working for them." Good point. I don't know the answer. But the fact is, people *make* you their business. Businesspeople want the really good, helpful, smart people to succeed and the dumb, unhelpful people to fail. That's all there is to it.

MAKING PHONE ALLIES
So how do you make instant allies and fans (who are going to prove essential to your future success)?

Be Cheerful and Energetic. The fact is, people like happy people. People respond to happy people. Answering your phone all serious-like, with a serious, grown-up business voice, doesn't open up the door to conversation. Which is what you have to do. When you're new on the job, the people who are used to calling your office are going to be like, "Who's this new person?" They're going to want to know who you are. Business is not all business; it's personal, too. If you've got your supergeek business voice on, they'll probably leave a message, hang up the phone, and say, "What a bonehead." If, however, you answer the phone real friendly-like, they're much more apt to open up to you and treat you like a peer rather than a message taker.

Be Calm and Collected. A lot of entry-levelers think it's cool to come off as if they're really, really busy. They're often short, snappy, and unhelpful on the phone. I'm sure you've come across people like this. What this person is saying (not literally, but by his tone) is, "Listen, the duty of answering the phone while I'm trying to get work done is just too much pressure for me and is too much for my little brain to handle; therefore, I'm short, snappy, and pissed-off." When you're anything but cool and charming, you're basically telling the world of callers that the simple duty of answering the phone is too much for you.

Be Helpful. When someone calls for your boss, they almost always need something. If someone asks for your boss and he's not there, instead of just taking a message, say, "I'm sorry, he's not here right now. Is there anything I can help you with?" If they say no, that's okay, then tell them what time you expect your boss back and ask if it's all right if they get back to them then. Let them know that you realize that their phone call is very important and that you're available to help them in any way. (You don't say, "I'll help you in any way"; it all comes through in the tone of your voice and your attitude in taking the message.) It is refreshing when you get a helpful person on the line who gives a shit. Believe it or not, it's really rare.

GIVING GOOD PHONE GOT HIM A BETTER JOB
This is how Michael went from being an assistant for a casting director in New York to landing a casting director gig in L.A. Every day these casting directors in L.A., whom Michael's

boss was working with, would call his office. Instead of just passing the call on to his boss (who was fortunately very busy), Michael would deal with them directly and answer their questions. "They would talk to *me*, and I would tell my bosses what the situation was. I was like a point man," says Michael. After a year of dealing with Michael, they liked and trusted him enough to offer him a job with them in L.A.

I asked Michael, "Did you know that's how things worked—that that's how you wind up getting jobs, from people that you talk to on the phone?" "No," he said. "At first you don't realize it. And it's funny because you *do* burn bridges because you don't know who certain people are and you *do* give them some attitude. Or you don't do the job as well as they want you to, and you have no idea who they are."

HOW GIVING BAD PHONE CAN COST YOU YOUR JOB
This is the story of my calling my friend, who is the vice president of a $55-million-a-year clothing company, to see if he wants to have dinner.

"Hi, is Joe there?" I ask the receptionist in the New York office. "No, he's not," she replies. Silence. "Is he out of town or just out for the day?" I ask. "I think he's out of town," she says. Silence. "So he won't be in today?" I ask. "I don't think so, but don't quote me on it," she says. (I'm starting to think this is a prank.) "Is he in the main office in Pennsylvania?" I ask. "I don't really know. Do you want me to find out?" she asks. No, I want to go back and forth like this for the next half hour, you stupid twit.

Fun, huh? I think this is a wonderful little portrait of the type of person who will always be answering phones—and that's if she's lucky. Yeah, it's quite obvious that immediately she should have said, "Hold on a minute, and I'll find out where he can be reached." Her bigger mistake, though, was demonstrating her utter incompetence to me, the caller, someone she didn't know.

I, being friends with Joe, her boss, felt obliged to tell him what a complete moron she was and begged him to fire her. (Two weeks later she was gone, hopefully partly because of me.)

Maybe you're saying, "What's the big deal? Man, this Charlie guy is a real prick." Well, maybe I am, I don't know. I just know that if I were my friend, I would be very upset that the receptionist I employ is lazy and useless.

Be Like Men

"I think the biggest problem with women is how they behave in the office. Say there's a male boss. And say there's a young woman and a man that work for this man. The young guy will go into his office and say, 'I have this great idea,' and he tells him the idea. The woman will have the same idea, and she'll go into his office and say, 'I don't know whether you're going to think this is dumb but . . .' Now why does she say that? Why doesn't she just say, 'I've got a great idea'? You have to act like a guy in certain respects, and women don't know how men act. They've never studied that. They haven't been raised to act like men."

—Lisa Katselas, entertainment lawyer and film producer

COVER YOUR BOSS'S ASS

Whether you're an assistant or a forty-five-year-old vice president, it's your job to cover your boss's ass and to protect him from his enemies within the company. Just try to make him look good. If he's out playing a round of golf on Friday afternoon and the president calls for him, cover his ass and say he's out at a meeting. And if you get caught for covering your boss's ass, you most likely won't get in trouble for it. You'll most likely be respected for it.

Quick story. This guy I know who worked in real estate hated his supervisor. Apparently, the guy was a real jerk. Totally abusive. Well, one day while his supervisor was at lunch with his fiancée, the president of the company (a real hard-ass himself) came by my friend's desk and asked where his boss was. He told him at lunch. "With who?" the president asked. "I believe with his fiancée." Wrong answer. Later that day, when the president of the company met with my friend's boss, he told him to fire my friend. The president said my friend had "breached the confidentiality" of his boss's whereabouts. In other words, he didn't cover his boss's ass.

definition

LUNCH HOUR:
That space of time reserved for running lengthy errands and purchasing lottery tickets.

FEED HIM INFORMATION

In chapter 26, I said you should feed information (about competitors and anything that relates to your business that is in papers and magazines) to up-and-comers you want to suck up to. You need to do this for your boss as well. Leave articles in his in-box that will be helpful or interesting to him that *he* in turn will leave in *his* boss's in-box.

Important note: Do not try to bypass your boss and impress *his* boss by putting it in *her* in-box. You're treading on very shaky territory here. There is a chain of communication and command that needs to be respected. The reason I said it's okay to feed information to up-and-comers in other departments is that they are outside of this chain of command.

Become an Expert

Besides clipping out articles for your boss that might be helpful, you should also be reading every maga-

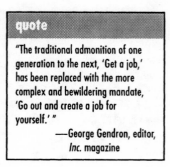

quote

"The traditional admonition of one generation to the next, 'Get a job,' has been replaced with the more complex and bewildering mandate, 'Go out and create a job for yourself.'"
—George Gendron, editor, *Inc.* magazine

zine and sections of the paper that relate to your business in order to become a source of facts and information. In other words, even as an assistant or low-level "associate," you need to become an expert in your field.

For instance, say you work for a producer or a talent agent in Hollywood. You should be reading the trade magazines every day (*Variety* and the *Hollywood Reporter*) to keep yourself abreast of what's going on. You should know every deal being made, who just got hired to direct what movie, what movies are coming out the following weekend, how the top movies did over the weekend, who's sleeping with whom, etc. You should be a walking encyclopedia on your industry so that your boss comes to *you* when he has a question about anything. It's all about making yourself indispensable.

ASK FOR WORK

You can do what's asked of you, do it well and on time, and keep your job. But if you want to impress your boss, you need to go up to him *looking* for work. Listen, you can goof off and try to have fun, but how much fun can you really have at work? My attitude is, since you're stuck there at the job, you might as well work. This is your company's attitude as well. If you don't have enough to do, think up a project, do it, and show your boss after you've completed it. Remember, your boss has his *own* work to do. It's not his job to keep you busy and entertained.

"Information, Please"

"Information is everything. And it's only by having relationships with your colleagues and talking to them that you get information. It's the exchange of information that makes the world go round. You can sit in your office and be the best little worker bee, but so what? You're never going to get anywhere. It's those little tips that you get, and those little favors that people do for you, that get you places."

—M. Lan, interior designer

Chapter 34

OKAY, YOUR BOSS LOVES YOU. NOW WHAT?

All right, let's say you've done, or are doing, all this stuff mentioned in the preceding chapters. You work your ass off. You get there early, you stay late, you ask for assignments, you hand them in on time, etc., etc. Will this get you promoted? Unfortunately not. "What? Being a superstar won't get me promoted?" you ask. No. Being a superstar is about getting your boss to love you. Getting promoted requires doing something more.

GRAB RESPONSIBILITY

One reason you need to get your boss to love you is so, when the time comes, he'll pull for you to upper management. But more important, it's so he'll *trust* you and *allow* you to do some of the things that he does. And unless he allows you to do some of the stuff that he does, you'll never prove you are capable of doing it, and you'll spend the rest of your life answering phones and sending E-mails.

But don't expect your boss to say, "You know, if you're interested in advancing here, then you should be asking me for some responsibility." It's not going to happen. He probably won't *want* you to do more than what your job description says. So you've got to start grabbing responsibility and making things happen on your own.

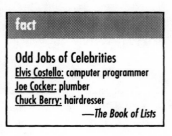

fact

Odd Jobs of Celebrities
Elvis Costello: computer programmer
Joe Cocker: plumber
Chuck Berry: hairdresser
—*The Book of Lists*

When Ray Rogers started at *Interview* magazine, nobody handed him writing assignments. Even though he had good writing credits from past internships at other magazines, *Interview* already *had* plenty of people on staff who were hungry and, frankly, more experienced. He was a low-level editorial assistant, so nobody really cared if he ever wrote anything. So getting his first record review was a bit of a struggle. "I was real persistent," he says. "If I hadn't pushed for that, they wouldn't have given me anything. You know, they're not going to come to you with a little silver platter and say, 'We would be honored if you would do a review of this new record.' Or, 'We would be honored for you to write our next feature story on music.' You know, they're not going to come to you and do that. So you've got to fight."

PICK UP THE SLACK

Keep your eyes open for projects that are falling through the cracks or aren't getting the attention they deserve and do the work yourself. For example, when Jennifer (interview on pages 89–93) was an assistant at a public relations firm that did PR for movies, she noticed that a client (a film) wasn't getting the attention it deserved. "Somebody dropped the ball on this film, so I took it upon myself to do the publicity campaign for the film. And out of that campaign came pieces in *Vanity Fair*, a four-page piece in *Interview*, a piece in *Premiere*. I said, 'Well, if no one's going to do this properly, I'll do it.' So I took the opportunity and ran with it."

HOARD WORK

The name of the game is about making yourself indispensable. It's about taking on responsibility for so many little things so that everybody has to come to *you* when they need something done. Sure, it makes your life busier, but so what? This is one of the main reasons why Greg Drebin says he moved up the ladder at MTV. As he says:

[It was about] never saying no in terms of work. And never saying "I can't do that" or "That can't get done." Even if it means that I've got to drop everything and do something else, and it's a little, minor job. You know, nothing is too small. As soon as you start saying "I'm too big for that," that's when you become disposable. [You don't want people to say] "Well, I don't need to talk to Greg anymore about this because I get that information from somebody else now." [If somebody says] "I don't need to run that by Greg because he doesn't help me with that anyway; he always refers me to somebody else," then what do you need me to do? What am I here for? If there's something that *you're* not doing, then somebody *else* is doing it, and then you're not needed anymore.

INCLUDE YOURSELF AND RAISE YOUR PROFILE

Being a low-level new hire at a company is like being a ten-year-old boy who is never included by his older brother. You never get to do any of the fun stuff. You have to sit there at your desk picking your nose while the big kids get to do all the fun stuff like attend important staff meetings, take lunches with prospective clients, and go to cheesy weekend conferences at three-star hotels in Houston.

You might be wondering how you're supposed to learn and grow in the job if you're constantly shut out of all the action. Here are a few ways:

Offer to Take Meeting Notes

Is there a weekly or biweekly meeting that you want to be a part of but aren't because you're just a peon? Tell your boss or the person running the meeting that you'd like to take meeting notes. There might not be anyone doing this job, and if there is, it might be a career secretary who isn't good at it and who doesn't really want to do it anyway. Doing great meeting notes is a fantastic way to show your boss and other important people these things:

- That you get the big picture. Taking meeting notes requires that you understand what's important and what's not. You have to synthesize all that you hear into precise, easy-to-understand bulleted points. Likewise, if you include irrelevant things discussed in the meeting that no one really gives a shit about, you're going to look like an idiot. So there is risk involved here.
- That you can write clearly and that you can produce a good-looking, professional document. Likewise, this is another opportunity to blow it and look like an idiot.
- That you can be trusted with a task and a deadline. Taking meeting notes requires that you find the time in your day, or after your day, to write them up and distribute them to the necessary people by the next day.
- That you're savvy enough to find a way to attend a meeting you shouldn't be attending.

Besides the fact that you'll be impressing people in the ways just mentioned, it also benefits you in the following ways:

- Your boss's peers and his bosses get to know who you are. One of the biggest challenges of being a peon is getting people to know who you are. This is a great way for people to match your name with your face. It is generally okay, if not necessary, that you include your name on the first page of the minutes.
- It gives you an opportunity to impress them with your knowledge. Though you probably won't be called upon to voice your opinion, if you know something that relates to what they're talking about that no one else seems to know, you should say it. It could be knowing what the capital of Spain is or what movie made the most at the box office last weekend or who the Mets' backup catcher is.
- It gives you a chance to do independent research that might assist the higher-ups. Say you're doing minutes at a weekly meeting at a marketing company and you keep hearing the same question: "Who directed *that* commercial?" Something you might want to think about doing is compiling a list of the most recent commercials airing on TV and who directed them, and make this list available to everybody.

Offer to Pay Your Own Way

Is there a big booksellers conference happening in Chicago that your boss is going to or a huge Internet trade show in Miami that you want to go to but won't be sent to because you're too low on the totem pole? Well, don't accept that you can't go; invite yourself. First, ask if you can attend. If they say no, offer to pay your own way. Or say you'll fly yourself to the conference if they'll put you up.

Why bother? Industry conferences are great ways to meet people from other companies and collect business cards. They're also a great opportunity to schmooze with higher-ups in *your* company in a more relaxed atmosphere over drinks, dinner, strippers, and crap tables.

The president of Troma Films, Lloyd Kaufman, told me about an intern who said he would fly himself to the Cannes Film Festival in France and help out if they gave him a floor to sleep on. As Lloyd says about this kid, "He understands that the Cannes Film Festival is like a crash course in the movie business and the making of movies, too. Everybody's there. He'll meet all sorts of people, from the heads of major Hollywood studios to underground filmmakers."

"Extra Work? Sure"

While Rob was working as a junior copywriter at a hot, midsize advertising agency, he volunteered his time on a project that sounded interesting to him. The project was coming up with some ads for products being advertised on the Internet. Since Rob had never written "Net ads" before, he thought it might be a fun challenge. So, after getting his boss's permission to work on a few ads for the Internet group, Rob wrote some that they loved. A month later, when the parent company started a new Internet company, they recruited Rob and gave him a promotion because (a) he had volunteered (and they liked his ideas), and (b) in their opinion, he now had Internet experience. Proof that volunteering your time isn't a waste of time at all.

Why You Must Raise Your Profile

The reason you must become known and liked by your boss's associates—why you must be the star of the assistants—is that your future promotion rests on it. If you're well liked, then your promotion will be a popular move for your boss to make. If you're not, then your boss will, in effect, lose popularity herself for promoting you. Plus, very often, your boss's associates have a say as to whether or not you should be promoted as well.

Case in Point

My first job in Hollywood was as a production assistant on a CBS reality-based series. I did all sorts of things, from taking turns answering the phones to driving around town doing errands to fetching bagels to basically doing whatever any of the many producers asked us to do. I was one of three PAs who all shared the work and divvied up the assignments. We all had the same boss, but she gave us the freedom to divide the work the way we wanted.

Luckily, the other two guys I worked with were slugs. Whenever a producer came over to where we hung out and asked if somebody could do something, the other two guys would just sit there.

---

definition

U.S. ARMED FORCES:
What you'll fantasize about joining, immediately prior to either becoming homeless or moving back in with your parents.

On my second day on the job, one of the executive producers on the show needed a bookshelf put together in her office. I instantly volunteered. I wanted this producer to know who I was. I figured that, by my spending a few hours in her office, we might wind up talking. I was right. While I was working, she said, "So you're a new face. Who are you?" I introduced myself and said that I had just moved from New York. She asked me what I had done there, and I told her. She seemed impressed.

A few days into the job, I had heard that they hadn't hired a travel coordinator yet. This person is responsible for arranging all the flights and hotel rooms for the crews—sometimes four crews were out at a time—that were out shooting segments. At around eight P.M., when it was quiet, I went to my boss and told her that I would be really interested in the travel position. She told me that they were having a staff meeting the next day and that she'd bring my name up.

The next day at the meeting, they were discussing people for the job, and my boss mentioned my name. People said, "Who?" "He's the new production assistant from New York," she said. "The one who built my bookshelves?" the executive producer asked. "Yeah, him." "Oh, I like him. He's a smart guy. Let's give it to him."

So after not even one week, I doubled my salary and became travel coordinator, much to the chagrin of the other two production assistants, who had been with the company for over a year.

HAVE AN OPINION

When you're new on the job, you should want nothing more than to please your boss. But in doing so, it can be easy to lose your identity. You find yourself agreeing with him about the stupidest things. From hating the movie that he saw last weekend (which you actually liked) to hating mayonnaise on bologna

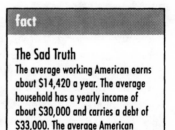

fact

The Sad Truth
The average working American earns about $14,420 a year. The average household has a yearly income of about $30,000 and carries a debt of $33,000. The average American household falls behind $3,000 a year.
—Michael Moore, *Downsize This!*

sandwiches as well. With one boss, I actually took the time to say, "Yeah, I hate mayo on bologna, too." It's like I was on a never-ending date with my boss, always afraid of hating or liking the wrong things. Your boss is going to respect you and think you actually have a brain if you disagree with him once in a while.

Not only that, if you *don't* disagree with him once in a while and show him that you have an opinion, he will never come to you and ask you for one. This is bad.

One thing that separates the people who move up the ladder from those who don't is an opinion. Do you have one or not? You can be the best assistant in the world—always on time, very organized, willing to stay late to complete a project, always cheerful and energetic. These are great and absolutely necessary qualities to have to get ahead. But they don't mean anything if you, as a person, don't have your own sense of taste, convictions, and ideas—all of which I will classify as having an opinion.

What If You're Wrong?

You could say that there might be a problem with having an opinion. Hell, yours could be wrong. You

> **quote**
>
> "A large income is the best ingredient for happiness I ever heard."
> —Jane Austen

know what? It doesn't matter. Better to have an opinion and voice it than not have one at all. Your bosses are bosses just for this reason: They have opinions and ideas, which they then carry out.

So if you ever hope to move up the ladder in your company, you must be willing to assert your opinion and stick to it—just as your boss would. Even if they don't agree with you, at least they know that you're thinking, that you have ideas, that you're someone who's not interested in being an assistant or a receptionist all your life.

While some employers don't really care if you have an opinion or not—they just want their lives made easy—others expect it. Laurence Schwartz, a film producer, says, "I look for people who have ideas of what to make films about."

I love that quote. It's so simple. He's an executive at a film company who is responsible for getting films made. And if you're going to get a film made, you have to have a subject, an idea. That means having an opinion about what would make a good film.

The simplicity of that quote can be applied to every job. If you work for a newspaper and want to move up, you have to have ideas of what's newsworthy and ideas of what to write about. But as Neal Justin, pop culture critic of the *Minneapolis Star Tribune*, says, "I hear a lot of young people say to me, 'I want to be a reporter.' And you ask them 'What story ideas do you have?' and they go 'Ummm.' They often don't have any."

Money-Back Guarantee

"I went to the library and researched who the most interesting people to work for would be. I sent a direct-mail piece to 322 people, saying, 'Would you consider hiring me for 90 days. No obligations, no nothing.' " He got 125 responses.
—Peter Barton, president and chief executive, Liberty Media Corporation,
New York Times, May 15, 1996

THE ARROGANCE FACTOR

When you talk about having an opinion and expressing it, it requires a bit of arrogance. Because when you say "I think we should do this instead of this"—whatever it is—you're saying that your way is right and someone else's way is wrong. No matter what business you're in, whether it's washing cars or designing children's books, if you have an opinion—which you must—then you're going to come head-to-head with someone else with a different (and often lame) one. And whoever's opinion is accepted moves one step up the ladder of success.

Consider Robin Danielson's thoughts on what makes a successful advertising copywriter:

> It's generally a group of extremely egotistical young men, and the system makes them that way. Because in order to get work sold in a bull-pen environment, it's the person who says "I've got the biggest dick" that's the guy who wins. A lot of times the work is relatively equal. The stuff that gets through is very often just somebody who's willing to say, "I am king of the fucking world." So successful creatives are trained to be assholes.

IMAGE MATTERS

Did anyone ever tell you how it doesn't matter what anyone thinks of you—it's how you think of yourself that matters? Well, they were

wrong. In the business world, image is everything. Whatever someone thinks of you, that is what you are. If the vice president thinks
you're an idiot with a bad haircut who will never be promoted, then
you *are* an idiot with a bad haircut who will never be promoted.

A lot of this whole business thing is a game. It's posturing. It's a
matter of giving people a certain impression. Making them think
that you're smart, that you're on the ball, that you're promotable. A
lot of this is done by how you present yourself—clotheswise
and attitudewise. It's in the way you carry yourself. When you and
a thirty-five-year-old vice president are talking while waiting for
an elevator, an outside observer shouldn't be able to tell that you
don't have the same job as the afore-
mentioned bald guy next to you.
You see, it's not only about looking
neat and clean, it's also about looking
important.

Here's the deal: dress for the job
you want, not for the job you have.
Here's Robin Danielson on this point. Listen up.

> **quote**
>
> *"You have to be scrappy to survive."*
> —Bob Stein, new-media guru and
> founder of the CD-ROM publisher
> Voyager

The thing about advertising is, the first question is, "Can you go
to the client?" If you want somebody to feel like they can trust
you to do the job of the person who's above you, then every day
you should *look* like they could trust you to do the job of the person who's above you. Even if you think you know what you're
doing that day and don't think you need to be dressed up to be
doing any of it. The first time you might get the chance to do
something is when it's spontaneous, not when it's planned—
when somebody says, "Oh, shit, who can do that?" I had a girl
who worked as an account assistant, and she basically got herself
stuck for a good six months longer than she needed to, purely on
the basis of the way she dressed. I mean, people are not going to
pull you aside and tell you, "Cut it out." People aren't going to be
that nice to you.

The Real Skinny with . . . Michael Katcher, Casting Director

WHY HE GOT PROMOTED EARLY IN HIS CAREER FROM "ASSISTANT" TO "ASSOCIATE":
I took the initiative without them having to tell me what to do. I was very eager, without being annoying. I've worked with people who are eager *and* annoying, and you don't want to work with the person. I grabbed responsibility, and they gave it to me. They saw that I wanted it, and they saw that I was confident.

STANDING YOUR GROUND:
[This is when Michael started at his second casting job.] I was fired the first week I started working for her. I basically got blamed for something that wasn't my fault because I was the low guy there. And I was thinking, "This is fucking ridiculous." So I said, "Look, this is what I want if I stay." I turned it around on her. I said, "You have to give me the freedom to think and be creative. You can't just expect me to sit there and get coffee and do this shit for you. I'm not going to do it. I'm there to make you a good casting director." And I was. I was there to make them look good, which is what any good assistant should do.

THE SHITWORK:
[You] shouldn't think about making money when you start. You're not going to make any money. You have to be willing to wipe people's asses. I mean, seriously, you have to be willing to do the shitwork.

WELCOME TO HOLLYWOOD:
I was really busy and in a pissed-off mood because there was no help. [Michael had been begging his bosses to hire an assistant.] So I literally ripped the phone out and threw it against the wall and said, "Fuck it, I'm leaving," and walked home. And I was thinking, okay, they're going to call me. They didn't call me. They didn't call me! So I was like, fuck, I'll go back to the office. So I went back and we had it out.

LOOSE LIPS:
It's a really small town. Anything you say always gets back to the person. They'll always find out what you said. I've learned to just keep my mouth shut, just grin and bear it. It's just a job, you know what I'm saying?

Chapter 35

THAT ELUSIVE INTERNAL PROMOTION

THE END OF THE LINE

I hope it's pretty clear to you that there is no promotion line. Nobody is going to come up to you and say "Thanks for being patient. Here, you're promoted." You can work and work and work, prove to your boss you have a brain, an opinion, are capable of doing his work, etc., and nothing might happen. In fact, it probably *won't* happen. This is when a lot of people say "Screw it," pack up, and get another job at another company at the same level. I've seen people do this all the time. I've done it, too.

Getting your company to go that next step in promoting you is by far the most challenging and elusive thing any young worker faces. It's one of the mysteries of life. You don't know how and when it's going to happen; it just happens. Or else it doesn't.

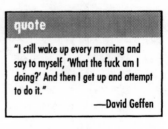

quote

"I still wake up every morning and say to myself, 'What the fuck am I doing?' And then I get up and attempt to do it."

—David Geffen

THE CATCH–22

In order to get promoted, not only do you have to prove that you are *capable* of doing the work of the position you will be promoted to, but you have to actually be doing it. Your company is not going to say, "Gee, we *think* Charlie will be able to do this job. Let's give him a shot." No, they're going to give it to me if, and only if, I've proved that I can do it. And how do you prove that you can do it? You have to actually do it.

This is hard for a lot of young people to understand. They'll ask, "How can I do the job above me when I already have my own job to do and when they won't *allow* me to do it?" That's a good question. But it's the way it works. Here's the deal. Until you actually start to add to the profitability of the company, you will remain an assistant. Figuring out how to do this is the key to success. Here's how:

JUST DO IT: CREATING YOUR POSITION

I can best explain this point by giving an example. A friend of mine is an assistant at one of the top three talent agencies in the world. He works for a literary agent whose job is to find and nurture screenwriters and then sell their scripts. For four years he's worked his ass off for his boss, staying until eight P.M. every night and often coming in on Saturdays. He's worked as hard as or harder than all the other assistants and has a great attitude to boot. If anybody were to be promoted, it would be him. But here's the question: Why *would* they promote him? What would he do? Well, he would represent writers. But what writers? The writers at the agency already *have* agents.

After three years he woke up and realized that his fate was in his own hands. If he wanted to be an agent, he had to start acting as an agent, start working with writers and selling their scripts. He realized he had to do this even though it was basically against company policy. Assistants aren't allowed to solicit scripts like agents do. But only the assistants who solicit scripts and start bringing money into the company are promoted. The catch-22.

---

definition

STAFF MEETING:
Machiavellian gathering of office workers designed for face-to-face finger-pointing and other highly personal apportioning of blame.

Once my friend realized what he had to do, he wound up selling three scripts in six months, two for over $200,000. Since his own efforts were basically paying his salary, they said "Okay" when he went to the powers that be and told them he needed to stop working for his boss so he could concentrate on selling more scripts. As he says, "If I hadn't walked in there and told them to give me an office and find someone else to take my [assistant] job, I'd still be an assistant."

The Tao of Just Doing It (as Shown by the Aforementioned Story)

· **Nobody told him to just do it.** It took him three years to realize that he had to just do it, that he had to create his own position. Nobody told him. Why? Because (a) they didn't want to lose him as a valuable assistant, and (b) nobody really cared if he moved up or not.

· **It was actually against company policy.** If just doing it is not actually *against* company policy, it will most likely be frowned upon. Say you're working as an assistant to a book editor. The only way you're going to become an editor is to find writers of merit and convince your company to buy their manuscripts. When you bring them a manuscript and say "Here, read this. It's great," at first they might say to themselves "That's not his job. He's only an assistant; he shouldn't be working with writers." But if the writer you found is good, they'll say "Well, it doesn't matter if he should have been doing this or not. Let's buy this writer's book!"

· **Just doing it meant contributing to the profitability and success of the company.** As long as you do something that contributes to the company's profitability and success, it doesn't matter if you're a serial killer. Well, maybe it does, but not much. In the end, money and profitability are all that matters. How you get these things is secondary.

· **Just doing it meant telling <u>them</u> you're promoted.** Just because you're now making the company money or are somehow adding to the company's success (more than by just being a great assistant), don't expect them to come to you and promote you. You have to go to them and say, "I've been doing this, this, and this" and actually show them, on paper, what you've done. I love the way my friend said it to his bosses in the preceding story. He told them he needed to stop working for his boss so he could concentrate on selling scripts—making the company more money. He didn't say promote me or give me a raise. He said free me up so I can make the company even more money.

TAKE A DEPARTING PERSON'S JOB

This is an easier way of moving up the ladder than creating your own position. Somebody else has done the work for you by expanding the department (unless they themselves inherited the position), and now you are simply stepping into their shoes. A lot of people think this is the way they're going to get promoted. They'll hang in there long enough until somebody packs up and leaves or dies. This can work, but *only* if you've demonstrated that you can do this person's job. This is how you do this:

· **Make a friend.** Get to know somebody in the department you want to work in so they'll let you hang out and observe what they do—and let you help.

· **Come in on weekends.** It's hard to learn someone else's job when you've got your own to do. It's going to require giving up your weekends and/or evenings. This is how Farrah was promoted to assistant stylist at *Elle* magazine a few years back. "During the year when I was an assistant to the senior editor, I would volunteer to assist one of the stylists when they needed help," she says. So when the assistant stylist position became available, Farrah got it because she already knew how to do it.

· **Make sure you're in the know.** You don't want to be surprised when someone whose job you want leaves. This is why being a wallflower can be detrimental to your career. It should be your mission to know the comings and goings of all the people in the office. You need to know who is about to get promoted, fired, who is unhappy and about to quit, and whose drug habit is getting a little too out of hand.

· **Pounce on it.** As soon as you hear someone is leaving—assuming you've learned their job and have done everything mentioned in the last forty or so pages—immediately go to their boss and tell them you want the job. Save them the hassle of having to interview a bunch of people. And do it early, before they've had the *opportunity* to interview anyone.

 • **Don't take no for an answer.** If they tell you that they're going to interview a bunch of people for the position but you know that *you* would be great for the job, then tell them so. Tell them how much you want it. Ask them to give you a shot. Ask for a trial run.

This is how I got promoted from house manager to theater manager at a Broadway theater I was working at. The theater manager, this thirty-four-year-old guy (I was twenty-four), gave his notice, so I went to my boss and told him I'd like to be considered for the job. He basically brushed me off. I knew he thought

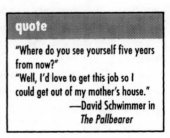

quote

"Where do you see yourself five years from now?"
"Well, I'd love to get this job so I could get out of my mother's house."
—David Schwimmer in
The Pallbearer

that I was too young for the job, and maybe I was. Either way, I knew I could do it. A week before this guy's last day, I went to my boss again and said I wanted the job. Again, he blew me off. "We'll see," he said. I told him, "Listen, I know I'm young and all, but why don't you give me a chance? Give me three weeks. If I haven't caught on in three weeks, you can get somebody else." "Let me think about it," he said. But he wasn't thinking about it. He was too busy with other stuff. So the next day, I got a little more ballsy and went up to my boss and said, "Listen, how about I start interviewing people for my job and line someone up so, if I wind up taking over the theater manager job, we won't be stuck." Again, out-of-his-mind busy, he said, "Yeah, sure, go ahead." That week I had the theater manager show me everything I needed to know, and when he left, I simply started doing his job. My boss never said, "The job is yours." I just took it.

Chapter 36

YOUR LIFE IS OVER. THEY WON'T PROMOTE YOU

Sometimes it just doesn't matter what you do; you will never be promoted at that company. Or so it seems. The problem is, you can never be 100 percent sure. Most entry-levelers get discouraged and quit too early. But the reason they get discouraged and quit is that they see other people sail past them—namely, the stars who are doing all the extra stuff I've talked about. So the people who get discouraged and leave aren't leaving too early. The fact is, it doesn't matter how long they stay; they will never be promoted.

But let's assume you're not one of these pathetic losers; you're a certified workaholic star who is not getting your due, and you are afraid you never will. Now, assuming you are somehow contributing to the success and/or profitability of the company, *beyond* what your job title says you should be doing, what should you do? Besides telling everybody to screw off and look for another job outside of the company (which is the subject of the next chapter).

CHANGE WHAT YOU DO

Before you quit, try to pinpoint what it is you don't like about your job and try to solve it. For example, maybe you can hire an intern to do all the crap you hate doing. Or maybe some of your mindless work could be given to the receptionist, who doesn't do anything but sit on his fat butt all day.

But there's no point shedding the crappy work if you're not, at the same time, taking on more managerial responsibilities.

The Job Title Game

What do you do when you reach the top of the pay scale for your position? Accept the fact that you'll never get a raise again, or find another job? You don't have to do either.

Linda was working as the assistant to the president of a TV production company. She wanted more money but was told that for that position she couldn't make more than she was making. She didn't want to leave, though, because she liked the job and needed the security. So she did some research and came up with the title of manager of special projects. "I still do pretty much what I've been doing," says Linda. "But now they pay me more money for it because I have a new title other than executive assistant."

GO TO YOUR BOSS

Before you start interviewing, give your boss the opportunity to pull some strings by telling him that you plan on leaving. When you tell him you're going to leave unless something happens, if he really loves you,

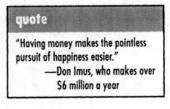

quote

"Having money makes the pointless pursuit of happiness easier."
—Don Imus, who makes over
$6 million a year

he might *make* something happen. Once he's faced with the prospect of really losing you, then, and only then, might he get off his butt and make your appeal to the powers that be. It's like a relationship. Sometimes it takes breaking up with someone to get what you want.

If your boss tells you to hang in there or to be patient, ask him for how long. Tell him you need to know when. If you don't make him commit to a date, he will string you along forever.

GO TO HR

In chapter 28, I mentioned how you should make friends with someone in human resources. This is why. They often know about job openings—in your department and others—before anybody else does. If you have a good relationship with someone in HR, they might tell you about the job before they post it on the job board.

CHECK OUT THE JOB BOARD

If you don't have a friend in HR willing to give you insider information, then check out the job board. Most companies are required to list all the internal job opportunities before they interview people from outside the company. If you see a job you're interested in, the notice will tell you to go to HR to apply. Don't. Go directly to the person in the department who is hiring and let them know of your interest. Drop by in person, don't call. Try to catch them at the end of the day so you can get to spend some time with them. Don't worry about bothering them. Believe me, this person would love to not have to interview a bunch of strangers for this position. If he likes you, you're going to save him a lot of time.

CHANGE DEPARTMENTS

Just because your boss is a jerk and your department hasn't promoted anybody in years doesn't mean you should necessarily bail out of the company. What about working in another department? I've posed this question to frustrated worker bees, and a common response I get is this: "I've slaved for two years as an assistant. I'm not going to be an assistant again in another department in the same company. Screw that. This place sucks."

It's never different. Every company sucks. It's the same everywhere. But at the same time, every company doesn't suck. Including yours. So don't look for greener grass in another company, as most dissatisfied young workers do. Use your advantageous position (the fact that you work there gives you inside info) and look for the green grass in *your* company. Start to get to know, schmooze, and help someone in another department where you'd like to work.

Take a Step Backward

You've got to get out of the "title and money" mind-set and into the mind-set of "What do I really want to do?" You can't be afraid to say, "I did this for a year or two, and now I know the department I *really* want to work in, so I'm going to take a step backward and go there." This is what Greg Drebin did at MTV. After two years of working his way up to the title of "publicist"—a real title—he quit to take a lower-level job in the acquisitions and programming department. While others might have thought he was crazy at the time, the move paid off. Now as senior vice president of programming, he has much more influence over the channel than he ever would have had if he had stayed in publicity.

Warning!

Don't be surprised when—because it's gonna happen—your boss freaks out when he hears that you're leaving him for someone else.

Notice that I did not say that your boss will freak out when you tell him you *want* to transfer to another department. Nope. Don't breathe a word of it to your boss until the deal is done. They'll take it personally that you're leaving and will probably try to sabotage the deal.

Chapter 37

Moving On: Moving Up the Ladder by Switching Companies

Once you've explored all of your options at your company and have decided (a) there's no other department you'd rather work in and (b) there's absolutely no way they're going to promote you, then perhaps it's time to move on. When you've absolutely made up your mind that you're leaving, then, and only then, do the following:

Ask Your Boss for Help

Get your boss involved in your job search. There's nothing worse than trying to go out on interviews behind your boss's back. Make it easy on yourself and make him your ally in this, not your enemy. You never know, maybe he'll get on the phone and get you a couple of great interviews with friends at other companies. Plus, he might give you a better reference if he feels like a part of your life and job search.

---

definition

BOARD MEETING:
Assemblage of well-to-do citizens who convene for the purpose of exchanging insider-trading information.

Perseverance

When Chris got out of school, he got a job as an accountant. Although the money was decent, Chris wasn't really into it. After three years with the same Chicago firm, he had had enough. He needed a change. He *wanted* to go into film producing, but he didn't know anybody in film. So he put two and two together and figured he'd get his foot in the door of a studio through the accounting department.

Again, not knowing anybody, he called one of the major studios in Los Angeles and asked to be transferred to accounting. When the person in accounting answered the phone, he said, "Hi, I'm Chris _____, from the accounting firm of so-and-so. Could you please tell me who the responsible accountant is for the film so-and-so?" The person gave Chris the guy's name, assuming it was a legitimate business call, and transferred him. When the accountant picked up the phone, Chris introduced himself and told the gentleman he was working in Chicago as an accountant and wanted to move to Los Angeles to work in film. The guy said jokingly, "Why would you want to move to Los Angeles the way the Lakers are playing? Chicago's the team. I'd stay there." The guy told Chris there wasn't much he could do for him being that he lived in Chicago.

When they hung up, Chris called someone who knew someone who worked for the Chicago Bulls and managed to get a signed jersey, which he sent to the accountant at the studio two days later. The next week Chris called the guy up and said he was going to be in Los Angeles on business in two weeks—which he wasn't—and asked if he could meet with him. Since Chris had sent the guy a signed jersey, he couldn't really say no.

Chris flew out to L.A., met the guy for lunch, and told him flat out that he didn't have business to do there, he had flown out only to meet with him. The guy said, "In that case, why don't I introduce you to a couple of other people in the department to make it worth your while." Chris went back to Chicago without a job offer but called the guy every month for seven months, checking to see if any job had become available. Finally a job opened up, Chris flew out there, interviewed, and got a job.

ASK YOUR COWORKERS FOR HELP

This is where having coworker friends really pays off. Make your coworkers' contacts *your* contacts. Let them help you. You never know what information they might have about a job opening.

CALL THE PEOPLE YOU DO BUSINESS WITH

Most people's second, third, and fourth jobs come from people at other companies they did business with. Hopefully, while you were at your job, you made friends with people at other companies as talked about in chapter 29, "Networking Outside of Your Company." If you've done it right, you should have at least a few people who will set up interviews for you.

But hopefully you've done better than that and have made a couple of fans out there who have said to you "If you ever leave your job, call me. I'd love to hire you over here." Don't think this is so unusual. I've had this offer a few times, and I don't think I'm that special.

CALL A RECRUITER

Talk to former colleagues who have gone on to new jobs to see what recruiter placed them. Or see if your trade association endorses any

---

Beware of the Headhunter

After graduating from Arizona State, Brooke moved to Seattle hoping to find work. With no connections and uncertain as to what she wanted to do, she hit the old classifieds. One job, listed by a headhunter, looked interesting. It was for an administrative assistant position with a sportswear design company. Brooke interviewed with the headhunter (who was hired by the sportswear company to fill the position), then with the company, and landed the job. "The headhunter was great," she says. "She was like a personal trainer and a cheerleader. She gave me lots of information on how to answer questions in interviews, the kind of questions they're going to ask you, and ways to present yourself."

Brooke soon learned, however, that headhunters have a bottom line—money. "Ultimately, headhunters are salespeople," she says. "They're trying to sell you on a *job*, and they're trying to sell *you* to an employer because they're going to make money on the deal. I found that everything was misrepresented. She said it was going to be all these things that it wasn't. I stayed there for just under a year and ended up having a fairly bad experience."

particular recruiter or recruiters. If a recruiter wants to charge you a fee or percentage of your salary for their services, tell them to take a hike. Reputable recruiters are paid by the company that is looking to hire someone, not by the someone looking to be hired.

CHECK YOUR REFERENCES

Before you give someone as a reference, you might want to consider having a friend dummy-check it for you first. There's a company that will actually do this for you—for a fee, of course. They are Taylor Review at (810) 651-0286.

LOOSE LIPS SINK SHIPS

Don't tell anyone where you're interviewing. Not even your good friends. You have no idea whom they innocently might tell. For instance, you'll tell Bobby that you have a great interview coming up with the local alternative rock radio station, and he'll mention it to his sister Cindy. Then, later on that night, Cindy mentions to her friend Lucy that WBOS is looking for someone. "Really?" says Lucy. "How do you know?" "Because Bobby's friend has an interview with them." "Hmm," says Lucy to herself. "I'm gonna get *me* an interview there, too." Voilà, now you've got competition for this job from Lucy and all Lucy's friends' friends. Seriously, when it comes to an interview, do not tell anyone. If I'm in an office and overhear that someone has an interview at a place where I want to work, you can be damn sure I'm going to try to weasel an interview there myself. It's human nature.

DON'T JUMP AT THE FIRST OFFER

Yes, you're miserable at your job. Yes, you want to slice and dice your boss. Yes, you'd rather—well, you've got the idea. As unhappy as you are, don't jump at the first crappy job that you're offered.

And you will get offers. The fact that you have a job makes you much more attractive than most of the slouches you'll be competing with who don't have jobs. Guys, it's like attracting women. When you've got a girlfriend, that's when the girls want you. When you don't, they don't.

LEAVE ON GOOD TERMS WITH EVERYONE

People have a funny way of reappearing. Especially ex-coworkers who, years later, have the final vote on whether or not to hire you at the new company where they're vice president. This happens all the time. In fact, people get a kick out of putting a dent in someone's career. I've had the pleasure of doing it myself. It felt great. This guy who was not particularly mean to me, but was never quite nice to me either, was up for a job at a company I had been at for over a year. He should have been nicer to me, because it didn't take much to convince my boss that he should continue interviewing people and not hire this guy.

But not only will you run into ex-coworkers at different companies down the line, there is a good chance that you might try to return to an ex-company itself. If you leave on good terms with

---

"Um, Hi Again"

You're working at a job when you find a new, more *exciting* job. So, what do you do? It's "See ya!" to the old job. You'll never see those jokers again. Or will you?

When Dorothy quit her nursing job on Martha's Vineyard to move to Connecticut, she didn't expect she'd ever see any of her old cohorts again. She was wrong. After three years she decided to move back to the island—without a job. As she says, "Luckily, I didn't burn any bridges when I left. I hadn't made any enemies, so there was no one that could poison the atmosphere when I returned and tried to get my job back. No one could say 'Oh, she did this and this.' Whenever I leave a job, I'm really careful to make sure that I do so on great terms. If I'd tarnished my reputation on the Vineyard even a little, people would not have welcomed me back."

everyone by continuing to do your job well up to the last day, by giving adequate notice and wishing everyone well, the door is going to be open to you. If not, you're screwed.

The Real Skinny with . . . Claire Raskind, Film Publicist

ON HAVING THE RIGHT ATTITUDE—NO ATTITUDE:

I remember one time the president of Orion Pictures walked up to my cubicle and handed me his jacket. And I said, "Oh, do you want me to hang this up?" and he said, "No, I want you to sew a button on for me." And I was like, you know, it's that moment where you can either go, "I'm not going to do that," or you can just swallow your pride for a minute. He wasn't doing it to degrade me; he had a meeting and he needed a button on his jacket. He has enough pressure. He's running the company. It's a lot of pressure.

ON STANDING YOUR GROUND AND MAKING ENEMIES:

Now another time, an executive came up to my desk, handed me his lit cigarette, and said, "Can you put this out for me?" And I said to him, "No, I don't smoke. I can't." And he was furious. He basically hated me the whole rest of the time I worked there.

ON INTEGRITY:

They told my boss [at Orion] in one room that she was getting fired and told me in the other room that I was getting promoted, and I just thought the whole thing really sucked basically. They had just kicked my boss out on the street who had been doing a great job there for sixteen years. How did I know they weren't going to do the same thing to me after they learned how everything was done?

ON DEALING WITH THE CONSEQUENCES OF HAVING INTEGRITY (SEE PRECEDING QUOTE)—I.E., BEING OUT OF WORK:

I got completely obsessive. I took my Rolodex and I went through and I wrote a letter to everybody, even if I thought we never really clicked. I thought, someone must know of a job opening in publicity. After three weeks I got a job.

Chapter 38

KEEPING YOUR JOB ONCE YOU'RE PROMOTED

PROMOTE TO FIRE

You've just been promoted. After a few years of slaving for your boss and the company, they've rewarded you with a title change and your own office. "You like me. You really like me," you think to yourself.

You might be wrong. This is not very common, but sometimes a company will promote you in order to get rid of you, hoping and expecting you'll fail. That's why some people call it "promote to fire." It can work in two ways:

1. **Premature promotion:** This is when you're promoted way too early, before you know enough to be able to succeed on the job. When you're an assistant or a low-level employee, they may not have a good reason to fire you. But if they give you your own office and a lot of things to do that you have no idea how to do, then they can rightfully fire you when you screw up.

2. **Guilt or split-vote promotion:** This is when you've been at the company for years and everybody's hoping you'll just quit and find a job elsewhere because they don't think you're really worth promoting. When they're convinced that this isn't going to happen, they'll promote you either out of guilt or loyalty or because one person way up the food chain likes and believes in you. "Fine," the others say. "We'll promote him and give him six months." Whereas they might give someone they really wanted to promote a year or two to prove themselves, they'll give you the minimum.

No Yanking Allowed

The next time you're thinking about masturbating at work, remember this story, told by my friend Paul, who works at a law firm in New York.

"A guy I worked with at my law firm was caught masturbating in the conference room and was fired. Some of us talked about it and decided that had he been having sex with someone, he might not have been fired. I think this is the thing that disturbed everyone—the fact that . . . he was yanking *himself*. The consensus was that if he was just having sex, he probably wouldn't have been fired."

CONSIDER YOURSELF ON TRIAL

I don't think you need to worry about whether or not you were a "promote to fire" victim. Chances are, you weren't. However, you should consider yourself one anyway. You should think of yourself as being on trial. People are going to be watching you closely, sussing out whether or not you'll make the cut. And whether you realize it or not, your boss and other people above you are talking about you behind your back. Some of these people are going to hope you succeed, and some are waiting for you to drop the ball on something.

Why? Who knows? Maybe they don't like the college you went to or how you dress, or maybe they simply think you're an idiot based on something they heard about you. Most likely, though, it's because they're afraid and threatened by you.

PULLING YOUR WEIGHT

So don't assume you're all set because you now have your own office. The work has just begun. As an assistant or a trainee, you weren't responsible for the success or failure of the company. As a person with a real title, you're either going to pull your weight and keep your job or get fired.

Some people right out of the gate don't realize this and are surprised a year later when they're canned. They thought they could just do a good job and that would be enough. They didn't realize that others were expecting them to figure out ways to grow or improve the company.

When Lauren Marino was promoted from assistant editor to full editor at Hyperion Publishing, she was hit with the reality of profit responsibility right away. "All of a sudden my job completely changed. Now all the responsibility was on me. My entire career was now based on what I acquired and how well my books sold in the marketplace," says Lauren.

JOB SECURITY: AVOIDING DOWNSIZING

Getting a good job and a promotion is great. Keeping it is even better. No matter what business or company you're in, chances are, they're going to downsize—a more civilized way of saying they're going to fire a lot of people and absolutely crush their lives. Fortunately, downsizing victims' names aren't indiscriminately drawn from a hat. You *can* increase your odds against being downsized. Here's how:

Stay Motivated

Once you've been promoted, there's not going to be anyone leaning over you as there was when you were an assistant or a trainee. Now, when you have a project or a job to do, you've got to motivate yourself.

You'll soon realize that there is a minimum of work that you can get away with doing. There are minimalists in every company, some who have been surviving as such for years. If you don't aspire to greater money and responsibility, you can give the minimalist approach a shot. Just realize that when your department is eliminated or scaled back, you'll be the first to go. Knowing this should motivate you enough not to be a minimalist.

Ensure Your Employability

There's a saying at Apple Computers: "Your sense of security will come from your employability." Ask the thousands of "downsized" Apple employees what they think of this cute little saying and they'll probably beat the shit out of you. Nevertheless, I think there's a lot of truth in the saying, and I think you should keep it emblazoned somewhere inside your brain. Here are a few ways to ensure and increase your employability:

Keep Up with Technology

Oh, that technology. Who can keep up with it? I'll tell you who *must*. You, of course. Even if your job doesn't require you to be familiar with the Internet, you should be up on it. Not only might it help you do your job better, it's simply something every white-collar worker must know. With some careers, like accounting and finance, it's essential that you're Net savvy so you can keep up with the new software that changes every six months. Just keep in mind that even though your current job may not require knowledge of certain programs, your next job might. Be aware that there's a "Skills" section at the bottom of your future résumé that your future employer is going to be looking at.

Keep Up with What's Going On

Be aware of the latest trends and happenings in your industry by:

- Attending seminars
- Joining your industry's professional organization
- Reading every trade magazine
- Taking classes

Increase Your Butt–Kissing Range

Unfortunately, your direct boss's butt isn't the only butt that needs kissing. Hell, he might get canned by *his* boss. Therefore, you need to kiss butt at higher levels so that if your department gets eliminated, they decide to keep one person: you. Try to become friendly with your boss's boss—without your boss knowing it. (This will threaten your boss.) Here are a few ways to kiss his butt and stand out separately from your boss:

- Try to weasel your way into a golf game.
- Go to the same restaurant when you know he's going to be there and drop by his table.
- Walk by his office when he's there real late and comment on how late he's working. Ask him how things are going and if he needs a hand with anything. (After all, since he's there late, maybe he needs some help.)

> **quote**
>
> "Power is an illusion. No one is powerful, really, finally. In my business, you often end up a beggar: 'Please sign with us.' "
> —David Geffen, talking about the record business

Get Credit for Your Work

You work your ass off, you come up with brilliant ideas, you save the company buttloads of money, and you hope someone notices. Hoping isn't good enough. You've got to let people know how damn good you are—people other than your boss—the people who can fire your boss and everyone under him.

How is your boss's boss supposed to know that it was *your* idea to relocate your widget plant from Mexico to Asia, saving the company millions of dollars, unless *you* tell him? How is your boss's boss supposed to know that it was *your* idea to use the elephant in the Clio Award–winning commercial instead of a giraffe? Your boss is going to try (and rightly so) to take credit for every brilliant thing you do. The degree to which you stop this from happening is directly proportional to the degree to which your ass is safe from downsizing. Now, doing this without freaking out your boss is a delicate matter. Here are a few ways to consider:

- **Give your ideas via paper and E-mail instead of over the phone.** If you mention a great idea to your boss over the phone, it's a lot easier for her to forget that the idea came from you. She'll think it came out of a conversation *with* you, and therefore, the idea is really partially hers. (Make sure you save all correspondence so you can prove later on that it was your idea.)

• **Cc others whenever possible.** This is tough to do, but you want to get in the habit of cc'ing your boss's boss on all correspondence of importance. If your boss is insecure, she'll resist the practice, thinking you're looking to get credit from above (which, of course, you are). This is a very tricky thing to do, and I can't say that your boss won't hate you for doing it, but if you can pull it off, it will benefit you greatly.

• **Play dumb.** If you've given an idea to your boss that you know was received well from her boss, ask her boss casually in passing, "I was just curious what you thought about my idea of moving the plant to Asia?" You already know he thinks it's a great idea; now he knows it was *your* idea.

THE GRAND FINALE: ABUSING YOUR POWER— DECIDING WHAT KIND OF BOSS YOU'RE GOING TO BE

Now that you've been promoted, you get your own assistant, whom you can abuse, talk down to, torture, and send out for lunch. Or not. In fact, it might behoove you to treat them like you wish you had been treated. It's my opinion that assistants work harder for people they like and who treat them well. Here are some ways to treat your assistant well. When you're promoted, I hope you remember this little chapter and help to make the work world a better place for all.

• Say "Good morning" when you arrive and pass by your assistant's desk. It gives them the impression that you are glad that they're there.

• Tell them not to be afraid to ask questions. This will free them up from nerves and help them to relax, knowing that if they don't know something, all they have to do is ask. Also, encourage them to ask any questions they might have about the work you yourself are doing—things they don't necessarily need to know to do their job but will need to know if they ever hope to be promoted.

• Include them in your work. Tell them to keep an eye out for information that might be helpful, such as magazine or newspaper articles that relate to what you do. If you're smart, your assistant will be constantly feeding you information that will help you in your job.

• Give them the impression that you're interested in their opinion. How? Ask them for it once in a while.

• Take them out to lunch once every six months. The fact that you are willing to be seen with a peon like them will score you many points.

• Only ask them to pick up your dry cleaning in case of an emergency.

• Never make them schedule a date for you with your mistress.

• Give them tickets or gifts that you receive that you either can't use or don't want. I had one boss in the entertainment industry who constantly got passes to film premieres and interesting lectures. Whenever she couldn't use the ticket herself, she would have me call her son, who worked as an assistant at a competitor of ours. Not once did she ever offer a ticket to me. She was a mean, mean woman.

If you *want* to be a jerk and abuse your assistant, make sure you hide it from others in the company (if that's even possible). It's gotten pretty politically correct and litigious out there. Abuses you could heap on your assistant in the eighties are difficult to get away with in the nineties.

I was talking to a friend of mine last night who told me about an executive at his company who just got canned, apparently partially because she was an abusive nightmare to her assistants. "Why, what did she do?" I asked. "Her last assistant was her size, and she'd make her go try on dresses for her, buy a bunch, bring them back for a look-see, and then return the ones she didn't want." Apparently, the big cheeses at the company didn't like this one and canned her ass.

So there you go. That's it. Work hard until you die. But remember, an unexamined life is not worth living.

POWER VERBS: WRITING YOUR EXPERIENCE

Management Skill Verbs

Allocated funds for various bird-watching programs.
Determined campaign policy regarding the acceptance of gifts.
Directed a team of assistants and volunteers on the Kapoulie Project.
Elected treasurer of the Polar Bear Club two consecutive years.
Enlisted the help of twenty Santa Clauses to help save Christmas.
Formed a group of surfers to study wave differentials in Malibu.
Founded a bipartisan special-interest group dedicated to exposing teachers who give low grades.
Governed the class of '97 all four years of college.
Hired a contractor to rebuild fraternity's roof.
Initiated the use of television cameras in arbitration hearings.
Inspired group to begin recycling old beer bottles.
Instituted a policy of "don't ask, don't tell" among enlistees.
Led a group of ragtag soldiers through Disneyland.
Managed a discotheque frequented by more than two thousand people on Friday nights.
Moderated a debate between pro-life and pro-choice supporters.
Operated a $500-a-week lawn-cutting business for five consecutive summers.
Oversaw the washing of cars for the junior class Car-a-Thon.
Pioneered the use of the expression "Live life live."
Presided over weekly staff meetings.
Produced the 1997 senior class play *The Crucible*.
Recruited and hired seven Elvis impersonators for Sophomore Slump Week celebration.
Represented Students for a Free Tibet at the Whole Earth Peace Conference.
Selected caterer and band for senior picnic.
Spearheaded efforts to restrict the use of alcohol at frog-jump tournaments.

Sponsored a bill that gives victims the opportunity to participate in the trial of their assailants.

Staged a protest against fur outside the faculty's annual fund-raising dinner.

Started a student-led pro-life group.

Supervised a group of fifty-five volunteers.

Organizational Skill Verbs

Arranged housing for the entire visiting cast of *Cats*.

Assembled and distributed press kits to all the local papers and television stations in the area.

Catalogued the shoe collection of Ivana Trump.

Centralized organ-donor files, thus increasing the ease with which a donor can be found.

Collected outstanding monies owed the theater department.

Coordinated the "Mean People Suck" benefit concert, which raised over $2,300 for charity.

Disseminated pamphlets on pro-life to high school students.

Distributed over a thousand lunches to poor people every Saturday afternoon from 1996 to 1997.

Enforced the fraternity's laws and regulations fairly and consistently.

Executed plan to rid the campus of all mice, rats, and roaches.

Formalized hazing policies for the National Fraternity Organization.

Implemented a policy that outlawed discrimination based on sexual preference.

Installed Lotus Notes and Solitaire on all laptops in the library.

Maintained database of onetime and ongoing investors.

Organized the sailing team's spring break cruise to the Bahamas.

Planned a two-day seminar on the Zen of in-line skating.

Prepared a list of names and addresses of people interested in receiving free back rubs.

Processed over 1 million applications for the Meet Michael Stipe essay contest.

Recorded minutes at weekly staff meetings.

Reorganized the firm's filing system.

Scheduled monthly meetings between student board and faculty board.

Updated list of potential investors.

Communication Skill Verbs

Acquainted freshmen with their academic supervisors.

Answered the media's questions with respect to the expulsion of the president.

Apprised staff of all ongoing changes to the network system.

Briefed the president on the legalities of fund-raising from the office.

Conducted seminars on how to fend off an attacker for second and third graders throughout the state.

Contacted print and electronic press prior to each demonstration.

Demonstrated the effects of marijuana use by smoking three consecutive joints.

Drafted contracts for visiting musicians and performers.

Educated high school students about the dangers of drug use.

Familiarized incoming freshmen with the university's honor code.

Handled vacation requests for the entire company.

Informed staff of daily economic changes in Eastern European countries.

Instructed new employees in how to use the internal network system.

Lectured visiting students on the subject of drug use.

Listened to parents' concerns and calmed their fears.

Presented new marketing ideas to company board.

Reported findings about the influence of rap culture on sneaker sales.

Responded to users' complaints with respect to new version of MS Word.

Spoke about the buying habits of teenagers in the 1990s.

Summarized the findings of two independent councils on teenage suicide.

Taught beginning and intermediate windsurfing three consecutive summers.

Trained staff in how to deal with customer complaints.

Wrote end-of-the-year summary of camp's activities and accomplishments.

Analytical Skill Verbs

Analyzed handwriting samples from first graders from different economic backgrounds.

Assessed workers' sexual harassment claims to determine possible common themes.

Audited financial records of First National Bank.

Compiled a list of the restaurants and hotels the company's employees prefer the most.

Consulted on the design of an entertainment center.

Documented the history of rock and roll in Japan.

Edited company's monthly newsletter.

Evaluated the effectiveness of disciplining staff by fines.
Examined supermarket fish to determine salmonella bacteria levels.
Gathered data about the mating habits of kangaroos.
Identified areas susceptible to flooding.
Interpreted scientific data and wrote reports for laypeople to understand.
Interviewed people on the street for various CBS polls.
Researched the relationship between junior high school boys and their parents.
Searched Macon County for Civil War artifacts.
Surveyed random New Yorkers about what they liked about the movie *Private Parts*.
Tested elementary school kids in various social skill exercises.

Creative Skill Verbs

Authored three articles on how to sew a couture dress.
Conceived of the idea of installing microwaves in every room.
Conceptualized a virtual shopping village for the Internet.
Created a late-dinner menu for four-star restaurant.
Designed an after-school program for homeless kids.
Devised a plan to rid Mammoth Lake of all pollutants.
Established a network of hospital volunteers.
Invented a battery-operated iron.
Originated the use of soy at the chocolate factory.

Helping Skill Verbs

Aided the psychologically impaired in finding suitable housing.
Assisted former employees in finding jobs.
Attended to the needs of lowerclassmen.
Collaborated on book *Jobs That Don't Suck*.
Contributed to the successful implementation of a new playground.
Counseled "troubled" students to keep them in school.
Facilitated the construction of a gym in the freshman residence hall.
Fostered the growth of the after-school program.
Guided first-year interns in their transition from medical school to hospital work.
Helped victims of hurricane Hugo rebuild their lives.
Instilled confidence in a ragtag group of volunteer firefighters.
Provided moral support to teenage rape victims.
Settled housing disputes among first-year students.
Treated patients suffering from HIV and AIDS.

Selling Skill Verbs

Arbitrated a settlement between condominium owners and student renters.

Convinced owner to implement "two-for-one night," resulting in 20 percent profit for said night.

Dissuaded disgruntled staff from filing lawsuits.

Encouraged student union to make campus 100 percent wheelchair-accessible.

Marketed senior class yearbook, resulting in beating projected sales by 15 percent.

Mediated racial conflicts.

Negotiated contracts for all actors, directors, and designers for off-Broadway show *Jay Street*.

Persuaded administration to create a child-care facility.

Publicized all major sports events via radio, flyers, and bus ads.

Resolved disputes between players and coaches.

Secured new business by cold-calling and mailers.

Sold vintage clothing to used-clothing stores in New York City.

Solicited donations from union members and all concerned citizens.

Additional Power Verbs

Adapted curriculum on a person-by-person basis so nobody would be left behind.

Awarded the Riley Award for academic excellence two years in a row.

Boosted net sales by 75 percent within first sixteen months.

Broadened AIDS awareness on campus and in community.

Catered breakfast, lunch, and dinner for fifty people for six weeks.

Decreased staff turnover by 50 percent by increasing morale and incentives.

Developed TV show *Fantasy Island* for the stage.

Eliminated all profanity from elementary school reading curriculum.

Exceeded yearly sales projections by 15 percent the first year and by 20 percent the second year.

Excelled at four sports, achieving letters in all of them.

Expanded restaurant chain by adding five new stores in two years.

Financed 100 percent of college education by working full-time on campus.

Gained experience with laser monitoring technology.

Generated student interest in World Awareness Day.

Improved Web browser technology single-handedly.

Increased AIDS awareness by public speaking engagements throughout Charlottesville.

Launched a campaign to save the swamplands.

Modernized day-care facilities by adding computers and Internet service.

Published two books of poetry by age eighteen.

Raised two children while attending college full-time and working a full-time job.

Revamped the "senior citizen workout" by adding *Rockin' with the Oldies*.

Revitalized an ailing sailing program by procuring new sails.

Saved employer $500 a week in payroll by trimming sales staff without affecting sales.

Strengthened ties with Eastern European universities through exchange program.

Supplemented the diet of campers to include complex carbohydrates.

Utilized Quark and Photoshop to design newsletter.

INDEX

CHARLIE DROZDYK'S résumé is a veritable list of jobs that don't suck. He has worked on Broadway as a theater manager, in Los Angeles in film and TV, and in cyberspace, where he created and produced Web sites. He has also appeared on national TV as an expert on youth culture and business. Drozdyk lives in New York City, where he works in advertising as a strategic planner.

Printed in the United States
97030LV00003B/9/A